No. 19. Pullman and Baggage Car.

No. 7. Nickel and Brass Locomotive and Tender.

No. 303. Summer Car.

No. 3. Vestibuled Car.

No. 10. Interurban Motor Car.

No. 8. Pay-as-you-enter Car.

2. Summer Car.

No. 1910. Locomotive Outfit.

No. 13. Cattle Car.

No. 12. Gondola,

No. 1912. Locomotive.

THE LIONEL MFG. CO.

Wrap-around front and back covers of 1910, 1911 and 1912 Lionel catalogs.

SECOND EDITION
TCA LIONEL BOOK COMMITTEE

Compiled And Written By:
LIONEL BOOK COMMITTEE
TRAIN COLLECTORS ASSOCIATION

DONALD S. FRALEY, M.D., Editor
MALCOLM R. BERGER
ROBERT A. BOYER
JAMES J. BURKE, JR.
DAVID G. FELMLEY
VINCENT G. GIOVANNITTI
CYRUS HOSMER III
MELVIN H. NELMS
LOUIS J. REDMAN

SECOND EDITION

Printed in the United States of America

Library of Congress
Catalog Card Number 89-50826
ISBN 0-917896-02-5

The Committee dedicates
this book to the purposes
of the
TRAIN COLLECTORS ASSOCIATION
"providing educational and informational material to the membership and historians and other interested persons regarding the manufacture and history of tinplate trains"(*)

IN APPRECIATION
The Committee wishes to recognize
the role of its editor

DONALD S. FRALEY, M.D.

whose perseverance saw this edition
through to its completion.

(*) From the Articles of Incorporation,
Train Collectors Association,
March 15, 1957

Preface

THE LIONEL BOOK COMMITTEE

Seated (l to r): Jim, Don, Lou.
Standing (l to r): Vince, Malcolm, Mel, Dave and Cy. Not Present: Bob.

The production of this 2nd Edition was authorized by the TCA Board of Directors in 1986. During the years since the 1st Edition information had accumulated toward a 2nd Edition. That information, plus week-to-week work the past three years, has resulted in:

- Changing major errors and photos in the original printing
- Correcting minor errors in a new ERRATA Section
- Creating an ADDENDA Section for new information
- Producing an entirely new ACCESSORIES Section
- Completely re-writing the NUMERICAL Section to cross-reference the original and the new sections
- Changing the color-chip chart from 2 pages to 3

Although the film for the 1st Edition has about reached the end of its useful life, technical changes in the printing industry have resulted in improved reproduction from that film.

The preface to the 1st Edition mentions the general lack of comprehensive, accurate reference material on toy trains. Much material has been published since the 1st Edition, by many persons; but we believe this Edition will again be the reference book that sets the standard in the train collecting world. The original Lionel Book Committee accepted the challenge to produce a 2nd Edition, knowing full well the time and labor that would be required. This book, as was the first one, is a labor of love for trains.

The Lionel Number List was originally published by the T.C.A. in 1956. Over the years it was updated and revised as members contributed corrections. Finally in 1962 Don Fernandez and Lou Redman co-authored an illustrated, bound 2nd edition of the *Lionel Number List, T.C.A. Catalog Series I-A — I-D.* This complimented the *Picture Catalog of Lionel Standard Gauge Trolleys, T.C.A. Catalog Series I-E* published the year before. But the 1000 copies of the 2nd edition sold quickly and have long been out of print. In 1968 a list of revisions preparatory to a third edition appeared, but most train collectors do not even have knowledge of this work. So, though the hobby has rapidly grown over the last decade there has been a disturbing lack of comprehensive, accurate reference material written about toy trains. Other than articles in the *Train Collectors Association Quarterly,* the hard to locate old books by Louis Hertz, and a few currently available books that present an overview of a specific outstanding collection, very little information is available to the newer collector. And with the rapid proliferation of repainted items, altered trains and reproductions, it was felt that a comprehensive encyclopedia of Lionel trains was needed.

In 1972 train collectors in the Pittsburgh area hosted the 18th National Convention of the Train Collectors Association, and subsequently formed the Fort Pitt Chapter of the Eastern Division, T.C.A. One of the first committees to be organized within the chapter was the Historical Committee with Cyrus Hosmer, III as chairman and the other seven members shown listed on the title page. Utilizing the card file from the previous Lionel number list, which had been maintained through the years by Lou Redman, the work to produce a new number list was begun. This was not undertaken without some fear and trepidation on our part — who were we to think we could knowledgeably write a book about all of early Lionel? The research alone has taken us over two years, partially because of the rigorous restrictions we have placed on ourselves. The catalogs were thoroughly reviewed, all items personally examined, and some previously listed items dropped because of doubtful authenticity. Each section was checked and rechecked to minimize errors but obviously a book of this nature can never be absolutely complete since we are now decades after the actual production of these trains and records from Lionel are no longer available. Following the two years of research, another year has been spent in the actual production of this labor of love. Fortunately modern printing and color reproduction techniques have permitted us to include color photographs of all items and a color chip chart, something previously discarded because of the cost.

As in the previous *T.C.A. Catalog Series I* this book spans only the period 1900-1943. However, many areas such as 00, 2⅞", and streamliners, have been added. A comprehensive numeric listing for 1900 to 1969 is provided in the book with a dual purpose — to serve as an index for this book and to provide some insight into Lionel's logic and consistency in numbering. We have employed a series format to demonstrate the relationship of construction, detail and color of cars within each series.

The material in this book derives from innumerable contacts and conversations over many amassed years of train collecting, however acknowledgement of the following people is due:

Members who contributed to the early editions and revisions of the number list:
Harry Albrecht, James Ashby, Harold Ashley, Bill Ball, Michael Cann, Ken Cook, Peter Detmold, Leon Eggers, Don Fernandez, Ed Fisk, Robert Gaston, Russ Hafdahl, Robert Hahn, Frank Hare, Robert Heffner, Rex Heflin, Joe Henrichs, Harry Highfield, Robert Hornish, Cy Hosmer, John Inghram, Tom Johnson, Malcolm Kates, John Kelly, Frank Leslie, Roy Lister, Burton Logan, Walt Maiersperger, Lawrence Marquette, John Marron, Bob Marshall, Brandon Martin, Ray Melzer, George Miller, Sam Miller, Herb Morley, Dan Moss, Henry Navratil, C.P. Nicholas, Robert Poley, George Powell, Joe Ranker, Lou Redman, G.A. Robinson, Herb Rost, LaRue Shempp, Ken Sherer, Ben Smith, H.W. Steiner, Lloyd Taaffe, Horace Taylor, Fred Tucker, Martin Visnick, Dick Wagner, Fred Weber, Ed Wichmann, William Wiles, Jack Windt, Howard Worley, Dave VonGillern, and George Yohe.

Members who contributed information and ideas for the First Edition of this book:
Carl Abinanti, Michael Adair, Harry Albrecht, Dave Allen, James Ashby, Bill Ball, Bob Baron, Joseph Barr, Alvin Beck, John Boate, George Boon, R. L. Carver, Jim Cenname, Irving Chandler, Joseph Cirillo, Antonio Consoli, Al Cox, Frank Cox, John Cox, James Crone, Dave Crowley, Neil Curran, Dave DeCarlo, Major Donovan, Clyde Easterly, Dalas Ewing, Don Fernandez, Donald S. Fraley, Sr., Wes Frye, Vince Giovannitti, Howard Godel, Clarence Haney, Frank Hare, Henry Harte, Joe Henrichs, Paul Hill, Gordon Hinkle, Fred Hoffman, Chet Holley, Thad Howard, John Inghram, Ed Jones, John Kelly, Barry Kline, Sue Kline, Ward Kimball, Max Knoecklein, John Kresse, Hugo Kuehn, Bill Kus, Birkby Leip, Sam Lenhart, Ray Lew, Roy Lister, Russell Lucy, Walter Maiersperger, John Marron, George Miller, Ed Minkoff, Herb Morley, Robert Muschlitz, Herb McBride, Ernest McKee, Doug Nash, Freeman Orr, Harry Osisek, Edwin O'Leary, Paul Palmer, Al Pfaff, Ed Prendeville, Arnold Reiling, Bob Robinson, G.A. (Doc) Robinson, Jerry Rubenstein, Marvin Rukin, Tom Sage, Paul Scandrol, Tom Sefton, Bob Sell, LaRue Shempp, Ken Sherer, Don Spiedel, Ted Sommer, Aaron & David Steinberg, Harman Sterner, Glen Stinson, Martin Visnick, Lee Waddell, Eugene Wagner, Milt Walsh, Charles

Weber, Frank Werner, Ed Wichmann, Carey Williams, Howard Worley, George Yohe, and Cliff Anderson. We also wish to thank the staff of the New York Research Library, the Newark Public Library, and the New Haven Public Library for their help.

Finally, a special thanks to our wives who have suffered through these years of all night meetings, never ending phone calls, and photographic trips, and to Mrs. Elaine R. New for preparation of the many drafts of these pages.

Members who contributed information for the Second Edition:
Harry Albrecht, Cliff Anderson, Francis Audia, Gary Baldwin, William W. Ball, Ed Basse, Jr., Al Bennett, John J. Birdas, William Blystone, John Boate, George W. Boon, Bob Breneman, John Brewer, Robert S. Butler, Howard E. Carman, Dave Christianson, Richard T. Claus, John W. Coniglio, Bob Conner, Richard A. Cowan, Allison M. Cox, John A. Cox, John P. Daniels, John A. Daniel, Harry Daum, Harry Degano, Terrence J. Dotson, Jules Duda, Jim Dugas, Jay Duke, William Eidem, Paul C. Engelmann, Joe Ervin, Charles W. Feyh, Jr., Arthur S. Filbert, James E. Flynn, Jr., George J. Foss, Bruce T. Fowler, Glen Frazee, Joseph Freed, John D. Frisoli, Wesley F. Frye, Joel P. Fugazzotto, Joseph Gaidus, Edward N. Gerson, Philip Giles, Howard J. Godel, Steven Goldberg, Henry S. Golis, James Goyer, Dennis Graulich, Ronald A. Griesbeck, Paul Haidvogel, Charles Haney, Henry S. Harte, III, Robert Hartmann, John P. Hathcock, Fred Heimann, Fred Heinz, John Henderson, Jr., Chester Holley, Lawrence S. House, John R. Inghram, Gordon A. Janvrin, Greg Jones, Robert D. Jones, John T. Kelly, John A. Kiefel, Robert M. Kirchner, Barry Kline, Max Knoecklein, Richard H. Knowles, Robert Knox, George Koff, William J. Krone, Wilfred L. Kus, II, Robert Lakemacher, Don LaSpaluto, Harold J. Lauritano, Samuel H. Lenhart, Leonard B. Lenzen, James W. Madden, Jr., Gary Magner, Walter Maiersperger, William R. Martin, Frank Mazzarella, Herbert D. McBride, Tom McComas, Andrew McIntyre, Donald E. Mengle, Frank L. Merrell, George A. Miller, Robert B. Moler, Ernest F. Monck, Daniel J. Mordell, Herb Morley, Lee Morris, Ronald S. Morris, Raymond E. Myers, John S. Newbraugh, Louis H. Niederlander, Charles Nine, Joseph A. Palermo, John H. Pease, Clement A. Perschon, Ed Pinsky, Ed Prendeville, Joseph Ranker, John P. Rash, J. Trip Riley, Philip O. Ritter, Don Robbins, Robert C. Robinson, Jr., Stewart P. Robinson, Gerard Robinson, Robert R. Rockwell, John Rodino, Christian F. Rohlfing, Thomas S. Sage, William A. Sanchez, James M. Sattler, W. Paul Sauls, Jr., Frank Schopfer, Jr., Warren Schuch, Thomas W. Sefton, Harold W. Seitz, Robert C. Sell, Larue Shempp, Kenneth E. Sherer, Bill Shuppner, Donald G. Simonini, Fred Sipple, Jr., Ben Smith, Bradford H. Smith, Earl A. Smith, Glenn Snyder, William F. Spence, Jr., Frank Steele, Robert C. Steinis, Robert A. Strauss, Carl H. Sturner, J. Gerard Teater, A. Gordon Thomson, Michael A. Toth, Eugene Trentacoste, James Tuohy, Jack Turner, Richard E. Vagner, Martin Visnick, Jerry Wagner, Todd Wagner, Milton A. Walsh, Paul Wasserman, Alan T. Weaver, Charles W. Weber, Willis E. Weikert, Sr., Cliff White, Dave White, Edward H. Wichmann, Cary Williams, W. Keith Wills, Gordon L. Wilson, Wen Winegar, and Cecil L. Yother. We also wish to thank the staff of the Public Affairs Department, Sears National Headquarters, the staff of the Science and Technology Department, the Carnegie Library in Pittsburgh and Mrs. Carolyn Wells for preparation of the manuscript.

THE LIONEL BOOK COMMITTEE
Donald S. Fraley, M.D.
Editor

Contents

Continued on next page.

CONTENTS (cont.)

Introduction

This book covers Lionel trains from their first appearance in 1901 through 1943. The cutoff date is both logical and natural as Lionel actually stopped making trains during World War II. When production resumed after the war, the trains were markedly changed with knuckle couplers, new realism, and mostly molded plastic bodies. Truly, the era of "brass plates" and "tinplate" was gone. In addition, interest in collecting Lionel trains increased many-fold after World War II, with both catalogs and information readily avaiable. It was, therefore, felt that post war information need not be included in this volume. However, as can be noted in the COMPREHENSIVE NUMERICAL LISTING, Lionel continued to use the same master numbering list up to 1969. They would often go back many years later and fill in the blank numbers in the list. This numerical section, then, is as complete as possible through 1969.

Joshua Lionel Cohen, the founder and namesake of the company that produced the Lionel line of trains, was granted his first patent on November 7, 1899 for a device called a flashlamp. This was designed to ignite a small quantity of flashpowder as used by photographers of that era. The device as described and pictured embodied all the principles of the now-familiar dry-cell flashlight, so that anyone wishing to market a flashlight would have to acquire the patent or rights to it. According to the Lionel Corporation a man named Hubert did just that and founded the Eveready Battery Company. Mr. Cohen's next invention was an explosive fuse for which he was granted a patent on November 13, 1900. With the manufacture and sale of this fuse to the U.S. Navy, he had enough money for the launching of a small manufacturing company. To our good fortune, Mr. Cohen decided to manufacture small electric motors and to power toy railway vehicles with them. He and his partner, Harry C. Grant, began the manufacturing of these products. And it is H. C. Grant whose name appears on the first series of patents either granted or assigned to the Lionel Manufacturing Company. These first patents were filed in 1907 and granted in 1909. They were assigned to the "Lionell Mfg. Co." (obviously a misspelling) which at that time was a Connecticut-based company. The patents covered the four-wheel trolley truck, the three rivet, flat-sided (solid) car truck, electric motors, and Standard gauge track construction including the machine to form the rails. From the patent drawings it is apparent that Lionel experimented with various track construction, including T-shaped rail and split-pin connections which consisted of a half-pin in each opposing rail. Some early standard gauge track has been found equipped with these half-pins, but it is doubtful if this T-rail was ever made. Many of the 1910 patents were granted to Mario Caruso, one of many Italian craftsmen hired by Lionel, who rose to a position of prominence in the firm. He assigned these patents to The Lionel Mfg. Co. which was still a Connecticut business. About this time Joshua Lionel Cohen legally changed his last name to Cowen as a patent granted on November 22, 1910 notes this change. The Lionel company even patented a method for track construction which included roadbed, cross ties, and running rails stamped from a single piece of sheet metal. It seems unlikely this track was ever produced.

In July 1918 the Lionel Manufacturing Company was incorporated, and allowed to sell shares of stock. Though all of the Lionel advertising leads one to believe that they started in the train business in 1900 we have been unable to find evidence to support this claim. In fact, *Moodys' Industrial Manual,* which derives its information from the data supplied to the Securities and Exchange Commission by the companies themselves, states that Lionel Corporation was "incorporated in New York in July 1918, as successor to Lionel Manufacturing Company a New Jersey corporation organized in 1906. Business founded in 1901." Thus, not withstanding our doubts that Lionel actually made trains in 1900, we have nevertheless employed their famous slogan "Standard of the World since 1900" in our title.

All dating of items has been done from the consumer catalogs, and the dates are noted at the end of each description. An *uncataloged* item or set is one which either was never pictured in a consumer catalog, or which differs from the cataloged item or set because it is made of a consist of cars unlike the one pictured, made up of cars which were not cataloged in the period the set was produced, made up with differences in consists that are not likely to have been due to switching in the store, or found in original boxes with numbers not found in catalogs. Further definition of "specials", in particular Department Store Specials (DSS), is discussed in a SPECIALS section. Mention should be made here of the term "X" as used by Lionel. "X" on the car or set box means only that the item so marked was different from normal production in some way — trim, journal boxes, color, couplers, etc.

All major variations of each item are detailed. However, not all minor variations are included. By the study of the developmental charts and components list, many of the minor differences are readily appreciated. The committee felt that in-depth studies of minor variations in each series are not the domain of this book, but should be appropriately published as articles in the *T.C.A. Quarterly.*

A succinct but highly functional format has been employed throughout. Following the introductory paragraph on the section, each item is presented by number, car type, color, lettering detail, wheel arrangement, length and, finally, dates cataloged. Each descriptive statement is separated by a comma except catalog dates, which are set off by a period. If the item is known to have been made in more than one color, the colors are listed in chronologic order of appearance. The most common color variation (or variations) is italicized. If no color is clearly the most common, none is italicized. Early cars and most engines are entirely one color and listed as such. Later freight cars are generally listed by two colors — body/roof color — except cabooses where the window trim is added. Most passenger cars are listed by three colors — major body color/roof color/window trim color. Doors when different are also noted.

A color-chip chart is included, and all color designations herein refer to our assigned name, not Lionel's. *All items pictured in this book are original finish* and, in general, the most unusual variation of each item has been shown.

Occasionally, the description of a train will be followed by the designation — SPECIAL, DSS, or UNIQUE in parentheses. This should alert one to the fact that a more detailed description can be found in the SPECIALS section.

Additional Brief Notes:

1. All car and locomotive lengths are actual measurements over the frame or car body and do not include the couplers. The measurements given therefore may not agree with the lengths stated in the catalogs.

2. "Chugger" units were used in steam locomotives from 1933 to 1936.

3. The first year of the electric whistle in tender was 1935.

4. The last year of the electric-style locomotive was 1936.

5. The two position, Lionel-patented, E-unit reverse was used from 1925 to 1932. In 1932-33 Lionel began using an improved modification of the Ives drum-type, three position reverse. After 1933 all cataloged sets had three-position E-units whether steam or electric style, and plates so designated, "E". By 1939, all locomotives had E-units, the "E" designation was dropped from the plate. Most early locomotives were hand reverse (HR), but some cheaper locomotives — such as a 33, 261, 248, early 250 electric, 257 — had no reverse (NR).

6. Abbreviations:

BJ black journals
Br brass trim
CJ copper journals
DSS Department Store Special
E remote control unit, either two or three position
HR hand reverse
N nickel trim
NJ nickel journals
NR no reverse
NM never made, as far as can be determined
RS rubber stamped
T tender
Uncat uncataloged
W whistle
Wh wheel

O Gauge Locomotives

1915-1942

The O gauge locomotive section is a composite of material gleaned from old catalogs, study of available trains, and review of the data in the second edition. Though 1915 is the year Lionel first cataloged O gauge trains, three lines of evidence would indicate production began much earlier — perhaps as early as Christmas, 1913. The first of these three points is that the late Irving Shull, who was in charge of Lionel's service department and curator of its museum, stated some years ago that O gauge locomotives were made in 1913. Secondly, the 1920 catalog discusses the O gauge chassis and motor and their development in 1913. Finally, flecked red window material was used in Standard gauge cars up through 1913 but no later and several early O gauge passenger cars have turned up with this material. While the question of the start of O gauge production cannot be absolutely answered, 1942 represents without a doubt the end of prewar O gauge production. Dates given here are the dates when the item was cataloged, and do not necessarily reflect when the item was actually made. The list includes all cataloged numbers, whether manufactured or not. Those numbers for which no item has been found are listed as never made (NM) as far as is known. This obviously cannot prove that they were never made. It only serves as a notation that the item has never been seen to date.

The O gauge locomotives have been subdivided into six series based on similarities of construction, numbering, and the period of manufacture. Two additional series appear at the end — WINNER LINES and MACY LOCOS. Comments made in this introduction to O gauge locomotives are referable to all the subdivisions. More specific comments are made at the beginning of each section about the locomotives in that group. All 0, 027, and 072 articulated streamliners and their motor units are discussed in a separate section — STREAMLINERS. As noted in the introduction, specials and unique items are listed herein but are discussed in more detail in the SPECIALS section.

Early locomotives are generally a single color with black frame and are designated only by the body color. Later locomotives — particularly electric style — often have different colors for body, frame, and trim. These are listed in the following manner — body color/ frame color/ window trim color. Color designations are as shown in the color-chip chart, with the exception that the use of black underwent a series of changes with time. Black locomotives prior to 1934 had a glossy finish, from 1934 through 1938 had a semigloss (satin) finish, and after 1938 had a flat (dull) finish. The locomotive color is black if none is listed.

The types of couplers and their usefulness in dating a locomotive or car are discussed in detail in the O GAUGE CARS section, but some additional points are worthy of note here. All 700/150-series electrics have hook couplers, while all 250-series electrics have latch or combination latch couplers. From 1935-37 non-automatic box couplers were used on the larger O gauge tenders, but latch couplers were still used on the cars until 1936. The automatic box coupler was first used in 1938. Finally, while all the electric-style locomotives have two couplers, of the steam engines only the scale "Hudson" (700E) and Pennsy style switchers have two. The rest of the steam engines have only the coupler on the tender, though a knuckle coupler is often simulated in the pilot of the die-cast locomotives.

A discussion of the many small changes in motor design for O gauge locomotives is not within the scope of this book; twelve types are known for the 700/150-and 248- series alone. As mentioned in the introduction, early locomotives either are equipped with a hand reverse (HR) lever or are non-reversing (NR). Later locomotives, both steam- and electric-style, have remote control reverse — the E-unit. After 1933, all cataloged sets had E-unit locomotives and were so marked until 1939. After 1939 the "E" was dropped from the plates.

Though variations in the types of simulated pantographs, whistles, bells, and headlights are extremely useful in dating Standard gauge locomotives, the relative lack of change in these items over the years of O gauge production limits their usefulness. With the exception of the non-operating Standard gauge pantograph, and the operating pantographs on the 256, all O gauge electric-style locomotives had small stamped-metal pantographs. Similarly, the brass ornamental whistle on all later O gauge electric-style locomotives was the same (7-16" high), except on the 256 where the Standard gauge size (9/16") was used. Bells were used on early electric-style locomotives and all were of one type. However, small steam-type locomotives had a turned simulated bell while larger steam-type locomotives had a nickel-plated swinging bell in a U-shaped bracket. The most useful piece of trim on O gauge electric locomotives is the headlight. Pedestal headlights were used up to 1918, followed by nickel-plated strap headlights from 1918 through 1926, and O gauge size die-cast headlights from 1927 on.

Following the color description of each engine, the type of plates or lettering on the locomotive is listed. The various types are:

- Early rubber stamped (RS) lettering — 1915-25
- Brass plates (Br) — 1926-34
- Nickel plates (N) — 1935-39
- Late rubber stamped (RS) lettering — 1940-42

These designations do not refer to the type of journals or other trim on the locomotive, but only to the number plates. The dating of the journal types and trim is detailed in the O GAUGE CARS introduction.

FIGURE 1

DEVELOPMENT OF LIONEL O GAUGE ELECTRIC LOCOMOTIVES

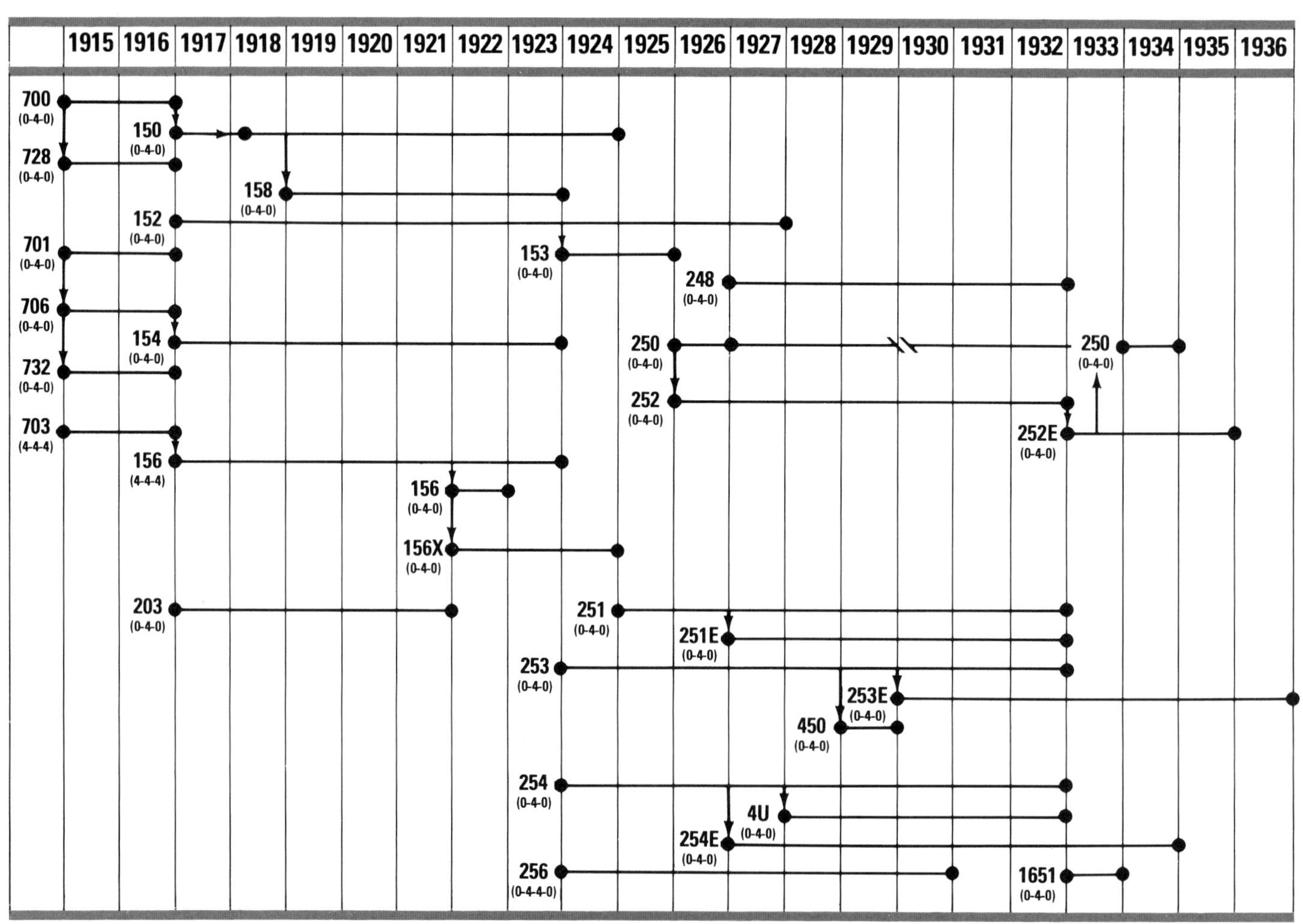

Additional Short Notes

1. Steam type locomotives are not designated as such but show just the wheel arrangement. All have eight wheel tenders unless otherwise noted.

2. All electric-style locomotives are designated by (Elec) in the description.

3. The "Chugger" is found in only one O gauge steam-type locomotive-the 260E.

4. Teledyne couplers are automatic box couplers on Pennsy-style switchers that operate on the whistle relay.

5. Remote control section (RCS) track is the special track section for unloading or uncoupling cars.

6. The 1934 motor plates and catalogs spell gauge — GUAGE — useful in dating production.

7. Early castings of 238E and 250E steam locomotives had weights inside, while later models had a heavier casting but no weights.

8. Some locos stamped inside "Made in U.S. of America" presumably export sets.

9. Abbreviations:

CW clockwork
CM&StP body style like 254 electric-style locomotive
ME Magic Electrol (DC reversing coil)
NH body style like 253 electric-style locomotive
NYC body style 248 electric or S-class outline of 156 electric-style locomotives.

FIGURE 2

DEVELOPMENT OF LIONEL O GAUGE STEAM LOCOMOTIVES

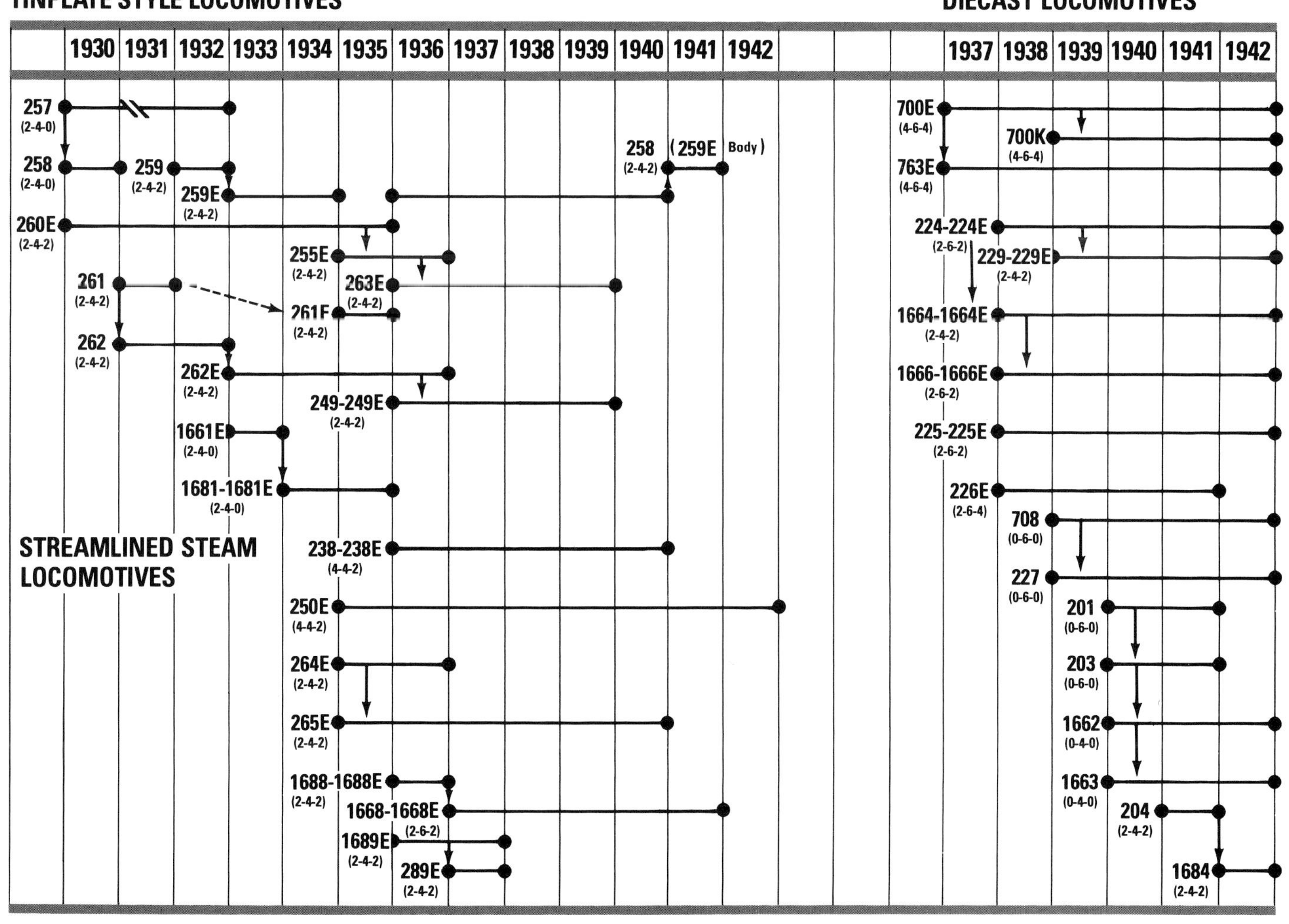

EARLY PERIOD LOCOMOTIVES
1915-27

From the beginning of cataloged O gauge locomotives until the change to later styles in the mid 1920's, all the locomotives manufactured were electric outline, resembling the New York Central "S"-type cabs. A steam type 0-4-0 was cataloged in 1915 and another in 1921 but neither was ever made (NM). The earliest electric-style locomotives were the 700 series (700, 701, 703, 706) of 1915-16. All locomotives of the 700-series were dark green with red window trim, had pedestal headlights, and hook couplers mounted to the frame by a rivet. The two years of production are easily distinguished by the gilt-painted ventilators and cast-iron wheels of 1915, and dark green (no gilt paint) ventilators and die-cast wheels with nickel rims in 1916. In 1917 Lionel renumbered the locomotives as the 150-series but production changes were few. However, in July, 1918, when Lionel Manufacturing became Lionel Corporation, the 150-series production changed to strap headlights, hook couplers mounted in slots in the frame, and the appearance of other body colors. Most of the locomotives of the early period had no reverse (NR), but a few had a hand-reverse (HR) lever. Automatic reverse did not appear until later on the 250-series. Finally, it should be noted that the locomotives of the early period have been measured two ways — by cab lengths (in parentheses) and by the frame length — to show better the relationships between these engines.

150 **Elec.** (early), 0-4-0, NYC, same body as 700 elec., NR, dark green, RS-NYC oval, (5¾″ cab), 7″. 1917.

150 **Elec.** (later), 0-4-0, NYC, NR, RS-NYC oval, (5″ cab), 6″. 1918-25.
dark green; brown; *maroon;* dark olive green; mojave; peacock

151 **Steam-Type,** 0-4-0, with 8-Wh tender, cataloged 1921 but NM. 1921.

152 **Elec.,** 0-4-0, NYC, early-NR, later-punched hole in end for reverse rod-HR, RS-NYC oval, (5¾″ cab), 7″. 1917-27.
dark green; dark olive green; dark gray; light gray; peacock; mojave

153 **Steam-Type,** 0-4-0, same as 151 but brass and nickel, cataloged 1921 but NM. 1921.

153 **Elec.,** 0-4-0, NYC, same as late 152 with hole punched in end for reverse rod, HR, RS-NYC oval, (5¾″ cab), 7″. 1924-25.
dark green; dark olive green; gray; mojave

154 **Elec.,** 0-4-0, NYC, HR, RS-NYC oval, (6″ cab), 8 or 8½″. 1917-23.
dark green; dark olive green.

156 **Elec.,** 4-4-4, NYC, HR, RS-NYC oval, (7″ cab), 10″. 1917-23.
dark green; maroon; olive green; gray

156 **Elec.,** 0-4-0, NYC, HR, dark green, RS-NYC oval, (7″ cab), 10″. 1922.

Note: Same as 4-4-4 but no pilot trucks

156X **Elec.,** 0-4-0, NYC, HR, catalog number for 156 with no pilot trucks but RS-156 and NYC oval, (7″ cab), 10″. 1923-24.
maroon (flat or gloss); olive green; gray

158 **Elec.,** 0-4-0, NYC, NR, same as 150 (later) but with two dummy headlights and no bell, RS-NYC oval, (5″ cab), 6″. 1919-23.
gray; black

203 **Elec.,** 0-4-0, armored loco with guns, NR, gray, unlettered 7½″. 1917-21.

Note: Early armored locos had cast iron wheels, later had die-cast wheels.

700 **Elec.,** 0-4-0, NYC, NR, dark green, same body as early 150, RS-NYC oval, (5¾″ cab), 7″. 1915-16.

701 **Elec.,** 0-4-0, NYC, NR, dark green, RS-NYC oval, (6″ cab), 8″. 1915-16.

702 **Elec.,** 2-4-2, NYC, HR, cataloged 1915 but NM. 1915.

703 **Elec.,** 4-4-4, NYC, HR, dark green, RS-NYC oval, (7″ cab), 10″. 1915-16.

704 **Elec.,** 2-4-2, NYC, HR, cataloged 1915 but NM. 1915.

706 **Elec.,** 0-4-0, NYC, same as 701 but with HR, dark green, RS-NYC oval, (6″ cab), 8″. 1915-16.

710 **Steam-Type,** 0-4-0, with 4-Wh tender, cataloged 1915 but NM. 1915.

728 **Elec.,** 0-4-0, NYC, dark green, same as 700 but RS-QUAKER 728, (5¾″ cab), 7″. Factory special, circa 1915-16. SPECIAL

732 **Elec.,** 0-4-0, NYC, dark green, same as 701 but RS-QUAKER 732, (6″ cab), 8″. Factory special, circa 1915-16. SPECIAL

150 (early) dark green

150 (later) maroon

152 peacock

153 dark olive green

154 dark green

156 olive green

156X maroon (flat)

158 gray

203 gray

700 dark green

701 dark green

703 dark green

706 dark green

728 dark green

732 dark green

LATER ELECTRIC STYLE LOCOMOTIVES
1924-36

Lionel introduced a new series of electric-style locomotives in 1924 patterned after prototype engines (CMStP&P, NYC, NH, B&M). These are referred to as "brass plate" electric locos, since all have brass plates with embossed lettering except as noted in the description. All have brass trim except for some nickel trim such as simulated springs on the 248, 251, and 254 engines. O gauge size stamped headlights were used on all early locos and O gauge die-cast headlights on all late locos, except the 256 which has Standard gauge headlights, both early and late. The color of these locomotives is designated by body color/frame color/windows and ventilator inserts color. Loco door color, if different is noted. All these locos have latch couplers except the very early 250, which has combination latch couplers. Journals follow the guidelines set forth in the introduction, with nickel (1924-30) followed by copper (1931-34). All these locomotives are hand reverse unless noted as non-reversing (NR), or E-unit sequence reverse (E).

4 **Elec.,** 0-4-0, CMStP&P, similar to 254 but with Bild-A-Loco motor and separate hand reverse slot in cab, 9¼". 1928-32.
orange/black/Br
gray with apple green stripe/black/Br

4U **Elec.,** 0-4-0, catalog number for 4 sold in kit form. Boxed set includes eight sections of track and can be used to build either the locomotive or stationary motor, orange/black/Br, 9¼". 1928-32.

248 **Elec.,** 0-4-0, NYC, NR, 7½". 1927-32.
- dark green/black/Br-ventilators and number boards, number RS or black plate etched with number (uncat. — circa 1926)
- orange/black/Br — RS or black plate with etched number
- dark green/black/maroon — RS (uncat. — circa 1927)
- *orange/black/peacock – RS*
- *red/black/cream – RS*
- red/black/Br
- olive green/black/orange — RS (uncat. — circa 1930)
- terra-cotta/black/cream — RS (uncat. — circa 1931)

250 **Elec.** (early), 0-4-0, NYC, NR, 8". 1926.
dark green/black/Br
peacock/black/Br
yellow-orange/black/Br

Note: No reverse slot in top of hood

250 **Elec.** (later), 0-4-0, same locomotive as 252E but with 250 plates, 8", uncat. Circa 1934.
yellow-orange/terra-cotta/Br
terra-cotta/maroon/Br

Note: Some have "E" stamped on doors, others do not. All have reverse slot in top of hood.

251 **Elec.,** 0-4-0, NYC, 10". 1925-32.
gray/black/Br
gray/black/red
red/black/ivory — with or without ivory stripe

251E **Elec.,** 0-4-0, same as 251, but E, 10″. 1927-32.
gray/black/red
red/black/ivory – with or without ivory stripe.

252 **Elec.,** 0-4-0, same as early 250 but HR, 8″. 1926-32.
dark green/black/BR
peacock/black/BR
olive green/black/BR
terra-cotta/maroon/Br — with or without cream stripe
yellow-orange/terra-cotta/Br
yellow-orange/black/Br
maroon/black/Br — cream stripe (DSS)

252E **Elec.,** 0-4-0, same as 252 but E, 8″. 1933-35.
terra-cotta/terra-cotta/Br (UNIQUE)
terra-cotta/maroon/Br
yellow-orange/terra-cotta/Br
Note: With or without RS — "E" on brass side door.

253 **Elec.,** 0-4-0, NH, 9″. 1924-32.
maroon/black/Br
red/black/Br
dark green/black/Br
dark green/black/orange
mojave/black/Br
peacock/black/orange
terr-cotta/maroon/cream
pea green/black/orange (uncat. — circa 1930)
Stephen Girard green/dark green/cream
red/black/orange(uncat. — circa 1931)
gray/black/Br (uncat. — circa 1923-26)
medium blue/black/Br (SPECIAL)
Note: Peacock and pea green locomotives come with or without orange stripe.

253E **Elec.,** 0-4-0, same as 253 but E. 1931-36.
peacock/black/orange
terra-cotta/maroon/cream
Stephen Girard green/dark green/cream
Stephen Girard green/black/cream
Note: Found with "E" RS on side of cab or embossed on number plates.

254 **Elec.,** 0-4-0, CMStP&P, 9½″. 1924-32.
dark green/black/Br
mojave/black/Br
olive green/black/Br – some with red stripe or red strip and red hatches
pea green/black/Br — with or without either orange stripe or orange hatches or both
pea green/dark green/Br
red/black/Br
apple green/black/Br
Note: Olive green 254 can be found with red celluloid and pea green can occasionally be found with orange celluloid behind ventilators.

254E **Elec.,** 0-4-0, same as 254 but E. 1927-34.
olive green/black/Br — with or without red stripe
pea green/black/Br — with or without orange stripe and orange hatches
orange/black/Br
Note: Found with "E" embossed on number plate or RS on side door. Orange 254E used in "Macy Special" but not marked differently than regular production.

256 **Elec.,** 0-4-4-0, B&M, twin motors, 11½″. 1924-30.
- *orange/black/Br — RS lettering, large nickel stamped headlights, non-operating pantographs*
- orange/black/Br — RS lettering, die-cast headlights, non-operating pantographs
- orange/black/pea green — rectangular brass-plate lettering, die-cast headlights, working pantographs — no border on plates
- orange/black/pea green — rectangular brass-plate lettering, die-cast headlights, working pantographs—black border on plate (two stripes)
- orange/black/pea green — rounded corner brass-plate lettering, die-cast headlights, working pantographs.

450 **Elec.,** 0-4-0, same as 253 except "R.H. Macy" on plate on pickup and Br plate — script letters MACY SPECIAL above ventilators, 9″. uncat. Macy DSS-circa 1930.
red/black/Br
apple green/dark green/Br

1651E **Elec.,** 0-4-0, NH, litho cab on 253 frame, sets only, red litho/brown roof/black frame/Br, lettered LIONEL-IVES, 9″. 1933.

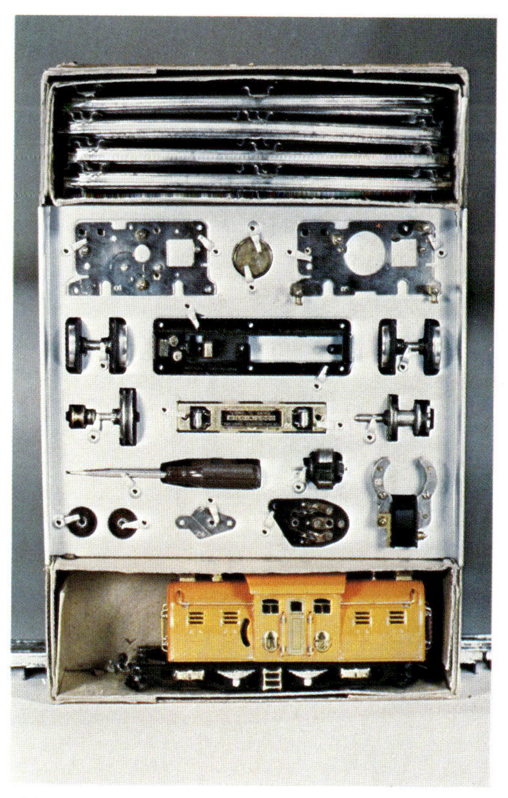

4U set box

4U orange

248 terra-cotta

250 (early) dark green

250 (later) yellow-orange/terra-cotta

251 gray

251E red/cream stripe

252 olive green

252E terra-cotta/maroon

253 maroon

253E Stephen Girard green

254 dark green

254E olive green

256 orange/pea green

450 red

1651E red litho/brown

MIDDLE PERIOD STEAM LOCOMOTIVES
1930-42

All of these locomotives have die-cast zinc frames and sheet-metal superstructures except the late 258, 259, 259E, 1661, 1681, and 1681E, which have sheet-metal frames. This series first appeared in 1930, one year after Lionel reintroduced steam engines in the Standard gauge line. These were the last of the truly tinplate locos and later gave way to die-cast boilers and scale detail. All the locomotives in this series are hand reverse (HR) unless otherwise noted. The black engines have a gloss finish prior to 1934; thereafter, a semi-gloss paint was used. Trim follows the guidelines described in the locomotive introduction with brass and copper from 1930-34, and nickel subsequently, except for the gunmetal 260E with nickel trim (1934) and the black 259E with nickel trim (1934). Engines with brass and copper trim have red-spoked wheels, while locos with nickel trim have black wheels. Numbers are found on brass (Br) plates, nickel (N) plates, or are rubber-stamped (RS) as noted. Tenders have two four-wheel trucks unless otherwise noted.

249
249E 2-4-2, same boiler and frame as 261/261E/262/262E but with added valve gear and marker lights, with or without whistle, with 265 or 225 tender, N, 9¾". 1936-37, and uncat. 1938-39.
gunmetal; black

255E 2-4-2, same boiler and frame as late 260E but no Chugger, with whistle, with 12-Wh 263 tender, gunmetal, N, 11⅝". 1935-36.

257 2-4-0, same boiler and frame as early 258, Br, NR, 8¼". 1930, and uncat. 1931-32.
- black with orange stripe, with 4 Wh 257 tender-black with orange stripe;
- black/no stripe, with 4-Wh 257 tender-black with or without stripe, or crackle black tender without stripe (uncat. — circa 1931-32)
- black/no stripe, with 2-Wh 259 tender—black/no stripe (uncat. — circa 1931-32)

258 **(early)** 2-4-0, same as 257 but HR, Br, with 4-Wh 257 or 8-Wh 258 tender, black with orange stripe and matching stripe on tender, 8¼". 1930.

258 **(late)** 2-4-2, same boiler and frame as 259/259E but with 027 motor, RS, with 1689 tender, 9⅞", uncat. Circa 1941.

259 2-4-2, same boiler and frame as late 258 but NR, with 4-Wh 259 tender, black, Br, 9⅞". 1932.

259E 2-4-2, same as 259 but E, Br or N, with or without whistle, $9\frac{7}{8}$". 1933-34, 1936-38, and uncat. 1939-40.
black with 4-Wh 259 tender (1933)
black with 8-Wh sheet-metal 262 tender (1934)
gunmetal with 1689 or 2689 tender
black with 1689 or 2689 tender
(uncat. — circa 1936-40)
black with 4-Wh 1588 tender (uncat. DSS — circa 1936-40)

260E 2-4-2, similar body and frame as 255E/263E, with Chugger 1933-35, Br or N, $11\frac{5}{8}$". 1930-35.
black/black frame/cream stripe in groove, with 8-Wh 260 tender with matching stripe on tender (1930)
black/green frame/no stripe, with 8-Wh 260 tender with matching green frame on tender
black/green frame/no stripe, with 12/Wh 260 tender with matching green frame on tender
dark gunmetal/dark gunmetal frame/no stripe, with 12-Wh 263 dark gunmetal tender (1934)
dark gunmetal/dark gunmetal frame/no stripe, with 12-Wh 263 dark gunmetal tender with whistle (1935)

261 2-4-2, similar boiler and frame as 249/249E, with 4-Wh 257 tender, black, Br, NR, $9\frac{3}{4}$". 1931.

261E 2-4-2, same as 261 but E, with 8-Wh 261 tender, black N. $9\frac{3}{4}$". 1935.

262 2-4-2, same as 261 but HR, with 8-Wh die-cast 262 tender, black, Br, $9\frac{3}{4}$". 1931-32.

262E 2-4-2, same as 261 but E, with 8-Wh die-cast 262, sheet-metal 262, or streamlined 265 (uncat.) tender, black, Br or N, $9\frac{3}{4}$". 1933-34, and uncat DSS — circa 1935-36.

263E 2-4-2, similar boiler and frame as 255E/260E, no Chugger, with whistle, with 12-Wh 263 tender in matching colors, N, $11\frac{5}{8}$". 1936-39.
gunmetal/gunmetal frame
blue/dark blue frame

1661E 2-4-0, same boiler and frame as 1681/1681E, with 4-Wh 1661 litho tender, black/red frame, motor plate lettered LIONEL-IVES, sets only, 8". 1933.

1681 2-4-0, Lionel Jr., with 4-Wh 1661 litho tender, HR, 8". 1934-35.
black/red frame (1934)
red/red frame (1935)

1681E 2-4-0, same as 1681 but E, sets only, 8". 1934-35.
black/red frame (1934)
red/red frame (1935)

2259EW Catalog number for 259E with 02689W tender with whistle and controller. 1938-39.

2263EW Catalog number for 263E with 2263W tender with whistle and controller. 1938-39.

249E gunmetal

255E gunmetal

257 black/no stripe

258 (early) black/orange stripe

258 (late) flat black

259 black

259E black

260E black/cream stripe

261 black

261E black

262 black (same as 262E)

263E blue/dark blue frame

1661E black/red frame

1681 black/red frame

1681E red/red frame/black tender

STREAMLINED STEAM TYPE LOCOMOTIVES
1935-42

Following the example of the prototype railroads, Lionel began producing streamlined steam engines in 1935. All of these locomotives have die-cast superstructures except the 264E and 265E, which have sheet-metal boilers and die-cast cabs. All have nickel plates, nickel trim and nickel journals except very late 1668 engines found with nickel plates on engine, and RS lettering and black journals on tender. As in other sections, lengths given refer to engine length only. Further, when two numbers are listed together, it signifies that the plates can be numbered either way. Whistles in the tenders began in 1935, and all tenders have two four-wheel trucks unless otherwise noted.

238
238E 4-4-2, PRR "Torpedo", with 265, 2225 or 2265 tender, with whistle, N, 10⅜". 1936-38, and uncat — 1939-40.
gunmetal; black

Note: Locomotives in cataloged sets are predominantly, possibly exclusively, gunmetal. Uncataloged sets have black locomotives.

250E 4-4-2, Milwaukee Road "Hiawatha", 072, with 12-Wh 250, 250X (drawbar) or 2250 tender, with whistle, Hiawatha orange and Hiawatha gray/black (gray tender top), N, 13¼". 1935-42.

264E 2-4-2, NYC "Commodore Vanderbilt", with or without whistle, with 261 or 265 tender, N, 9¾". 1935-36.
light red: *black;* light blue

265E 2-4-2, NYC "Commodore Vanderbilt", same as 264E but with added eccentric rods, with or without whistle, with 261 (black only), 261X (black only), 265 (black or gunmetal), 265X (light blue only), or 2225 tender, N, 9¾". 1935-40.
black; *gunmetal;* light blue

289E 2-4-2, NYC "Commodore Vanderbilt", same casting as 1689 but with O gauge motor, with 4-Wh 1588 tender or 1689 tender, with or without whistle, sets only, N, 9⅛", uncat. Circa 1937. black; gunmetal

1668 2-6-2, PRR "Torpedo," with or without
1668E whistle, with 1689 tender, N, 9½".
1937-41.
gunmetal; black

1688 2-4-2, PRR "Torpedo", same casting as
1688E 1688, with or without whistle, with 1689
1688E tender, N, 9½". 1936 and uncat.
1937-42. gunmetal; black

1689E 2-4-2, NYC "Commodore Vanderbilt", same casting as 289E, with or without whistle, with 1689 tender, N, 9⅛". 1936-37.
gunmetal; black

1698E Catalog number for 1689E with whistle tender, whistle controller, and transformer. 1936.

1699E Catalog number for 1688E with whistle tender, whistle controller, and transformer. 1936.

238 gunmetal

250E Hiawatha orange and gray

264E light red

265E light blue

289E gunmetal

1668 black

1688 gunmetal

1689E gunmetal

LATE PERIOD STEAM LOCOMOTIVES
1937-42

As a group, this represents the change from tinplate engines to more realistic locomotives. All of these locomotives have zinc alloy die-cast superstructures. Some have only minor attempts at detailing. Others, such as the 700EW or Pennsy 708 switcher, are scale models. All of these engines have E-unit reverse though in later years the "E" designation was dropped from the plates. Further, all have nickel plates (N) or rubber-stamped (RS) lettering as noted. Unlike the earlier semi-glossy black finish, all black engines in this group are flat black. Lengths given are actual measurements of the locomotives (not locomotives plus tender), and may not agree with the lengths given in the catalogs. The phrase "Magic Electrol" (ME) refers to the use of a DC coil-reversing mechanism. The PRR B6 0-6-0 switchers are all RS-8976 on the cab but have cast boiler fronts with the individual loco numbers (0, 227, 228, etc.) cast in.

There are some PRR B6 0-6-0 switchers with a zero cast in boiler front plate — can be otherwise identical to a 227, 228, 231, or 232. The 225 and 226 locos are occasionally found with no number plate but rather with plates lettered LIONEL LINES.

201 0-6-0, with ME, RS, with or without ringing bell, with backup lights, with 2201 slope-back tender, black, 8½″. 1940-42.

203 0-6-0, same as 201 but without ME, RS, with 2203 slope-back tender, black, 8½″. 1940-41.

204 2-4-2, same casting as 1684, RS, with or without whistle, sets only, with 1689 or 2689 tender, 9¼″, uncat. Circa 1941.
black; gunmetal

224 2-6-2, with or without whistle, N, 10⅛″. 1938-42.
224E
gunmetal with 2689 tender
gunmetal with 2224 die-cast tender
black with 2224 die-cast tender
black with 2224 plastic tender

225 2-6-2, with or without whistle, N, 10½″. 1938-42.
225E
gunmetal with 2225 tender
gunmetal with 2235 die-cast tender
black with 2235 or 2245 die-cast tender
black with 2235 plastic tender

226E 2-6-4, with whistle, with 12-Wh 2226 tender, black, N, 11¾″. 1938-41.

227 0-6-0, PRR, tubular track version of full scale 701, backup light, Teledyne couplers, tinplate tender trucks, with or without ringing bell, with 2227 slope-back tender, black, RS-8976 on cab, "227" cast in boiler-front plate, 9⅝″. 1939-42.

228 0-6-0, PRR, same as 227 but for use with 2800-series cars, with 2228 tender, black, RS-8976 on cab, "228" cast in boiler-front plate, 9⅝″. 1939-42.

229 2-4-2, with or without whistle, N or RS, 10⅛″. 1939-42.
229E
gunmetal with 2689 tender
black with 2689 tender
black with 2666 plastic tender

230 0-6-0, PRR, same as 227 but rear coupler operated by RCS track, dummy front coupler, black RS-8976 on cab, "230" cast in boiler-front plate, 9⅝″. 1939.

231 0-6-0, PRR, same as 228 but rear coupler operated by RCS track, dummy front coupler, black, RS-8976 on cab, "231" cast in boiler-front plate, 9⅝″. 1939.

232 0-6-0, PRR, same as 230 but with ME, with ringing bell only, black, RS-8976 on cab, "232" cast in boiler-front plate, 9⅝″. 1940-42.

233 0-6-0, PRR, same as 231 but with ME, with ringing bell only, black, RS-8976 on cab, "233" cast in boiler-front plate, 9⅝″. 1940-42.

700E 4-6-4, Scale NYC "Hudson", built to NMRA standards, for 072 T-rail track, with scale 12-Wh 700 tender, black, RS-5344 on cab and headlight, "700E" embossed on ashpan plate, 14⅛″. 1937-42.

700K 4-6-4, same as 700E but sold in kit form with major castings having only gray primer coat of paint, "700K" embossed on ashpan plate, 14⅛″. 1939-42.

701 0-6-0, Scale PRR, B6 switcher, built to NMRA standards, for 072 T-rail track, with scale slope-back 701 tender, with backup light, black, RS-8976 on cab, "8976" cast in boiler-front plate, 9⅝″. 1939-42.

763 4-6-4, similar to 700E but less detailed, for 072 tubular track, with whistle, N, 14⅛″. 1937-42.
gunmetal with 12-Wh 263 or 2263 tender
black with 12-Wh 2263 tender
gunmetal with 12-Wh 2226 tender
black with 12-Wh 2226 tender

Note: Also shown in catalog with "X" tender for T-rail track.

900 0-6-0, PRR, catalog number for 230, tender, and reverse controller. 1939.

900B 0-6-0, PRR, same as 900 but with ringing bell. 1939.

901 0-6-0, PRR, catalog number for 231, tender, and reverse controller. 1939.

901B 0-6-0, PRR, same as 901 but with ringing bell. 1939.

902 0-6-0, PRR, catalog number for 227, tender, and reverse controller. 1939-42.

902B 0-6-0, PRR, same as 902 but with ringing bell. 1939-42.

903 0-6-0, PRR, catalog number for 228, tender, and reverse controller. 1939-42.

903B 0-6-0, PRR, same as 903 but with ringing bell. 1939-42.

905 0-6-0, PRR, catalog number for 201, tender, and reverse controller. 1940-42.

905B 0-6-0, PRR, same as 905 but with ringing bell. 1940-42.

906B 0-6-0, PRR, catalog number for 232, tender, and reverse controller. 1940-42.

907B 0-6-0, PRR, catalog number for 233, tender, and reverse controller. 1940-42.

1662 0-4-0, switcher, with 2203 slope-back tender, back-up light, sold in sets only, black, RS, 8½″. 1940-42.

1663 0-4-0, same as 1662 but with ME, with 2201 slope-back tender, black, RS, 8½″. 1940-42.

1664
1664E 2-4-2, same casting as 1666, with or without whistle, N or RS 10⅛″. 1938-42.
gunmetal with 1689 tender
black with 1689 tender
black with 2666 plastic tender

1666
1666E 2-6-2, same casting as 1664, with or without whistle, N or RS, 10⅛″. 1938-42.
gunmetal with 2689 tender
black with 2689 tender
black with 2666 plastic tender

1684 2-4-2, same casting as 204, with or without whistle, with 1689 or 2689 or 2666 plastic tender, black, RS, 9¼″. 1942.

2224EW Catalog number for 224, whistle tender, and whistle controller. 1938-41.

2225EW Catalog number for 225, whistle tender, and whistle controller. 1938-42.

2226EW Catalog number for 226, 2226W tender, and whistle controller. 1938-40.

2226EWX Same as 2226EW but with 2226WX tender. 1941-42.

2229EW Catalog number for 229, 02689W tender, and whistle controller. 1938-40.

2229EWX Same as 2229EW but with 2666W tender. 1941-42.

2663T Catalog number for 1663, tender, and reverse controller. 1940-42.

2763EW Catalog number for 763, 2263W tender, and whistle controller. 1938-39.

2763EWX Same as 2763 EW but with 2263 WX tender. 1940.

5344 See 700E, NYC "Hudson", this number RS on loco cab.

8976 See 701, PRR, B6 switcher, this number RS on loco cab.

The two detail pictures presented below demonstrate the differences in boiler front castings on 0-6-0 switchers.

227 boiler front plate (227)

701 boiler front plate (8976)

201 black

203 black

204 gunmetal

224E gunmetal

225E black

226E black

227 black

228 black

229 black

233 black

700E black

701 black

763E gunmetal

1662 black

1663 black

1664 black

1666E gunmetal

1684 black

CLOCKWORK HANDCARS AND LOCOMOTIVES
1933-37

Lionel produced neither clockwork locos nor lithographed cars until after the absorption of the Ives Company in the early 1930's. Then for a few years these inexpensive sets appeared in the Lionel catalog.

1100 **"Mickey Mouse" Handcar,** red, maroon, apple green, or orange base, 7½". 1935-37.

1103 **"Peter Rabbit" Chick Mobile,** with flanges for track or without for floor operation, yellow base, 8⅞", uncat. Circa 1935-37.

1105 **"Santa Claus" Handcar,** green or red base, 8⅞". 1935-36.

1107 **"Donald Duck" Rail Car,** red base/white or orange house/green roof, 9⅜". 1936-37.

1506 0-4-0, with headlight, bell and brake, no whistle, with a 4-Wh 1509 "Mickey Mouse" stoker tender, light red, sets only, 7¼". 1935.

1506L 0-4-0, same as 1506 but with 4-Wh 1502 tender, black. 1933-34.

1508 0-4-0, "Commodore Vanderbilt" type, with light, ringing bell and brake, with 1509 "Mickey Mouse" stoker tender, light red, sets only, 7". 1935.

1508X Catalog number for 1508 with 1509 "Mickey Mouse" stoker tender only. 1935.

1508X Catalog number for 1508 with 1541 tender, NM. 1935.

1511 0-4-0, "Commodore Vanderbilt", type with whistle, with 4-Wh 1516 tender, sets only, 7½". 1936-37.
black; light red

1521 Catalog number for 1511 with 1516 tender. 1937.

1588 0-4-0, "Torpedo" Type, with whistle, with 4-Wh 1588 tender, same casting as 1688, black, sets only, 9½". 1936-37.

1100 red base

1103 flanged wheels

1103 non-flanged wheels

1105 red base

1107 orange house

1506L black/red frame

1508 light red

1511 light red

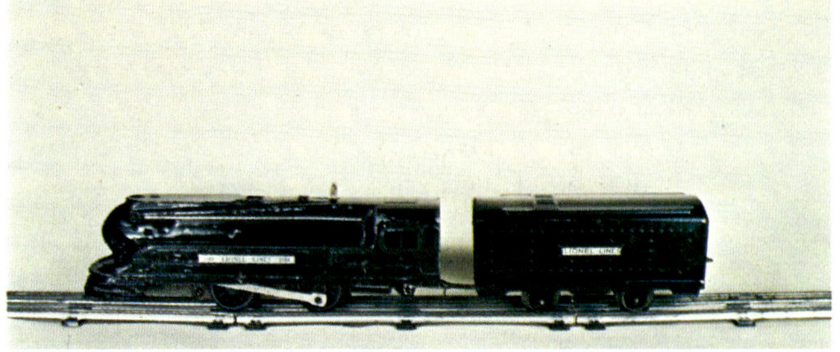
1588 black

WINNER LOCOS
1930-32

The Winner Lines was a subsidiary corporation of Lionel producing low cost electric trains in the early 1930's. Three separate catalog flyers are known, dating from late 1930, 1931 and 1932. The last was inserted in some of the 1932 Lionel catalogs. All the locos were 0-4-0 wheel arrangement and shared the same motor.

1000 **Elec.**, 0-4-0, NH, litho, lettered WINNER RAILWAYS, cataloged in 1930 Winner flyer but NM. 1930.

1010 **Elec.**, 0-4-0, NH, litho, lettered WINNER LINES, dummy headlight (same as on 158) on top, disc wheels, 5″, sets only, 1931-32 Winner flyers. 1931-32.
light orange/green/cream
tan/green/cream

1015 0-4-0, 4-Wh (1016) tender, black/orange trim, embossed spokes on wheels, no headlight, 7", sets only. 1931-32.

1030 **Elec.**, 0-4-0, NH, litho, lettered WINNER LINES, dark orange/green/cream, dummy headlight on top, operating headlight in front, embossed spokes on wheels, 5", sets only. 1932.

1035 0-4-0, 4-Wh (1016) tender, operating headlight, embossed spokes on wheels, 7", sets only. 1932.
black/red trim
black/orange trim

MACY LOCOMOTIVES

These locomotives were made by Lionel in special sets for the R.H. Macy and Company, New York. A more complete description of the sets can be found in the SPECIALS section.

252 **Elec.**, 0-4-0, NYC, HR, maroon/black frame/ cream stripe, 8", uncat. Circa 1930 (DSS)

450 **Elec.**, 0-4-0, NH, HR, same as a 253 except "R.H. MACY" on plate on pickup and BR plate-script letters "MACY SPECIAL" above ventilators, 9", uncat. Circa 1930 (DSS)
red/black frame/Br
apple green/dark green/Br

1010 light orange/green

1015 black/orange trim

1030 dark orange/green

1035 black/orange trim

252 maroon/cream stripe

450 apple green/dark green frame

450 red/black frame

O Gauge Cars 1915-1942

As in the other sections of this book, the O gauge car list has been compiled from catalogs and from extensive review of known items. Dates listed are the dates the item was cataloged, and do not necessarily reflect when the item was actually manufactured. Further, uncataloged items (i.e., not in the consumer catalogs or different in some way from the cataloged item) are noted as uncataloged, and an approximate date of production assigned. No attempt has been made to list all minor variations (particularly of trim), but by studying the enclosed charts, one can determine the possible variations from the components dating. Department store specials (DSS), such as the Macy trains and "one-of-a-kind" items, are listed here for completeness but discussed in more detail in the section — SPECIALS. Winner Line trains, a subsidiary corporation of Lionel from 1930-32, are discussed at the end of this section. All 0 and 027 streamlined and articulated cars are discussed with their power units in another section — STREAMLINERS.

Couplers. The type of coupler is in general very useful in dating the car. The pictures and descriptions in figure 3 readily identify the couplers. The type of couplers has not been detailed in the description of the cars but can be readily determined by the years of production. The latch coupler, introduced in 1924 as The "Lionel Automatic Coupler" had nothing automatic about it. The term "Latch" was first applied to this coupler by Lou Redman in a TCA Quarterly article in 1956. This term was both descriptive and convenient, and has gained universal acceptance among collectors. Cabooses were usually made with only one coupler, but can be found with two couplers and the carton marked (X). Cars with automatic box couplers have the prefix "2" added to the number.

Trucks — O gauge cars always have two four-wheel trucks (i.e. eight wheels) unless otherwise noted. Cars with only four wheels have no

FIGURE 3

Early Hook
(1915-27)

Inverted T-shaped hook

Combination Latch
(1924-28)

Latch coupler with additional tongue and slot for hook coupler attachment. Transition-period coupler.

Latch
(1924-42)

In later years used only on cheaper and uncataloged items.

Late Hook
(1933-37)

Straight hook — used on mechanical and four wheel electric-powered sets.

Box-Type I
(1935-42)

Larger box coupler with two parallel lines embossed on top. Can couple to latch type. Used on 810 series and later on other O gauge cars.

Box-Type II
(1938-42)

Smaller box-type with knuckle outline embossed on top. Used on all O gauge lines.

Automatic Electric
Box-Magnet Operated
(1938-39)

Earlier O gauge automatic box coupler.

Automatic Electric
Box-Solenoid Type
(1939-42)

Scale Couplers
(1940-42)

FIGURE 4

Type I
(1915-16)

Single semicircular hole in truck side frame, three embossed rivets at each end. Used on early passenger cars.

Type II
(1917-26)

Two cutouts in truck side-frame, two embossed rivets at each end, two embossed rivets at bottom. Early freight and passenger cars.

Type III
(1915-23)

Single semicircular hole in truck side frame, two embossed springs, four embossed rivets at each end. Artist conception of trucks for early 610 and 612 only but NM.

Type IV
(1933-42)

Small truck from the Lionel made "Ives" line of trains. Single oblong hole in truck side frame, embossed reinforcing bar, two embossed rivets at top and at corners of journal boxes, two slots for journal boxes. Used on most small and litho cars. Early trucks of this type have a narrow bolster bar at top, while later ones have a wide bolster bar.

Type V
(1923-35)

Large, heavy-duty truck, no cutouts in truck side frame. Early trucks of this type had no reinforcing bar while later ones had a reinforcing bar. Used only on 710 and 605-series passenger cars and four-wheel truck 260T tender.

Type VI
(1926-34)

Large, heavy-duty truck, central rectangular cutout in truck side frame, embossed reinforcement bar, three embossed rivets at bottom, single journal box slot. Used on medium sized O gauge passenger cars (607 type).

Type VII
(1933-41)

Former Ives heavy duty truck, two triangular cutouts in bolster, three embossed springs in center, single slot for journal box. Embossed reinforcing bar with nine rivets along top. Used on 800-series cars.

Type VIII
(1936-41)

Same as typo VII but with three rivets at each end along top of embossed reinforcing bar and bar broken in middle. Used on late 2000-series cars.

Type IX
(1933-42)

6-Wh truck, resembles double type V, two rectangular cutouts in truck side frame, embossed reinforcement bar, no embossed rivets, single slot for journal box. Used for 710-series, ex-Ives and scale-detailed passenger cars and 263 TW, "Hiawatha" tender and 226TW.

Type X
(1940-42)

Bettendorf-style scale truck, fully sprung. Used on all scale cars except caboose.

Type XI
(1940-42)

Leaf-spring, archbar scale truck, not sprung. Used on scale caboose.

Note 1: Type I trucks modified with removal of upper corners of truck for clearance of steps and fish belly frame on early freight cars. Truck may be left with one or two embossed rivets on each end.

Note 2: Type XI truck with no attached coupler used on front end of 701T and rear end of scale caboose.

TYPE I

TYPE VII

TYPE II

TYPE IX

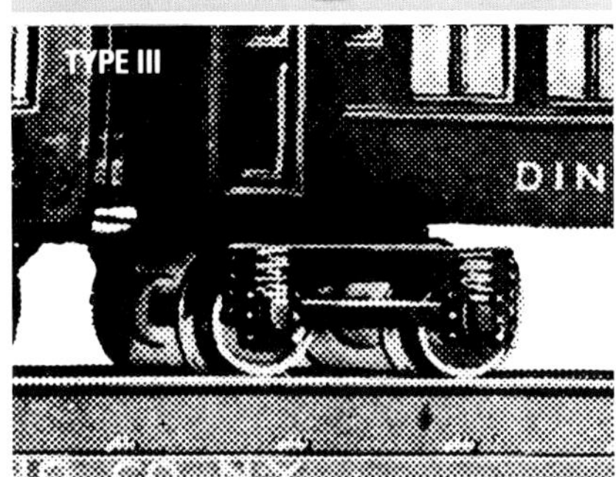
TYPE III

TYPE X

TYPE IV

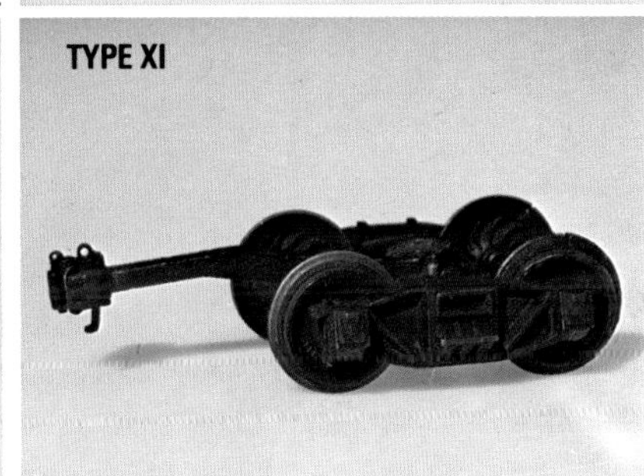
TYPE XI

TYPE V

TYPE VI

trucks but have the two axles mounted through the frame. Early cars have bushings on the axles to keep them from falling out of the frame. Three styles of frame embossing are found; early, with one embossed spring and no journal box slots, later with two embossed springs and no slots, and last with two embossed springs and two journal box slots. Over the years of O gauge production a number of truck styles were used, as identified in Figure 4.

Journal Boxes. An integral part of the trucks are the journal boxes. Like other components, the journal boxes are useful in dating a car. The types and general dates of production are as follows.

No journal boxes (no slots)	1915-25
Nickel journal boxes	1924-30
Copper journal boxes	1931-34
Nickel journal boxes	1935-39
Black journal boxes	1939-42
No journal boxes (slots punched) (uncat. specials)	1936-42

Color. In describing the cars, the colors are listed in chronological *order of appearance.* The most common color variation (or variations) is *italicized.* The colors listed are described in the color chart elsewhere in this book and do not necessarily correspond to the colors as designated by Lionel in the catalogs. Passenger cars are listed by three colors — major body color/roof color/window trim color. Doors, if different, are also noted. Freight cars are generally listed by two colors — body/roof, except for cabooses where the window trim is added. Early cars that are all one color are the exception to this notation and are listed with only one color. The color of observation railings is not noted unless more than one color railing is known. Similarly, railings on cabooses generally occur in only one color on each caboose variation; exceptions to this are noted. The frame on each car is black unless otherwise noted.

Lettering. After the color description of each car and separated by a hyphen, the type of plates or lettering on the car is listed. The various types are listed below.

Early Rubber Stamped lettering	1915-25
Brass plates	1926-34
Nickel plates	1935-39
Later Rubber Stamped lettering	1940-42
Decal lettering	1939-42

These designations do *not* refer to the other trim on the car, nor to the journal boxes but only to the number plates. In general, trim follows the chronology of the journals. Further, this does not apply to early-series cars where enameled inserts are RS but are not added on plates.

Additional Brief Notes

1. All car lengths given are actual measurements over the frame and car body and do not include the couplers. Measurements given may not agree with the lengths listed in the catalogs.

2. Lettering shown in capitals is as it appears on the car.

3. Aluminum roofed passenger cars are generally "specials" with the exception of the 613-series in O gauge and the 1630/2630/2640-series in 027 gauge.

4. The prefix "3" denotes operating cars with automatic-box couplers.

5. Up to 1928, actual railroad names were used on passenger cars; after that, only LIONEL LINES appeared on them.

6. The designation of "X", as used by Lionel, means only that the item so marked was different from the normal production run. Thus, it could mean two couplers on a caboose, no journals, a different color, different trim, etc.

7. Abbreviations:

Br	Brass nameplates
DSS	Department Store Special
N	Nickel nameplates
NM	Never made
RS	Rubber-stamped lettering
Wh	wheel

To show the development of each car series, the O gauge cars have been split into a number of sections of related cars. The order is passenger series, freight series, lithographed, and finally, Winner Lines and Macy Specials.

EARLY PASSENGER SERIES
1915-25

The early O gauge passenger cars were first cataloged in 1915, although reportedly they were made as early as Christmas, 1913. All were similar in construction, with arch windows, hook or combination latch couplers, no added nameplates or trim. Interior lights were used only in the larger cars after 1923. All cars have rubber stamped NEW YORK CENTRAL LINES lettering, except the 603-4 and 702 — all not road-lettered. All cars have eight wheels (two four-wheel trucks) unless otherwise noted. Early cars (1915-16) have type I trucks and later cars have type II.

600 PULLMAN, 4-Wh, RS-NEW YORK CENTRAL LINES, 5½″. 1915-25.
dark green; brown; *maroon*

601 PULLMAN, dark green/dark green/wood-grained window trim and doors, RS — NEW YORK CENTRAL LINES, 7″. 1915-23.

602 BAGGAGE, RS — NEW YORK CENTRAL LINES and between the doors RS — U.S. RAILWAY POST OFFICE, 7″. 1915-23.
dark green/dark green/wood-grained
yellow-orange/yellow-orange/wood-grained (uncat. — circa 1922)

603 PULLMAN, same as 601 and matches 602, yellow-orange/yellow-orange/wood-grained, 7″, uncat. Circa 1922.

603 PULLMAN (later), five paired windows, with or without interior lights, white celluloid in upper windows, hook or combination couplers, 6½″. 1920-25.
orange/orange/wood-grained
orange/orange/maroon
dark green/dark green/wood-grained (UNIQUE)

604 OBSERVATION (later), matches 603, 6¼″. 1920-25.

610 PULLMAN, RS — NEW YORK CENTRAL LINES, 8½″. 1915-25.
dark green/dark green/maroon or wood-grained
maroon/maroon/dark green
mojave/mojave/maroon or wood-grained

NOTE: Some of the earliest dark green cars have mottled red celluloid in window arches while other early and all late cars have mottled green celluloid.

611 MAIL, catalogued to match 610 but only prototype made.

612 OBSERVATION, matches 610. 1915-25.

702 BAGGAGE, for armored loco set only, same as 602 but gray — no lettering. 1917-21.

600 dark green

601 dark green

602 yellow-orange

603 yellow-orange

603 (later) orange

604 (later) orange

610 dark green

612 maroon

702 gray

MIDDLE SERIES SMALL PASSENGER CARS
1925-32

All cars of this series share the same body and frame. They have arch windows, no added journal boxes on early cars (but later cars have them), no trim, no brass nameplates, and no interior lights. One stamping for each side provides the contrasting color for window trim and nameboards. All cars are four-wheel except the eight-wheel "specials" noted below. In the early years of production the difference between the 529- and 629-series, as noted in the catalogs, was the absence of mottled green celluloid in the window arches of the 629 series. In later years both series had the celluloid material and differed only in the body colors available. All cars have latch couplers except very early 629-30 which have hook couplers.

529 **PULLMAN,** 4-Wh, 6½". 1926-32.
olive green/olive green/maroon
olive green/olive green/red
olive green/olive green/orange
terra-cotta/terra-cotta/cream — maroon frame

530 **OBSERVATION,** matches 529. 1926-32.

629 **PULLMAN,** 4-Wh, same as 529 except no mottled green celluloid in windows in early sets, 6½". 1924-32.
dark green/dark green/maroon
orange/orange/peacock
red/red/cream – 4-Wh or 8-Wh (SPECIAL — circa 1934)
light red/light red/cream — 8-Wh (SPECIAL — circa 1935)

630 **OBSERVATION,** matches 629. 1924-32.

529 olive green/orange

530 terra-cotta/cream

629 (4-Wh) red/cream

629 (8-Wh) light red/cream

630 dark green/maroon

MIDDLE SERIES LARGE PASSENGER CARS
1924-34

These large middle series passenger cars all had interior lights, greater detail than smaller cars, and either two four-wheel or six-wheel trucks. All had three-piece roof construction and longitudinal interior benches. The 610-series had one stamping for window trim, doors, and nameboards, while both the 605- and 710-series had one stamping for windows and another for doors. While the 610-12 cars had no added-on brass steps and non-swinging doors, the other cars in this series had operating doors and brass steps. All cars came equipped with latch couplers. These cars are found with large four-wheel trucks (types V or VII) or six-wheel trucks (type IX) as noted.

605 **PULLMAN,** RS — LIONEL LINES or ILLINOIS CENTRAL except gray sets which are lettered NEW YORK CENTRAL LINES or LIONEL LINES, 10¼″. 1925-32.
gray/gray/maroon
gray/gray/maroon/apple green clerestory stripe (uncat. — circa 1930-32)
gray/gray/red (uncat. — circa 1930-32)
red/red/ivory
orange/orange/cream
olive green/olive green/maroon (uncat. — circa 1931)

Note: Orange cars have cream doors except on MACY SPECIAL which has pea green doors. Olive green cars have olive green doors with long or short door-windows.

606 **OBSERVATION,** matches 605. 1925-32.

610 **PULLMAN,** RS —THE LIONEL LINES except mojave cars may be NEW YORK CENTRAL LINES, 8¾″. 1926-30.
mojave/mojave/maroon
mojave/mojave/red
olive green/olive green/maroon
olive green/olive green/red
olive green/olive green/orange
terra-cotta/maroon/cream (uncat. — circa 1933)
pea green/pea green/orange
light blue/alum/alum — scroll lettering (SPECIAL — circa 1936-37)
light red/alum/alum — block lettering (SPECIAL — circa 1936-37)
light red/alum/alum — scroll lettering (SPECIAL — circa 1936-37)

Note: Pea green cars may be found with white window shades.

612 **OBSERVATION,** matches 610. 1926-30.

710 **PULLMAN,** all RS — LIONEL LINES except orange sets which are RS — LIONEL LINES, NEW YORK CENTRAL LINES, or ILLINOIS CENTRAL, 11½″. 1924-34.
orange/orange/dark olive green — 4-Wh
orange/orange/dark olive green — 6-Wh
orange/orange/pea green— 4-Wh trucks
orange/orange/pea green — 6-Wh trucks
red/red/ivory – 4-Wh trucks
red/red/ivory — 6-Wh trucks
medium blue/dark blue/cream — 6-Wh trucks

Note: Red/red/ivory cars may have either Stephen Girard green or ivory doors; orange cars have maroon, wood-grained, or dark olive green doors.

712 OBSERVATION, matches 710, 11-½″. 1924-34.

605 olive green/red

606 orange/cream

610 light red/alum

612 terra-cotta/maroon

710 medium blue/dark blue/cream

712 orange/dark olive green

LAST SMALL SERIES PASSENGER CARS
1926-42

All these cars have one-piece roof construction and are variations of two body stampings (603 and 1630). Various number changes in the 600-series indicate production differences — i.e. 603-04 (no lights), 607-08 (interior lights), 609-II (SPECIAL-interior lights but no journals). Similar changes occur in the 1630-series with 1630-31 (latch couplers, no lights), 2630-31 (electric couplers, no lights) and 2640-series (electric couplers and interior lights). All cars have two longitudinal benches inside, a single stamping of contrasting color for window and door trim and nameboards, and no attached steps; they do have air tanks except as noted. Trucks on the 603-series are generally type VI, with type IV on the 1630-series.

603 **PULLMAN,** no interior lights, RS — THE LIONEL LINES, 7½". 1931-36.
red/black/cream
yellow-orange/terra-cotta/cream
Stephen Girard green/dark green/cream (SPECIAL)
light red/light red/white

604 **OBSERVATION,** matches 603. 1931-36.

607 **PULLMAN,** same body as 603, has interior lights, RS — THE LIONEL LINES except peacock cars which can also be found with RS — ILLINOIS CENTRAL, 7½". 1926-37.
peacock/peacock/orange
Stephen Girard green/dark green/cream
red/red/cream (SPECIAL)
maroon/maroon/cream (SPECIAL)

Note: All maroon 607-08 are without interior lights.

608 **OBSERVATION,** matches 607. 1926-37.

Note: Stephen Girard green cars can have brass or alum-painted observation railings.

609 **PULLMAN,** same body as 603, has interior lights, no air tanks or journal boxes, light blue/alum/alum, RS — THE LIONEL LINES, 7½", uncat. Circa 1937. (SPECIAL)

611 **OBSERVATION,** matches 609, uncat. Circa 1937. (SPECIAL)

1630 **PULLMAN,** no interior lights, RS — PULLMAN, 9½", sets only. 1938-42.
light blue/alum/alum
light blue/light gray/light gray

1631 **OBSERVATION,** RS — OBSERVATION, matches 1630. 1938-42.

2630 **PULLMAN,** same as 1630 but with electric couplers, no interior lights, RS — PULLMAN, 9½". 1938-42.
light blue/alum/alum
light blue/light gray/light gray

2631 **OBSERVATION,** RS — OBSERVATION, matches 2630. 1938-42.

2640 **PULLMAN,** same as 2630 but with interior lights, RS — PULLMAN, 9½". 1938-42.
light blue/alum/alum
State green/dark green/cream

2641 **OBSERVATION,** RS — OBSERVATION, matches 2640. 1938-42.

2642 **PULLMAN,** same as 2640, except tuscan/tuscan/92 gray, RS — PULLMAN. 1941-42.

2643 **OBSERVATION,** matches 2642, RS — OBSERVATION. 1941-42.

603 yellow-orange/terra-cotta

604 red/black

607 red/red

608 Stephen Girard green/dark green

609 light blue/alum

611 light blue/alum

1630 light blue/light gray

1631 light blue/alum

2630 light blue/alum

2631 light blue/alum

2640 light blue/alum

2641 light blue/alum

2642 tuscan/92 gray

2643 tuscan/92 gray

LAST LARGE SERIES PASSENGER CARS
1931-42

The last large passenger cars are found in two series, 600 and 613 — both with interior lights, applied handrails and steps, and removable roofs with spring latches. Corresponding cars with electric couplers are numbered for the 2600- and 2613-series. The roofs for cars in the 600/

2600-series are constructed from one piece of metal, while those of the 613/2613-series are made from two pieces. Late cars in both series have smaller trucks which are moved out further to the ends of the cars and steps removed.

600 PULLMAN, RS — PULLMAN, 9″. 1933-42.
light gray/red/ivory
light blue/alum/alum
light red/red/ivory

601 OBSERVATION, RS-OBSERVATION, matches 600. 1933-42.
Note: Light red cars may have either red or alum observation railing and light blue cars may have either nickel or alum railing.

602 BAGGAGE, matches 600, RS — LIONEL LINES. 1933-42.
Note: Light gray cars RS — THE LIONEL LINES or just LIONEL LINES.

611 COMBINE, terra-cotta/terra-cotta and maroon/cream, prototype but NM, uncat. Circa 1931-33.

613 PULLMAN, RS — THE LIONEL LINES and PULLMAN, 10¼″. 1931-40.
terra-cotta/terra-cotta and maroon/cream
light red/light red and alum/alum
blue/dark blue and blue/white (O gauge "Blue Comet")

614 OBSERVATION, RS — THE LIONEL LINES and OBSERVATION, matches 613, 10⅛″. 1931-40.

615 BAGGAGE, matches 613, RS — THE LIONEL LINES only, 10¼″. 1933-40.

2600 PULLMAN, same as 600, with electric-box couplers, occurs only in light red/red/ivory, 9″. 1938-42.

2601 OBSERVATION, matches 2600. 1938-42.
Note: Can have red or alum observation railing.

2602 BAGGAGE, matches 2600. 1938-42.

2613 PULLMAN, same as 613, with electric-box couplers, 10¼″. 1938-42.
blue/dark blue/white
State green/dark green/cream

2614 OBSERVATION, matches 2613. 1938-42.
Note: Blue cars may have blue or alum observation railing; State green cars may have State green or alum railing.

2615 BAGGAGE, matches 2613. 1938-42.

600 light red/red

601 light blue/alum

602 light gray/red

611 (preproduction) terra-cotta/maroon

613 (preproduction) terra-cotta/maroon

613 terra-cotta/maroon

614 blue/dark blue

615 light red/alum

2600 light red/red

2601 light red/red

2602 light red/red

2613 blue/dark blue

2614 State green/dark green

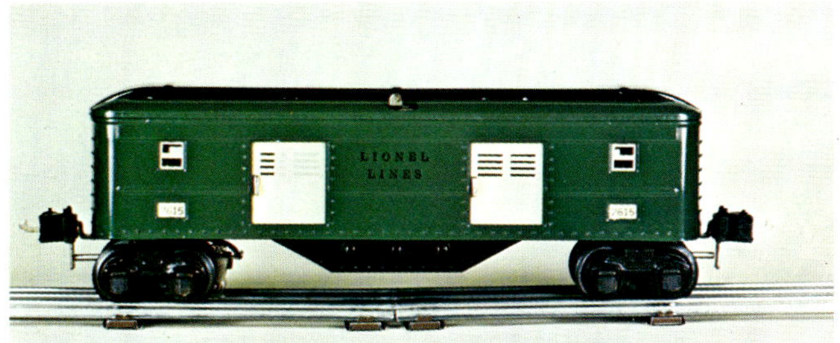

2615 State green/dark green

LARGE EX-IVES PASSENGER CARS
1933-37

These large passenger cars had interior lights and removable roofs with spring latches, but non-swinging doors and no added brass steps. Initially introduced in the "Ives" line in 1932, these cars were made with Lionel dies, were assembled in the Lionel Irvington plant, and after 1932, carried the LIONEL LINES name. Though produced for another five years, these cars never appeared in the Lionel catalogs.

1685 PULLMAN, 12", RS — LIONEL LINES, uncat. Circa 1933-37.
1685 gray/maroon/1685 cream — 6-Wh trucks
light red/maroon/cream — 4-Wh trucks
red/maroon/cream – 4-Wh trucks
light blue/alum/alum — 4-Wh trucks
vermillion/maroon/cream — 4-Wh trucks

Note: Black block lettering on gray, light blue, and vermillion cars; gold block lettering on red and light red cars.

1686 BAGGAGE, matches 1685, uncat. Circa 1933-37.

Note: Though commonly held that baggage cars were not made in all colors, original-finish cars have been found in all colors.

1687 OBSERVATION, matches 1685, uncat. Circa 1933-37.

1685 light blue/alum

1686 1685 gray/maroon

1687 red/maroon

SCALE DETAILED PASSENGER CARS
1941-42

These cars, made of phenolic plastic, were the best-scaled passenger cars Lionel made in O gauge. With interior lights, six-wheel tinplate trucks, undercarriage detail, spring-operated swinging doors, and automatic-box couplers, these were the top-of-the-line O gauge passenger cars. Both names have been found on the pullman, but no observations have ever been authenticated.

2623 **PULLMAN, IRVINGTON,** tuscan/tuscan/tuscan, white RS lettering, 14¼″. 1941-42.

2623 **PULLMAN, MANHATTAN,** same as IRVINGTON, uncat. Circa 1941-42.

Note: Though catalogs show IRVINGTON, in fact the MANHATTAN pullman is much more common.

2624 **PULLMAN, MANHATTAN,** same as above but RS-2624, uncat. Circa 1941-42.

2624 **OBSERVATION, MANHATTAN,** catalogued but NM. 1941-42.

2623 "Irvington" — tuscan

2624 "Manhattan" — tuscan

EARLY FREIGHT CAR SERIES
1915-26

These first cars were either 4-wh (5½″) or 8-wh (7″). All had hook couplers, no journal boxes or trim, and no light in cabooses. Three cars (800, 801, 802) were made in the 4-wh series initially. Early 4 and 8-wh cars had wide tread wheels; some 4-wh cars had spacers on the axles. The 900 boxcar for the armored loco appeared in 1917; the 901 gondola in 1919. Three cars (820-22) were made.

800 **BOX,** 4-Wh, all RS — PENN RR 4862 except some yellow-orange/maroon cars, RS — WABASH 6399, 5½″. 1915-26.
yellow-orange/maroon
yellow-orange/yellow-orange
green/green
orange/orange

Note: Other road names (Illinois Central, Union Pacific) appear in the catalogs but have never been found and are presumed NM.

801 **CABOOSE,** 4-Wh, 5½″. 1915-26.
brown/black — RS — WABASH RR 4390
brown/black — RS — script style NYNH&H, no number on side
maroon/black – RS – WABASH RR 4890

Note: May be found RS — 801 on side

802 **CATTLE,** 4-Wh, green, RS — UNION STOCK LINES on door, 5½″. 1915-26.

900 **BOX,** 4-Wh, same as 800, but gray for armored loco, no lettering, 5½″. 1917-21.

901 **GONDOLA,** 4-Wh, RS — LAKE SHORE (all colors) or PENNSYLVANIA (gray only), 5½″. 1919-27.
maroon; gray; dark green

820 **BOX,** RS — ILLINOIS CENTRAL or UNION PACIFIC 65784, or ATSF 48522, 7″. 1915-26.
yellow-orange/brown
yellow-orange/yellow-orange
orange/orange
orange/maroon
dark olive green/dark olive green — only Lionel car lettered ATSF

Note: Other road names (NYNH&H, NEW YORK CENTRAL, and UNION LINES) appear in the catalogs, but none have ever been found and are presumed NM.

821 **CATTLE,** green, RS — UNION STOCK LINES, 7″. 1915-16 and 1925-26.

Note: Though cataloged in 1915-16, probably not made until ten years later.

822 **CABOOSE,** RS — NEW YORK CENTRAL LINES in oval, 7″. 1915-26.
brown/black — vertical ribs embossed inward
maroon/black – vertical ribs embossed outward

Note: Shown in catalog RS — SANTA FE, but none have ever been found and are presumed NM.

800 orange/maroon

801 brown/black — NYNH&H

802 green

900 gray

901 maroon

820 orange- UNION PACIFIC

820 dark olive green — A TSF

821 green

822 maroon/black

LATER SMALL SERIES FREIGHT CARS
1927-34

Some overlap of this series with the earlier-series freight cars occurs. Both the early 803 hopper and early 804 tank were cataloged from 1923 on and sold in sets with the early series cars. All cars in the series were 6½″ and four-wheel only. They came with and without journals, and with and without attached number plates. In the absence of number plates, cars are RS lettered. Early cars had hook couplers and block lettering while later cars had latch couplers and serif lettering. Late cars may be found with many combinations of trim.

803 **HOPPER** (early), 4-Wh, dark green, RS — LIONEL. 1923-28.

803 **HOPPER** (late), 4-Wh, peacock — Br with added brass ladders and brakewheels. 1929-34.

804 **TANK** (early), 4-Wh, single brass dome, RS — LIONEL TANK LINES. 1923-28.
gray — RS
dark gray — RS
terra-cotta – RS

Note: Some early cars have red painted domes.

804 **TANK** (late), 4-Wh, three domes with added ladders and railings. 1929-34.
alum/no decal – Br
alum/Sunoco decal — Br or N (uncat. — circa 1934)
Shell orange/Shell decal — N (uncat. — circa 1939)
Shell orange/Shell decal — RS (uncat. — circa 1940)

805 **BOX,** 4-Wh. 1927-34.
cream/orange — Br
orange/maroon — Br
pea green/maroon — Br (uncat. — circa 1931)
pea green/orange – Br
orange/pea green — Br (uncat. — circa 1931)

806 **CATTLE,** 4-Wh. 1927-34.
pea green/terra-cotta — Br (uncat. — circa 1927)
orange/pea green — Br
orange/orange — Br (uncat. — circa 1931)
orange/maroon – Br

807 **CABOOSE,** 4-Wh. 1927-34.
peacock/dark green/red — Br (uncat. — circa 1928)
red/peacock/peacock – Br
light red/light red/cream — N or RS (uncat. — circa 1935-41)

809 **DUMP,** 4-Wh. 1931-34.
orange – RS
medium green — RS (uncat. — circa 1939-41)

831 **LUMBER,** 4-Wh. 1927-34.
black — 8 stakes
dark green — 8 stakes
dark green – 4 stakes
green — 4 stakes (uncat. — circa 1935-4l)

902 **GONDOLA,** 4-Wh. 1927-34.
dark green-Br
peacock – Br
Stephen Girard green — Br

Note: The 804, 809, 831, and 807 were made in uncataloged late colors with nickel or black journals after they were dropped from the catalog in 1934. Whether they were made intermittently or continuously for 1935-41 is unclear. See Specials list, loco 259 for further details.

803 (early) dark green

803 (late) peacock

804 (early) dark gray/red domes

804 (late) Shell orange

805 pea green/maroon

806 pea green/terra-cotta

806 orange/orange

807 peacock/dark green/red

809 orange

831 black/8 stakes

831 green/4 stakes

902 Stephen Girard green

LAST SMALL SERIES FREIGHT CARS
1934-42

These cars share the same 6½″ car body with the four-wheel small series freight cars but they are all eight-wheel cars. The chassis is always black unless noted otherwise, and the trim, number-plates, and journals follow the usual progression from brass to nickel to RS lettering/black journals in later years. The 650-series cars are found with latch or box couplers; the same cars with automatic (electric) box couplers were designated by the prefix "2" (i.e., 2650-series). In the later years of production of this series, several operating cars of the same size and with automatic couplers were introduced and were designated the 3650-series.

620 **FLOODLIGHT,** single light. 1937-42.
light red/alum light
light red/92 gray light
green/92 gray light — cataloged 1940-42 but NM

651 **FLAT,** green, 4 stakes, number RS on bottom. 1935-42.

652 **GONDOLA.** 1935-42.
yellow – N
burnt orange — RS

653 **HOPPER.** 1934-40.
Stephen Girard green – Br or N
black — RS — NM

654 **TANK.** 1934-42.
alum with Sunoco decal – Br or N
Shell orange with Shell decal — N or decal
light gray with Sunoco decal — decal

655 **BOX.** 1934-42.
cream/maroon – Br or N
cream/tuscan — N or RS (uncat. — circa 1939)

656 **CATTLE.** 1935-40.
light gray/light red — N — light gray or light red doors and door guides
burnt orange/tuscan — RS

657 **CABOOSE.** 1934-42.
red/red/cream — Br
light red/light red/cream – N or RS
light red/light red/white — RS
light red/tuscan/white — N or RS

659 **DUMP,** medium green — RS. 1935-42.

2620 **FLOODLIGHT,** single die-cast light, same as 620 except with automatic-box couplers. 1938-42.
light red/alum light
light red/92 gray light

2651 **FLAT,** same as 651 except with automatic-box couplers, green, 4 stakes. 1938-42.

2652 **GONDOLA,** same as 652 except with automatic-box couplers. 1938-42.
yellow – N
burnt orange — RS

2653 HOPPER, same as 653 except with automatic-box couplers. 1938-40.
Stephen Girard green – N
black — RS

2654 TANK, same as 654 except with automatic-box couplers. 1938-42.
alum with Sunoco decal — N
Shell orange with Shell decal – N or decal
light gray with Sunoco decal — decal

2655 BOX, same as 655 except with automatic-box couplers. 1938-42.
cream/maroon — N
cream/tuscan – N or RS

2656 CATTLE, same as 656 except with automatic-box couplers. 1938-42.
light gray/light red – N
burnt orange/tuscan — RS

2657 CABOOSE, same as 657 except with automatic-box couplers. 1938-42.
light red/light red/cream — N or RS
light red/light red/white — RS
light red/tuscan/white — N or RS

Note: Also made as 2657X with automatic box-couplers on both ends to be used with 0-4-0 switcher.

2659 DUMP, same as 659 except with automatic-box couplers, medium green — RS. 1938-42.

2660 DERRICK, cream/light red/green boom — N or RS. 1938-42.

Note: Boom is green plastic and does not match 45N color.

3651 LUMBER, operating, matches 2650-series, black — RS number on bottom. 1939-42.

3652 GONDOLA, operating, matches 2650-series. 1939-42.
green — cataloged 1939 but NM
yellow – N
yellow — RS (red or black lettering)

3659 DUMP, operating, matches 2650-series, number embossed in frame. 1939-42.
black/red hopper
black/green hopper — cataloged 1938 but NM

651 green/4 stakes

652 yellow

653 Stephen Girard green

654 Shell orange

655 cream/maroon

620 light red/alum

656 light gray/light red — light red doors

657 light red/tuscan/white

659 medium green

2620 light red/92 gray

2651 green/4 stakes

2652 burnt orange

2653 black

2654 light gray

2655 cream/tuscan

2656 burnt orange/tuscan

2657X light red/light red/white

2659 dark green

2660 cream/light red/green

3651 black

3652 yellow

3659 black/red

LATER LARGE SERIES FREIGHT CARS
1926-42

These freight cars were the top-of-the-line, brass-plate-period, O gauge cars with attached plates, journals and trim. All cars were 8⅞" long. The late cars in this series are found with RS lettering (no slots in car bodies for plates) and with the trucks moved further toward the ends of the cars. Corresponding cars with automatic-box couplers are designated with the prefix "2" (i.e., 2800), and matching operating cars by the prefix "3" (i.e., 3800). Most of the 810-series cars were first cataloged in 1926 using standard gauge 200-series catalog cuts. The 813 cattle and 814 box are found with large or small door handles, the large ones being earlier.

810 DERRICK, 8⅞" car but boom extends further. 1931-42.
terra-cotta/maroon/peacock boom – Br or Br and N
yellow/light red/green boom — N
Note: Windows can be brass or cream on terra-cotta/maroon derrick.

811 FLAT, RS — THE LIONEL LINES. 1926-40.
maroon
alum
green — cataloged but NM
black— cataloged but NM

812 GONDOLA. 1926-42.
mojave — Br
dark green – Br
Stephen Girard green — Br
green— N
burnt orange — cataloged but NM

813 CATTLE. 1926-42.
orange/pea green – Br
cream/maroon — N
tuscan/tuscan — RS

814 BOX. 1926-42.
cream/orange – Br
yellow/brown — N
cream/maroon — N
Note: Door guides normally match the roof color but can be found in peacock or pea green on cream/orange cars.

814R REFRIGERATOR. 1929-42.
ivory/peacock/black frame – Br
white/light blue/black frame — N
white/light blue/alum frame — N
flat white/tuscan/black frame — RS

815 TANK. 1926-42.
pea green/no decal – Br
alum/no decal — Br
alum/Sunoco decal – Br or N
Shell orange/Shell decal — N
Note: Pea green cars can be found with black or maroon frame.

816 HOPPER. 1927-42.
olive green — Br
red– Br or N
black — N
Note: Minor differences in red on these cars; some early cars lighter and some late cars darker red.

817 CABOOSE. 1926-42.
peacock/dark green/orange – Br
peacock/dark green/brass – Br
red/peacock/brass — Br
light red/light red/alum — Br or N
Note: These cabooses usually found with couplers on both ends but not marked X.

820 FLOODLIGHT, chassis RS — THE LIONEL LINES. 1931-42.
terra-cotta/black frame/brass lights
green/black frame/nickel-plated lights
green/black frame/92 gray die-cast lights
Note: Late base with die-cast lights is flat, not indented for light base.

2810 DERRICK, same as 810 but with automatic-box couplers, yellow/light red/green — N. 1938-42.

2811 FLAT, same as 811 but with automatic-box couplers, RS — THE LIONEL LINES. 1938-42.
alum — RS
black — cataloged 1940 but NM

2812 GONDOLA, same as 812 but with automatic-box couplers. 1938-42.
green – N
burnt orange — N or RS
black — cataloged 1940 but NM

2813 **CATTLE,** same as 813 but with automatic-box couplers. 1938-42.
cream/maroon — N
tuscan/tuscan — RS — cataloged but NM

2814 **BOX,** same as 814 but with automatic-box couplers. 1938-42; yellow/tuscan — N
cream/maroon – N; burnt orange/tuscan — RS

2814R **REFRIGERATOR,** same as 814R but with automatic-box couplers. 1938-42.
white/light blue/black frame — N
white /light blue/alum frame — N
flat white/tuscan/black frame — N or RS

2815 **TANK,** same as 815 but with automatic-box couplers. 1938-42.
alum/Sunoco decal – N
Shell orange/Shell decal — N or decal
Shell orange/no Shell decal — decal lettering
gray/Sunoco decal — cataloged 1941-42 but NM

2816 **HOPPER,** same as 816 but with automatic-box couplers. 1938-42.
red – N; black — RS

2817 **CABOOSE,** same as 817 but with automatic-box couplers, 1938-42.
light red/light red/alum – N
light red/tuscan/white — N
flat red/tuscan/white — N or RS

2820 **FLOODLIGHT,** same as 820 but with automatic-box couplers. 1938-42.
green/black frame/nickel-plated lights
green/black frame/92 gray die-cast lights
Note: Late base with die-cast lights is flat, not indented for light base.

3811 **FLAT,** operating, matches 2810-series, black — no lettering. 1939-42.

3814 **MERCHANDISE (BOX),** operating, matches 2810-series, tuscan — RS or decal — LIONEL LINES. 1939-42.

3859 **DUMP,** operating, matches 2810-series, black except red hopper bin — embossed number on frame. 1939-42.

810 terra-cotta/maroon/peacock

811 maroon

812 Stephen Girard green

813 tuscan

814 yellow/brown

814 cream/orange — pea green door guides

814R ivory/peacock

815 pea green

816 black

817 light red

820 green/nickel-plated lights

2810 yellow/light red/green

2811 alum

2812 burnt orange

2813 cream/maroon

2814 flat orange/tuscan

2814R white/light blue/alum

2815 Shell orange

2816 black

2817 flat red/tuscan/white

2820 green/92 gray lights

SCALE-DETAILED FREIGHT CARS
1941-42

These were low-priced, well detailed cars introduced just prior to WWII. After WWII the same cars were reissued with new numbers. All cars have automatic-box couplers.

2672 CABOOSE, PRR N5 style, no interior lights, no added window frames or smoke-stack, tuscan, RS — PENNSYLVANIA, 6⅜″. 1942.

2755 TANK, 9″. 1941-42.
92 gray/Sunoco decal – decal lettering
alum/Sunoco decal — decal

2757 CABOOSE, same as 2672 but with interior lights, attached window frames, smoke-stack and frosted windows, tuscan/red trim, RS — PENNSYLVANIA, 6⅜″. 1941-42.

Note: Available with automatic-box couplers on one end (2757) or on both ends (2757X).

2758 AUTOMOBILE (BOX), tucan, RS — PENNSYLVANIA, 9″. 1941-42.

3811 black

3814 tuscan

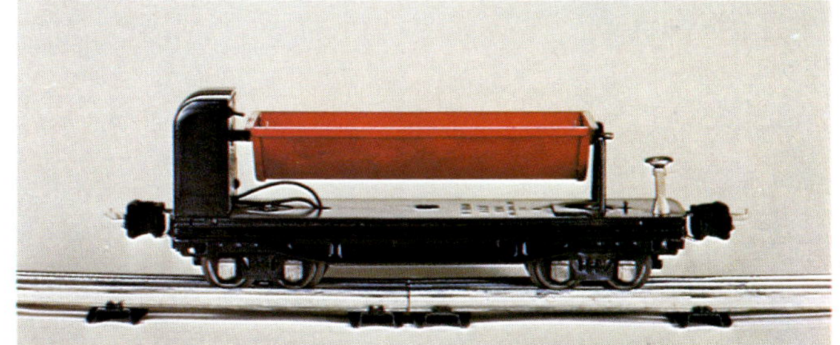
3859 black/red

2672 tuscan

2755 92 gray

2757 tuscan

2758 tuscan

714 tuscan

SCALE-SERIES FREIGHT CARS
1940-42

The four scale series cars were introduced in 1940 to be used with the scale "Hudson" and Pennsy B6 switcher, and were available in three separate series — 700 (NMRA scale couplers, sprung trucks), 700K (same but in kit form), and 2950 (electromagnetic couplers, tinplate trucks). The hopper was a zinc alloy die-casting, the caboose was a magnesium alloy die-casting, while the boxcar was of molded phenolic plastic and the tank car was a zinc die-casting. All cars had well-detailed attached trim — handrails, ladders, brakewheels, etc.

714 **BOX,** built to NMRA standards, tuscan, RS — PENNSYLVANIA, 10¾". 1940-42.

714K **BOX,** same as 714 but in kit form in primer paint only. 1940-42.

715 **TANK** built to NMRA standards, 9". 1940-42.
black with Shell decal — decal (1940)
black with Sunoco decal — decal (1941-42)

715K **TANK,** same as 715 but in kit form in primer paint only. 1940-42.

716 **HOPPER,** built to NMRA standards, black, RS — BALTIMORE & OHIO, 10½". 1940-42.

716K **HOPPER,** same as 716 but in kit form in primer paint only. 1940-42.

717 **CABOOSE,** built to NMRA standards, tuscan, RS — NYC, 8¾". 1940-42.

Note: Always has couplers on both ends.

717K **CABOOSE,** same as 717 but in kit form in primer paint only. 1940-42.

2954 **BOX,** same as 714 but with tinplate trucks and automatic-box couplers. 1940-42.

2955 **TANK,** same as 715 but with tinplate trucks and automatic-box couplers. 1940-42.

2956 **HOPPER,** same as 716 but with tinplate trucks and automatic-box couplers. 1940-42.

2957 **CABOOSE,** same as 717 but with tinplate trucks and automatic-box couplers. 1940-42.

715 black/Sunoco decal

716 black

717 tuscan

2954 tuscan

2955 black/Shell decal

2956 black

2957 tuscan

LITHOGRAPHED 027-SERIES CARS
1933-42

Lionel had never used lithography to market an inexpensive line of trains until after the complete takeover of the Ives company in the early 1930's. At that time several series of cars appeared with the IVES R.R. lettering and then remained in production under the LIONEL LINES herald until World War II. The three series were the 1510/1810 (four-wheel, hook couplers), 1670/1690 (small eight-wheel), and the 1710 (larger eight-wheel). Freight cars of both the 1670- and 1710-series were also available with automatic-box couplers with the prefix "2" (i.e., 2670 and 2710). These cars had no attached plates, very little attached trim, and no interior lights. Though originally marketed as "Lionel Junior", these trains were the first of what we now call 027. An interesting note is that under the Ives herald both the 1670- and 1710-series had cattle cars, but they were not carried over into the LIONEL LINES series, even though they shared the same body with the box car. Though rumored that a cattle car exists in the 1510-series, no car has been found, even under the Ives herald. Some of the cars of the 1670-series (1679, 1680, 1682) can be found with no journals and boxes marked 1679X, 1680X, and 1682X. These cars were dealer specials in the late 1930's. Finally, lithographed colors do not match the enamel colors given in the color chart but are described as closely as possible.

1512 **GONDOLA,** litho, 4-Wh, marked WINNER or NYC, 6″. 1933, 1936-37.
light blue; dark blue
Note: The 4-Wh lithographed freight series came with and without LIONEL LINES on the frame, with a black frame (1933-35), red frame (1936-37), and red frame and gold highlights (1937).

1514 **BOX,** litho, 4-Wh, 6″. 1933-37.
yellow/dark blue — ERIE markings
yellow/light blue – ERIE markings
yellow/light blue — ERIE upper left, BABY RUTH upper right, LIONEL lower left.
Note: May be found with orange, brown or black doors and door guides.

1515 **TANK,** litho, 4-Wh, 6″. 1933-37.
alum — FUEL OIL lower left, UNION TANK LINES upper left
alum – MOTOR OIL lower left, Sunoco herald, with or without LIONEL LINES below railing

1517 **CABOOSE,** litho, 4-Wh, marked WINNER or NYC herald, 6″. 1933-37.
dark red/brown/yellow
red/red/cream
red/red/cream/yellow cupola stripe — LIONEL along bottom edge.

1518 **DINER,** litho, 4-Wh, multi-colored Mickey Mouse lithography, sets only, 6″. 1935.

1536 **BAND CAR,** litho, matches 1518 DINER. 1935.

1536 **ANIMAL CAR,** litho, matches 1518 DINER. 1935.

1677 **GONDOLA,** litho, 8″. 1933-35, 1939-42.
peacock — LIONEL-IVES markings (cataloged 1933 but NM)
peacock — LIONEL LINES markings
red – LIONEL LINES markings

1678 **CATTLE,** litho, green/orange, cataloged with LIONEL-IVES markings but NM, 8″. 1933.

1679 **BOX,** litho, 8″. 1933-42.
yellow/dark blue — LIONEL-IVES markings (cataloged 1933 but NM)
yellow/dark blue – LIONEL LINES markings. no candy bar logo
yellow/medium blue — LIONEL LINES markings, with candy bar logo
yellow/light blue — LIONEL LINES, with candy bar logo
yellow/maroon — LIONEL LINES markings, no candy bar logo but lettered BABY RUTH
Note: Can be found with various combinations of brown or orange doors and guides.

1680 **TANK,** litho, 8″. 1933-42.
alum – MOTOR OIL lower left, Sunoco herald
Shell orange — PETROLEUM PRODUCTS lower left, Shell herald
alum — SUNX upper left, Sunoco herald
gray — SUNX upper left, Sunoco herald

1682 **CABOOSE,** litho, 8″. 1933-42.
dark red/brown/yellow — LIONEL-IVES markings (cataloged 1933 but NM)
dark red/brown/yellow — LIONEL LINES markings

light red/light red/cream – LIONEL LINES markings
light red/light red/cream/yellow cupola stripe — LIONEL LINES markings.
brown/brown/brown — NYC markings

Note: Can be found with couplers on one end (1682) or both ends (1682X).

1690 PULLMAN, litho, 8″. 1933-40.
dark red/brown/yellow — LIONEL-IVES markings (cataloged 1933 but NM)
dark red/brown/yellow — LIONEL LINES markings
light red/light red/cream – LIONEL LINES markings, with or without fishbelly and handrails

1691 OBSERVATION, litho, matches 1690. 1933-40.

1692 PULLMAN, litho, peacock/peacock/cream — LIONEL LINES markings, with handrails, no journals, no fishbelly, sets only, 8″, uncat. Circa 1937-38. SPECIAL.

1693 OBSERVATION, litho, matches 1692, uncat. Circa 1937-38. SPECIAL

1717 GONDOLA, litho, tan/burnt orange, 9½″, uncat. Circa 1933-40.

1719 BOX, litho, light peacock/blue, attached Br or N ladders, 9½″, uncat. Circa 1933-40.

Note: Can be found with various combinations of orange and brown doors and guides.

1722 CABOOSE, litho, 9½″, uncat. Circa 1933-40.
orange/maroon/yellow
orange-red/maroon/yellow
red/maroon/yellow

1811 PULLMAN, litho, 4-Wh, 6″. 1933-37.
light peacock/orange/cream — LIONEL-IVES markings (cataloged 1933 but NM)
light peacock/orange/cream – LIONEL LINES markings
light red/light red/cream — LIONEL LINES markings
gray/red and gray/ivory — LIONEL LINES markings

1812 OBSERVATION, litho, 4-Wh, matches 1811. 1933-37.

1813 BAGGAGE, litho, 4-Wh, matches 1811. 1933-37.
light peacock/orange/cream — LIONEL LINES markings
gray/red and gray/ivory — LIONEL LINES markings

2677 GONDOLA, litho, same as 1677, but with automatic-box couplers, red. 1940-42.

2679 BOX, litho, same as 1679, but with automatic-box couplers. 1938-42.
yellow/medium blue — LIONEL LINES markings, with candy bar logo
yellow/light blue — LIONEL LINES markings, with candy bar logo
yellow/maroon – LIONEL LINES markings, no candy bar logo but lettered BABY RUTH.

2680 TANK, litho, same as 1680, but with automatic-box couplers. 1938-42.
alum – MOTOR OIL lower left, Sunoco herald
Shell orange — PETROLEUM PRODUCTS lower left, Shell herald
alum or gray — SUNX upper left, Sunoco herald

2682 CABOOSE, litho, same as 1682, but with automatic-box couplers. 1938-42.
light red/light red/cream — LIONEL LINES markings
light red/light red/cream/yellow cupola stripe — LIONEL LINES markings
brown/brown/brown — NYC markings

Note: Available with couplers on one end (2682) or both ends (2682X).

2717 GONDOLA, litho, same as 1717, but with automatic-box couplers, tan/burnt orange, uncat. Circa 1938-42.

2719 BOX, litho, same as 1719, but with automatic-box couplers, light peacock/blue, uncat. Circa 1938-42.

2722 CABOOSE, litho, same as 1722, but with automatic-box couplers, uncat. Circa 1938-42.
orange/maroon/yellow
orange-red/maroon/yellow
red/maroon/yellow

1515 oil tank box

1512 light blue

1514 yellow/light blue

1515 alum/red frame with gold highlights

1517 red/yellow cupola stripe

1518 diner litho

1536 band car litho

1536 animal car litho

1677 peacock

1679X yellow/medium blue

1680X gray/SUNX lettering

1682 light red/yellow cupola stripe

1690 dark red/brown/yellow

1691 light red/light red/cream

1692 peacock/peacock/cream

1693 peacock/peacock/cream

1717 tan/burnt orange

1719 light peacock/blue

1722 orange/maroon

1811 light red/light red/cream

1812 light peacock/orange/cream

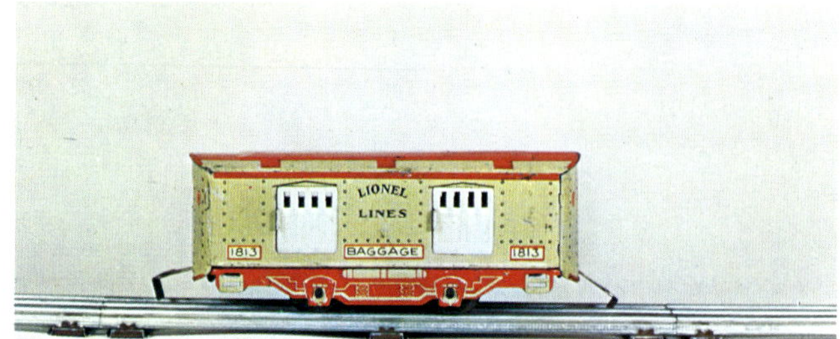

1813 gray/red and gray/ivory

2677 red

2679 yellow/maroon

2680 alum/MOTOR OIL/Sunoco herald

2682X brown/NYC

2717 tan/burnt orange

2719 light peacock/blue

2722 orange-red/maroon/yellow

WINNER CARS
1930-32

The Winner Lines cars are the same four-wheel, six-inch cars found in the Ives mechanical train sets (1931-32), the Ives "Yankee" electric sets (1931-32), and the Lionel mechanical sets (1933-37). All cars are lithographed; as noted elsewhere, lithographed colors do not correspond to the enamel colors in the color chart. Some cars have WINNER markings while others are indistinguishable from cars in the Lionel mechanical sets. All cars have late-style hook couplers.

1001 PULLMAN, litho, lettered WINNER RAILWAYS, cataloged in 1930 WINNER flyer but NM, 1930.

1011 PULLMAN, litho, lettered WINNER LINES, sets only. 1931-32.
light orange/green/cream
dark orange/green/cream

1019 OBSERVATION, litho, matches 1011, sets only. 1931-32.

1020 BAGGAGE, litho, matches 1011, sets only. 1931-32.

1512 GONDOLA, litho, lettered NYC, with or without WINNER lettering on chassis, sets only. 1931-32. light blue; dark blue

1514 BOX, litho, lettered ERIE, yellow/dark blue, sets only. 1931-32.

1517 CABOOSE, litho, lettered WINNER or NYC, dark red/brown/yellow, sets only. 1931-32.

1011 light orange/green/cream

1019 dark orange/green/cream

1020 dark orange/green/cream

1512 light blue

1514 yellow/dark blue

1517 dark red/brown/yellow

606 orange/orange/cream

MACY CARS

Regular production cars were made by Lionel for R. H. Macy and Company, New York, with special lettering and paint. A more complete description of these sets can be found in the SPECIALS section.

605 PULLMAN, orange/orange/cream, same as regular 605 but sold with specially marked 606, uncat, Circa 1930-32. SPECIALS

606 OBSERVATION, orange/orange/cream, same as regular 606 except with MACY SPECIAL brass plate on platform, uncat. Circa 1930-32. SPECIALS

607 PULLMAN, maroon/maroon/cream, same as regular 607 except RS — MACY SPECIAL, no interior lights, uncat. Circa 1931-32. SPECIALS

608 OBSERVATION, maroon/maroon/cream, same as regular 608 except RS — MACY SPECIAL and MACY SPECIAL brass plate on platform, no interior lights, uncat. Circa 1931-32. SPECIALS

610 PULLMAN, red/red/cream, same as regular 610 except RS — MACY SPECIAL in script lettering above windows, uncat. Circa 1926-30. SPECIALS

612 OBSERVATION, red/red/cream, same as regular 612 except RS — MACY SPECIAL in script lettering above windows, uncat. Circa 1926-30. SPECIALS

629 PULLMAN, red/red/cream, 4-Wh, same as regular 629 but sold with specially marked 630, uncat. Circa 1931. SPECIALS

630 OBSERVATION, red/red/cream, 4-Wh, same as regular 630 except with MACY SPECIAL brass plate on platform, uncat. Circa 1931. SPECIALS

606 (end) MACY SPECIAL plate

607 maroon/maroon/cream

612 red/red/cream

1717X gondola box

Paper Train

1943

Unable to produce tinplate trains during World War II Lionel designed and manufactured Set No. 50 "Lionel Wartime Freight Train" — a paper train complete with paper accessories and paper track. The only non-paper parts included were the 22 wood axles for the rolling stock. The paper locomotive is a close representation of a 224 and 2224 tender except for the lack of some valve gear. The 2812 paper gondola was modeled after the rubber stamped 2812 gondola but was bright red instead of burnt orange. The yellow 61100 paper automobile car was unlike any prewar car in color except the OO boxcar, but closely models the 2758 tuscan automobile car in shape and size. The 47618 paper caboose follows closely the lines of the 2757 caboose but is red instead of tuscan. The three freight cars carry the legend "BLT. 3-43". The set also contains 3 paper figures, crossing gate, crossing signal, three boxes, one board, and 198 inches of track.

Set No. 50 set box

224 and 2224 black

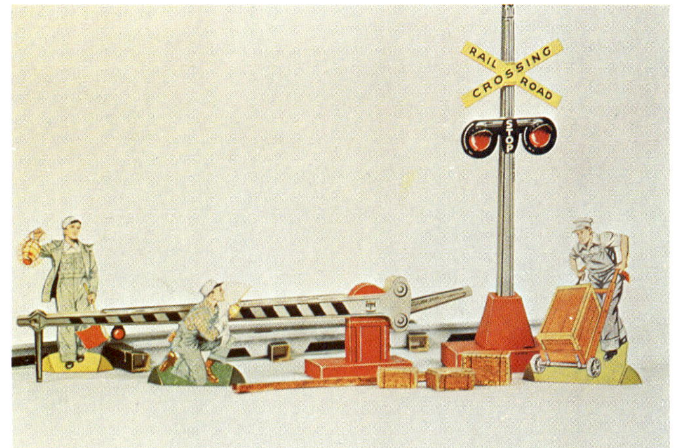

accessories

2812 red

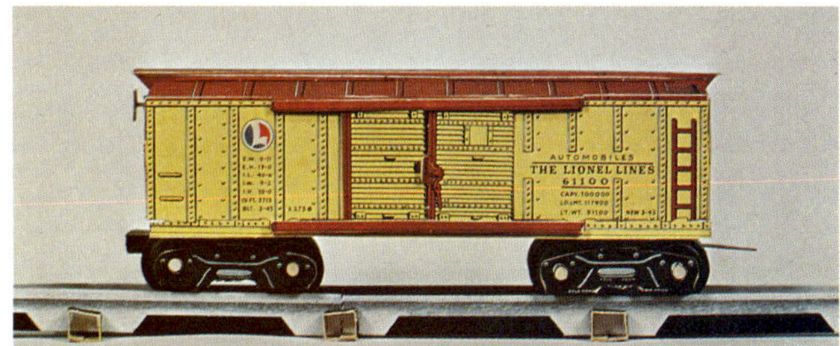

61100 yellow

47618 red

Standard Gauge Locomotives 1906-1939

Going by the catalogs, the last Standard gauge sets were offered in 1939, but some cars were still shown in 1940. When train production ceased with the start of World War II, Lionel swept out the factory and put together all the trains they could. It was possible, then, to buy a new Standard gauge set, freshly assembled, in 1942.

Although Lionel cataloged Standard gauge sets from 1906 through 1939, fewer numbers were used than in the O gauge line, making this section somewhat less involved. Unfortunately, fewer numbers over a long span of time means more variations of each number. No attempt has been made to list all the minor variations, but by studying the charts of the components and the listed variations one can determine most of the minor variations. Specials are listed here for completeness, but are described more fully in the SPECIALS section. Unique items, such as a pink 408E, are also noted but are again described more fully in the SPECIALS section. The following charts and photographs are provided to make easier the dating of the trains and the identification of the missing parts easier.

Wheels. Over the years of Standard gauge production solid cast iron, spoked cast iron, and die-cast wheels in a variety of wheel diameters and rim sizes were used on these locomotives. The wheel chart in figure 5 gives the wheel descriptions for the various locomotives. Realize, however, that the wheel diameter may vary slightly due to wear or growth of the metal.

Pilots. For identification purposes, note that pre-1926 steam engines used one of two separate types of cast iron pilots. On all other engine groups the pilot does not vary. This is not to imply that all other types of Standard gauge locomotives have the same pilot but rather that each locomotive is found with only one type of pilot.

Steam Locomotive Pilot Types

Early Cast Iron, 1906-17 3″ wide, 1¼″ high, 1″ mounting center, extends 1 11/16″; no coupler slot in pilot; used on 5, 5 Special, 6, 6 Special, 7, and 51

Later Cast Iron, 1918 On 3⅛″ wide, 1 5/16″ high, 1⅛″ mounting center, extends 1¼″, with coupler slot in pilot, used on 5, 6, 7, and 51

Headlights. The style of headlight can be very useful in dating the locomotive. Locomotives prior to 1925 or 1926 have a variety of sheet metal headlights as described in figure 6, while locomotives made from 1926 on have diecast headlights.

Motors. Four different motors were used in Standard gauge locomotives — a very early small frame vertical motor (1906-12), an improved large frame motor in early locomotives (1912-26), the Super Motor with large geared wheels (1923-25) and later two smaller geared wheels (1925-27), Bild-A-Loco with barrel commutator (1928-33) and finally a disc commutator (1934-39).

Reverse. All steam locomotives have either hand reverse or E unit reverse, while some electric style locomotives have no reverse. The ability to reverse is designated by the following abbreviations:

No reverse — NR in description
E unit reverse — E follows the locomotive number
Hand reverse — assumed if not designated, when necessary indicated by HR.

The reverse switch plate prior to July 1918 is stamped "The Lionel Manufacturing Co" or blank, thereafter, it is either blank or is stamped "The Lionel Corporation."

Trucks. The trucks on the tenders as on the cars are pictured and discussed in detail in the

FIGURE 5

1⁵⁄₁₆″ Dia. 	**Solid Cast Iron** 1910 (0-6-0) (4 tin wheels) (2 cast iron wheels) 1911 SPECIAL 53 (0-4-4-0)	**2⁵⁄₁₆″ Dia. Thin Rim** 	**Early Spoked Cast Iron** 5, 5 SPECIAL 51 6, 6 SPECIAL 7 42 54 1911 (0-4-0) 1912 1912 SPECIAL
1⁵⁄₁₆″ Dia. 	**Early Spoked Cast Iron** 53 (0-4-4-0) 1911 SPECIAL 33 (0-6-0) 34 (0-6-0) 1910 (0-6-0)	**2¼″ Dia. Thick Rim** 	**Early Spoked Cast Iron** 5 53 (0-4-0) 51 54 6 1911 (0-4-0) 7 1912 38 42 50
1¾″ Dia. 	**Early Spoked Cast Iron** 33(0-4-0)	**2⁷⁄₁₆″ Dia.**	**Die-Cast with Nickel Rim.** 8 318 10 380 50 402
1¾″ Dia. 	**Die-Cast with Nickel Rim** 33 (0-4-0) 34 (0-6-0)	**2⁷⁄₁₆″ Dia.** 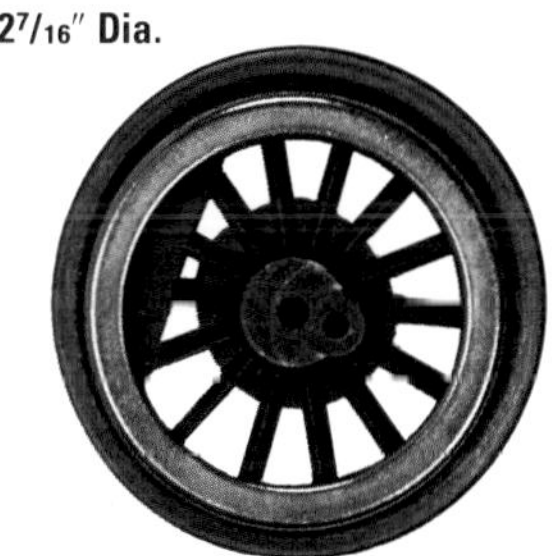	**Die-Cast with Nickel Rim** 8, 8E 385E 9, 9E, 9U 390, 390E 10, 10E 392E 318, 318E 400E 380, 380E 402, 402E 381, 381E, 381U 408E 384, 384E 1835E

FIGURE 6

Slide On 1906-13 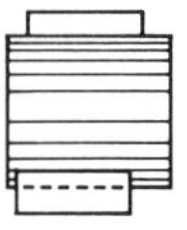 	Two variations — high or low vent soldered on top, slides over metal tab or punched guides on locomotive; used on early locos, also found as dummy headlight with no hole for wire in the back of headlight.	**Switch 1923-25** 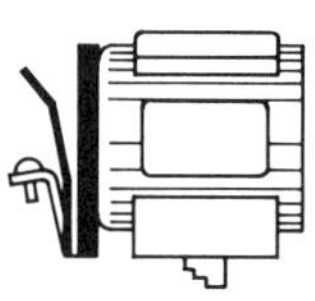 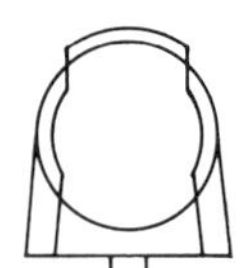	Switch on back to turn on and off, cut out sides of light for red and green celluloid, used only on 380 and 402 in Standard gauge, early 380's had this type but no switch.
Pedestal 1912-18 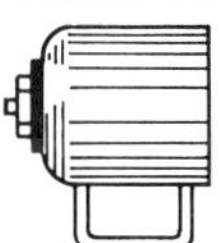	Two variations — with or without vent punched in the top, metal cradle underneath in the same axis as the light or at right angle to it.	**Die Cast 1926 on** 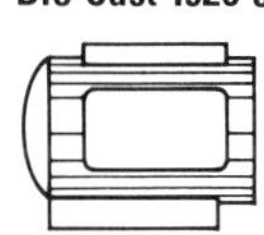	Casting threaded to accept mounting screw, fiber board and brass contact inserted; patented June 8, 1926.
Strap 1918-26 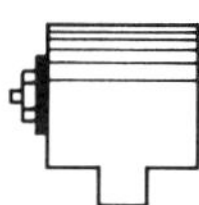	Two tabs extend through slots in locomotive.		

introduction to the STANDARD GAUGE CARS section.

Other Trim. Other trim such as bells, pantographs, and whistles appears on the locomotives, however, few changes on these items occurred over the years of production, and therefore, this trim is not very useful in dating the locomotive. Two different types of bells were used — a large, early bell mounted by two screws in the base (up through 1912), and a later, smaller bell with one screw in the base of the cradle (1913 on). There are four sizes of whistles: earliest is ¾″ tall, later 7/16″ size, still later ⅝″ high, and finally the ⅜″ tall whistle on steam locomotives.

Couplers. The changes in couplers over the years of Standard gauge production are depicted in a chart in the introduction to STANDARD GAUGE CARS but briefly the progression of types is as follows:

Short and long straight hook	1906-14
Short and long crinkle hook	1910-18
Hook with ears	1914-25
Combination latch	1923-28
Latch	1924-42

Box and automatic box couplers were never used on Standard gauge equipment as far as is known.

Additional Brief Notes

1. All color variations for each locomotive are listed in chronologic order of color appearance. If there is clearly a most common color, it is italicized.

2. The lengths given are actual measurements and may not agree with the stated lengths in the catalogs. For steam engines the length given represents the sum of the length of the engine (pilot tip to end of cab) plus the length of the tender (frame without couplers). The given lengths of electric style locomotives are measured from the tip of one pilot to the tip of the other pilot.

3. The frame on all brass plate electric style locomotives is black if not mentioned. Window trim on early electric style locomotives is red or green paint. Early electric style locomotives with cream window trim probably are all factory

FIGURE 7

DEVELOPMENT OF LIONEL STANDARD GAUGE ELECTRIC LOCOMOTIVES

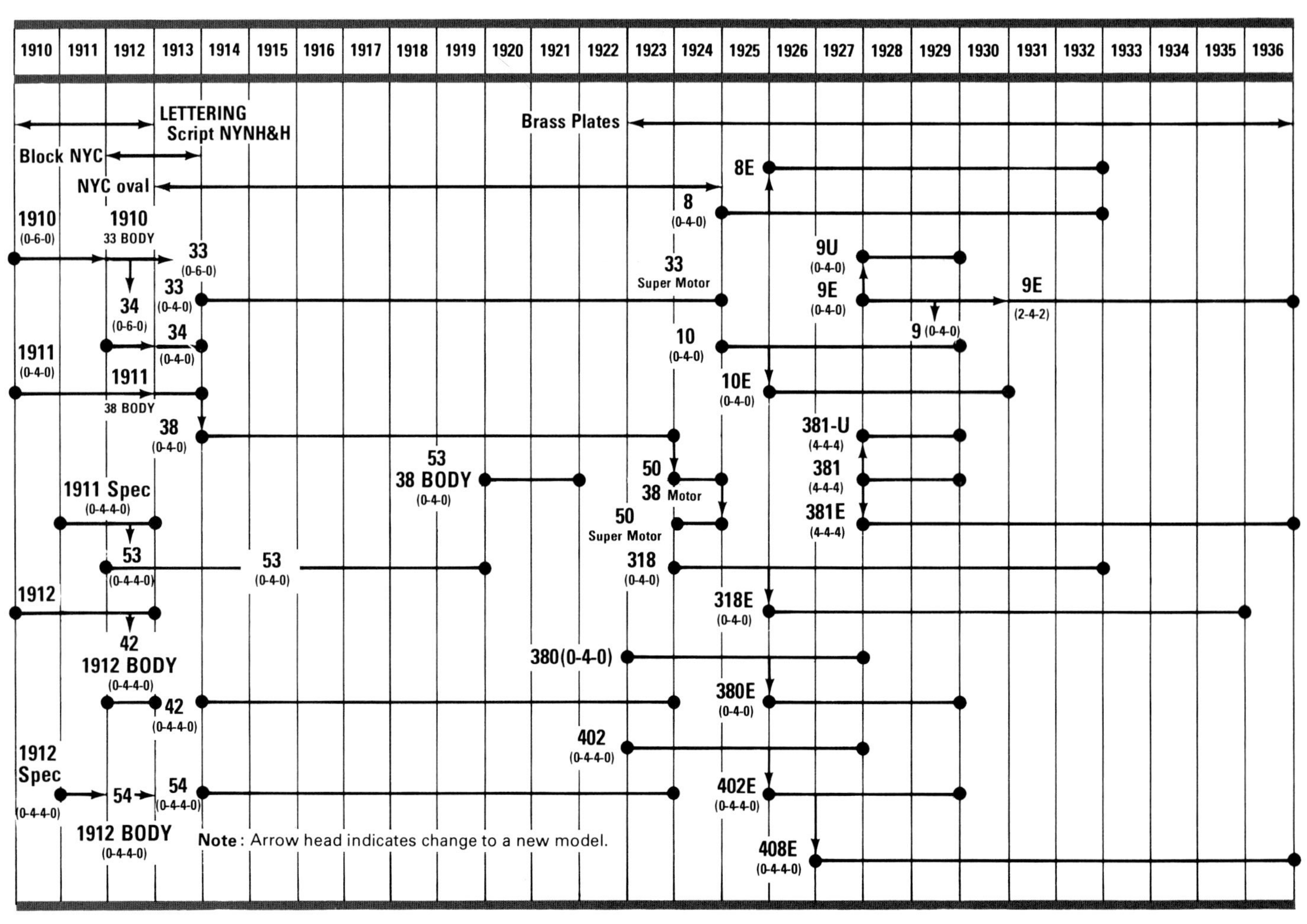

repaints. Window trim on later locomotives is brass (Br) if not noted. As mentioned in the COLOR CHART, the early colors vary markedly from item to item, and do not necessarily match the designated color on the chart.

4. NM — means "never made as far as known."

5. Electric style locomotives in colors used only after the locomotives were dropped from the catalogs may represent factory repaints — items repainted when sent back for repairs — or may have been continued as specials.

6. In the descriptions, most of the rubber stamped (RS) lettering of the early locomotives is given as it appears on the engines with the following exceptions:

- script NYNH&H — script lettering NEW YORK, NEW HAVEN & HARTFORD
- NYC oval — oval around NEW YORK CENTRAL LINES
- block NYC — block lettering NEW YORK CENTRAL LINES

7. Electric locomotives have MFG or screen plates up to 1918 and CORP plates thereafter on both the front and rear doors.

8. "Chuggers" were used on the 385, 392 and 400 steam locomotives from 1933 to 1936.

9. Early electric style locomotive had flat red primer paint on the inside.

FIGURE 8

DEVELOPMENT OF LIONEL STANDARD GAUGE STEAM LOCOMOTIVES

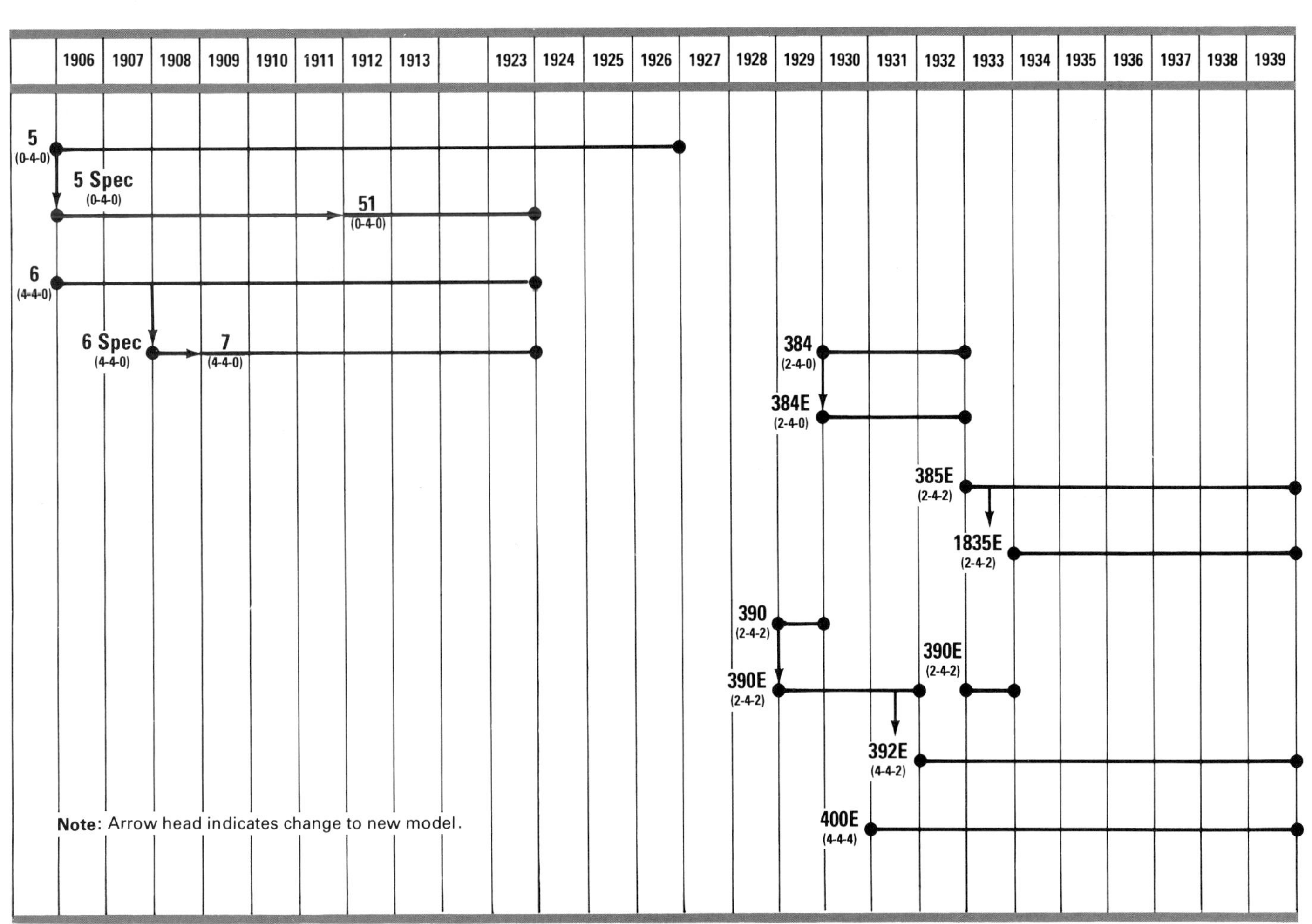

EARLY LOCOMOTIVES
1906-26

Lionel began Standard gauge production in 1906 after dropping the 2⅞" gauge line. All of the early locomotives were constructed primarily of sheet steel or brass, and soldered together. After two coats of enamel, window frames were painted red and added trim painted gold. Both the electric and the steam type locomotives were then rubber stamp lettered (RS) except the brass locomotives which remained unlettered. On the steam types the connecting rods, piston rods, cross-heads and guides are nickel plated steel; the boilers of the steam locomotives are made of Russian iron (blued finish) except on the 6 Special and 7, which are nickel and brass. Steam type locomotives were made completely of stamped steel except for the wood domes, stacks, cylinders, back-head, pilot beam and boiler fronts on the 5 and 6 locomotives and corresponding parts of brass on the 6 Special and 7. The electric type locomotive superstructures were copies of those that operated on electrified railroads; most commonly used was that of the New York Central class S-1. Early electric types from 1910-12 had sharp angled hood planes and a "square" body, while in general cabs from 1913 on had "rounded" hood corners except the 53 (0-4-0). Hand rails and steps, usually painted gold, were added to the electric style locomotives to give an appearance of completeness. All steam locomotives had a hand reverse controller, as Lionel referred to it; some electric style locomotives had no reverse (NR), while most have a hand reverse mechanism (HR).

STEAM LOCOMOTIVES

5 0-4-0, black, Russian iron boiler, nickeled trim with one boiler band, tall coal bunker, no tender, 11½". 1906-26.

Note: Earliest locomotives had a dummy headlight. Electric headlight first cataloged on 5 in 1910.

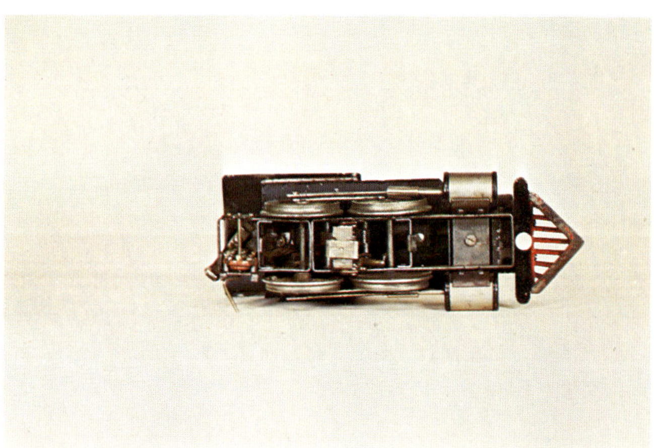

5 split frame detail

5 SPECIAL 0-4-0, same as 5 but with black, slope-back coal tender with a single 10-series truck, 18". 1906-09.

5 SPECIAL 0-4-0, same as 5 Special but with black, slope-back coal tender with two 100-series trucks, 18". 1910-11. (See also 51)

51 0-4-0, black, Russian iron boiler, same as 5 but with short coal bunker and with slope-back coal tender with two 100-series trucks, formerly a 5 Special, 18". 1912-23.

6 4-4-0, black, Russian iron boiler, nickeled trim with two boiler bands, black, rectangular coal tender with two 10-series trucks, 22". 1906-23.

Notes on the above locomotives:

1. Locomotive cab windows, ouside edge of tender floor, grab irons, and pilot were painted red.
2. Rubber stamp lettering on the above locomotives and tenders is generally NYC & HRRR but items may be found lettered PENNSYLVANIA or B&O RR. It is possible that other road names were used in limited quantity.
3. On earlier models a two-peice, loosely riveted frame was used so that the rear set of drivers was independent from the front, enabling all the wheels to rest on uneven track at the same time. This type of construction is called a "split frame" and was changed to a solid frame around 1912.
4. Early pilot wheels were cast iron while later pilot wheels were die-cast.

6 SPECIAL 4-4-0, same as 6 but body is brass and nickled, nickled brass rectangular coal tender, 22". 1908-09. (See also 7)

7 4-4-0, same as 6, brass and nickeled, with or without binding post inside cab, formerly a 6 Special, 22". 1910-23.

Notes on the above locomotives:

1. Interior and floor of tenders were painted red.
2. Pilot wheels, spokes of drive wheels, and centers of the tender wheels were painted red.

7 4-6-0, number originally used for locomotive advertised in 1907 but NM.

5 (early) dummy headlight

5 (later)

5 SPECIAL 1906-09

5 SPECIAL 1910-11

51

6 (early)

6 (late)

6 SPECIAL

7

ELECTRIC LOCOMOTIVES

33 **Elec.,** 0-6-0, NYC, NR, U-frame, RS — NYC oval or block PENN RR, dark olive green, 10⅜". 1913.

33 **Elec.,** 0-4-0, NYC, early models have U-frame and cast iron or die-cast wheels with NR, later models have a straight frame and die-cast wheels with HR, RS — NYC Oval or C&O, 10⅜". 1913-23.

dark olive green	red
midnight blue (DSS)	peacock
black	dark green
gray	red/cream trim
maroon	

33 **Elec.,** 0-4-0, same as above but with Super Motor, RS — NYC oval, dark olive green 10⅜". 1924.

34 **Elec.,** 0-6-0, NYC, NR, same as 0-6-0 33, RS — block NYC, dark olive green, 10⅜". 1912.

34 **Elec.,** 0-4-0, NYC, NR, RS — block NYC, U-frame, die-cast wheels, dark olive green, 10⅜". uncat. Circa 1913.

38 **Elec.,** 0-4-0, with side rods, NYC, RS — NYC oval or block NYC, 11⅛". 1913-24.

dark olive green	brown	pea green
black	red	olive green
gray	mojave	peacock
maroon	dark green	red/cream trim

42 **Elec.,** 0-4-4-0, with side rods, NYC — square body, RS — block NYC or NYC oval, dark olive green, 15½". 1912.

42 **Elec.,** 0-4-4-0, with side rods, NYC, RS — block NYC or NYC oval, 15½ to 16". 1913-23.

dark olive green

black	mojave
maroon	peacock
dark gray	gray
dark green	olive green

Note: Models made before 1918 have sliding side doors and three piece steps while those made during or after 1918 have fixed doors and one piece steps. Double motor model introduced in 1921 with two switches — one for hand reverse and one to change from AC to DC operation.

50 **Elec.,** 0-4-0, NYC, same body and motor as 38 but with headlight on each end, RS — NYC oval, 11⅛". 1924.
dark gray; dark green; maroon

50 **Elec.,** 0-4-0, same as preceding 50 but with Super Motor, no side rods, RS-NYC oval, 11⅛". 1924.
dark gray; dark green; mojave

53 **Elec.,** 0-4-4-0, with side rods, NYC — square body, spoked or solid wheels, formerly a 1911 Special, RS — script NYNH&H, block NYC or NYC oval, maroon, 12". 1912-14.

53 **Elec.,** 0-4-0, with side rods, NYC — square body, RS — NYC oval, 12¼". 1915-19.
maroon; dark olive green; mojave

53 **Elec.,** 0-4-0, with side rods, NYC, same body as 38, RS — NYC oval, maroon, 11⅛". 1920-21.

54 **Elec.,** 0-4-4-0, with side rods, NYC — square body, formerly a 1912 Special, but has hood punched with ears for the slide on headlight or later the hood had an added hole for the screw of a pedestal headlight, 15½". 1912.

Note: It is difficult to distinguish a late 1912 Special from an early square body 54 as Lionel just renumbered the set in 1912 to outfit 54. However, a square body brass locomotive with thick rim drivers and a pedestal headlight is most assuredly a 54, while a brass locomotive with thin rim drivers and a soldered on headlight bracket is a 1912 Special. The transition locomotive with punched ears for a slide on headlight could be either a 1912 Special or a 54.

54 **Elec.,** 0-4-4-0, with side rods, NYC, same as 42 but brass body, red spokes and ventilators, red cab door window frame, 15½ to 16". 1913-23.

Note: As on 42, early models have sliding doors and three piece steps, while later models have fixed doors and one piece steps. Locomotives from 1921 on have two motors and two switches — one for HR and one to change from AC to DC operation.

1910 **Elec.,** 0-6-0, NYC — square body, NR, RS — script NYNH&H, dark olive green, 9 11/16". 1910-11.

Note: The two center wheels are cast iron and are powered, the four end wheels are stamped steel and are non-powered.

1910 **Elec.,** 0-6-0, NYC, same body as a 33, NR, U-frame, RS — NYC oval, dark olive green, 10⅜". 1913.

1911 **Elec.,** 0-4-0, with side rods, NYC — square body, RS — script NYNH&H, NYC oval or block NYC, 11¼". 1910-12.
dark olive green; maroon

1911 SPECIAL **Elec.,** 0-4-4-0, with side rods, NYC — square body, RS — 1911 SPECIAL and script NYNH&H or block NYC, maroon, 12". 1911-12.

Note: This model generally comes with solid wheels but has been found with spoked wheels as on a 53.

1911 **Elec.,** 0-4-0, with side rods NYC, same body as 38, RS — block NYC, dark olive green, 11⅛". 1913.

1912 **Elec.,** 0-4-4-0, with side rods, NYC — square shape RS — script NYNH&H or block, NYC, dark olive green, 15½".1910-12.

1912 SPECIAL **Elec.,** 0-4-4-0, same as 1912 but brass body, red spokes and ventilators, soldered on bracket for headlight, 15½". 1911.

Note: Some 1912 Specials made later in 1911 have two punched ears in hood for slide on headlight and are indistinguishable from an early 54, though if equipped with thin rim drivers it probably is a 1912 Special.

38 maroon

33 (0-6-0) dark olive green

42 (square body) dark olive green

33 U-frame detail

42 maroon

33 (0-4-0) black

50 (open motor) gray

34 dark olive green

50 (super motor) mojave

53 (0-4-4-0) maroon

53 (square body) mojave

53 (38 body) maroon

54 (square body)

54 (42 body) 1913-18

1910 dark olive green

1911 (square body) maroon

1911 SPECIAL maroon

1911 (38 body) dark olive green

1912 dark olive green — 1910

1912 dark olive green — 1912

1912 SPECIAL

LATER LOCOMOTIVES
1923-39

In 1923 Lionel introduced its familiar "brass plate" line of trains. The electric locomotives were very popular as evidenced by the fact that Lionel had no steam type locomotives listed in their catalog sets from then until the introduction of the 390 in 1929. The 5 locomotive was shown in the catalog until 1926 but was not featured.

The electric style locomotives were facsimilies of prototype electric type locomotives with two railroads being represented: New York Central S and T classes, and the Chicago, Milwaukee, St. Paul and Pacific "Olympian" bi-polar class E. Bodies of these electric styles were made entirely of stamped metal. The doors, windows, ventilators, handrails, and other fittings were made of brass or nickel plated brass with the window frames, doors, and plates usually formed from a single sheet of metal. The frames were stamped from sheet steel, and the applied simulated springs and journals were made of brass or nickel-plated brass. Numerous rivets and other structural details were embossed in the frame. All the electric style locomotives had cast iron pilots except the 8, 9, 10, and 381; all had the Super Motor, unless noted to have a Bild-A-Loco type.

Lionel introduced its new Standard gauge steam style locomotive in 1929. The boilers and cabs were made of sheet steel and the frames, boiler fronts and steam chests were die-cast. Boilers were trimmed with brass, copper, or nickel-plated fixtures such as domes, stacks, cab window frames, hand rails, exhaust pipes, etc. The steam type locomotives were not copies of any particular prototypes although Lionel did try to capitalize on famous trains by using names such as "Blue Comet". All The steam locomotives had stamped steel pilots except for the cast iron pilots on the 390 and 400, and the pilot that is part of the die-cast frame on the 384. All the steam types were equipped with a Bild-A-Loco motor. Unless noted otherwise the tender color is the same as the locomotive. Further, the tenders usually had the same trim as the locomotives, although the plates may be brass when all the other trim is nickel.

STEAM LOCOMOTIVES

384 2-4-0, 8-Wh coal tender (384T), black with or without green stripe on the running board, 21". 1930-32.
Note: Pilot wheels are O gauge pilot wheels.

384E 2-4-0, same as 384, 21". 1930-32.

385E 2-4-2, 23½". 1933-39.
dark gunmetal/copper and brass trim — 384T (1933)
gunmetal/nickel trim — 384T (1934)
gunmetal/nickel trim — ex-Ives 385T (1935-39)

390 2-4-2, same tender body as 384 but RS — 390T, black with or without orange stripe on running board and tender, brass or mixed brass and copper trim, 22¼". 1929.

390E 2-4-2, same as 390, 390T (500 series trucks) or 390X (200 series trucks with stepped drawbar), 22¼". 1929-31 and 1933.
black/orange stripe
medium blue/dark blue frame/cream stripe-medium blue or red pilot
dark green/state green frame/orange stripe-state green or red pilot
dark green/state green frame/Stephen Girard green stripe on engine and either orange or Stephen Girard green stripe on tender
black/no stripe

392E 4-4-2, 25 or 27¼". 1932-39.
• black/brass and copper trim/domes and smokestack either copper or painted black — 384T with or without green stripe on tender
• black/brass and copper trim — crackle black 384T
• black/brass and copper trim — 12-Wh 392T tender

- black/nickel trim — 12-Wh 392T tender with nickel plates
- *gunmetal/nickel trim* – 12-Wh 392T tender

400E 4-4-4, with 12-Wh 400T oil tender, 31⅜". 1931-39.
black/brass and copper trim
medium blue/dark blue frame/with or without cream stripe/brass and copper trim
black/red stripe including tender/brass and copper trim
crackle black/brass and copper trim
dark gunmetal/brass and copper trim
light blue/dark blue frame/with or without cream stripe/nickel trim
gunmetal/nickel trim
all dark blue/red stripe/copper trim (SPECIAL)

1835E 2-4-2, same as 385E, 23½". 1934-39.
black/black and nickel trim — 384T (1934)
black/black and nickle trim – 1835W ex-Ives tender (1935-39)

384 black with green stripe

385E dark gunmetal

385E (late) gunmetal/nickel trim

390 black with orange stripe

390E medium blue/dark blue frame/cream stripe

392E black with 12-Wh 392T

392E (late) gunmetal/nickel trim

400E medium blue/dark blue frame/no stripe

400E (late) gunmetal/nickel trim

1835E black/black and nickel trim

ELECTRIC LOCOMOTIVES

8 **Elec.,** 0-4-0, NYC, 11″. 1925-32.
dark olive green
maroon
mojave
olive green
red/Br or cream window trim
red/cream stripe/cream window trim
maroon/cream stripe/cream window trim (SPECIAL)
peacock/orange stripe/orange window trim (SPECIAL)

8E **Elec.,** 0-4-0, same as 8, 11″. 1926-32.
mojave
olive green
red/Br or cream window trim
red/cream stripe/cream window trim
peacock/orange stripe/orange window trim (SPECIAL)
pea green/cream window trim (SPECIAL)

9 **Elec.,** 0-4-0, NYC, Bild-A-Loco motor held in place by four screws, dark green, 14½″. 1929.

9E **Elec.,** 0-4-0, NYC, Bild-A-Loco motor held in place by four screws or two latches, orange, 14½″. 1928-30.

9E **Elec.,** 2-4-2, NYC, Bild-A-Loco motor held in place by two latches, either old style E or drum type E (drum E has slot in roof), 14½″. 1931-36.
Stephen Girard green/dark green roof/brass trim
dark gunmetal/nickel trim

Note: The 2-4-2 9E had a one piece stamped roof with embossed center section and no handrails.

9U **Elec.,** 0-4-0, same as 9E orange except HR, brass plate marked 9U, sold in kit form for building either loco or stationary motor, boxed with eight sections of track, with or without weights on frame, orange, 14½″. 1928-29.

Note: Also sold in uncataloged sets with 428, 429, 430.

10 **Elec.,** 0-4-0, CMStP&P, 11½″. 1925-29.
mojave; gray; *peacock*
peacock/dark green frame/orange stripe — Super Motor (SPECIAL)
red/cream stripe (SPECIAL)

10E **Elec.,** 0-4-0, same as 10, 11½″. 1926-30.
gray
peacock
peacock/dark green frame/orange stripe — Bild-A-Loco or Super Motor (SPECIAL)
State brown/dark green frame/cream stripe (SPECIAL)
red/cream stripe (SPECIAL)

318 **Elec.,** 0-4-0, NYC, 12½″. 1924-32.
dark gray
mojave
gray
pea green
State brown/with or without cream stripe/cream window trim — red or State brown pilots

318E **Elec.,** 0-4-0, same as 318, 12½″. 1926-35.
mojave
gray
pea green
black
State brown/with or without cream stripe/cream window trim — red or State brown pilots —
Bild-A-Loco or Super Motor

380 **Elec.,** 0-4-0, CMStP&P, 13½″. 1923-27.
mojave
maroon
dark green

380E **Elec.,** 0-4-0, same as 380, with or without weights on frame, "E" either on plate or on side door, 13½″. 1926-29.
maroon; dark green

381 **Elec.,** 4-4-4, CMStP&P, Bild-A-Loco motor, dark State green/apple green subframe, 18″. 1928-29. (See 381 U)

381E **Elec.,** 4-4-4, same as 381, but State green/*apple green* or red subframe, 18″. 1928-36.

381U **Elec.,** 4-4-4, same as 381, catalog number for 381 hand reverse, sold as kit for building either the loco or a stationary motor, boxed with eight sections of track, dark State green/apple green subframe, 18″. 1928-29.

Note: 381U electric locomotives have been found with 381 or 381U plates.

402 **Elec.,** 0-4-4-0, NYC, two Super Motors, mojave, 17½". 1923-27.

402E **Elec.,** 0-4-4-0, same as 402, "E" either on plate or on side door, 17½". 1926-29.
mojave
cream (SPECIAL)
mustard brown (SPECIAL)

408E **Elec.,** 0-4-4-0, NYC, two motors, 17½". 1927-36.
mojave
apple green
dark State green
State green/dark green roof (UNIQUE)
State brown — Bild-A-Loco or Super Motors
State brown/dark brown roof — Bild-A-Loco or Super Motors
cream (SPECIAL)
pink (SPECIAL)
peacock (SPECIAL)
gray (SPECIAL)

Note: Six sample colors for 402E and 408E — mustard brown, State green/dark green roof, pink, cream, gray and peacock. State brown/dark brown roof 408E found with State brown or red pilots.

8 dark olive green

9 dark green

9E Stephen Girard green/dark green roof

9U orange

9U in set box (1928)

9U in set box (1929)

10 gray

10E peacock

318 dark gray

318E State brown/cream window trim/State brown pilots

380 mojave

381 dark State green/apple green subframe

381E State green/apple green subframe

402E mojave

408E dark State green

408E State brown/dark brown roof

MACY LOCOMOTIVES

These locomotives were made by Lionel in special sets for R.H. Macy and Company, New York. A more complete description of the sets can be found in the SPECIALS section.

8E **Elec.,** 0-4-0, same as any 8E, 11″. Circa 1930.
peacock/orange stripe/orange window trim
pea green/cream window trim

10 **Elec.,** 0-4-0, same as any 10, red/cream stripe, $11\frac{1}{2}$″. Circa 1930.

10E **Elec.,** 0-4-0, same as above 10, red/cream stripe, $11\frac{1}{2}$″. Circa 1930.

F.A.O. SCHWARZ LOCOMOTIVES

These locomotives were made for the F.A.O. Schwarz Company in New York. A more complete description can be found in the SPECIALS section.

60 **Elec.,** 0-4-0, NYC, same as 33 but RS — FAOS 60, black, $10\frac{3}{8}$″. Circa 1913-17.

61 **Elec.,** 0-4-4-0, with side rods, NYC, same as any early 42 with sliding side doors and three piece steps, RS — FAOS 61, black, 16″. Circa 1913-17.

62 **Elec.,** 0-4-0, with side rods, NYC, same as any early 38 but RS — FAOS 62, black, $11\frac{1}{8}$″. Circa 1913-17.

8E pea green/cream stripe — MACY SPECIAL

10 red/cream stripe — MACY SPECIAL

61 black — FAOS SPECIAL

Standard Gauge Cars

1906-1940

Much of what was discussed in the introduction to STANDARD GAUGE LOCOMOTIVES is equally applicable here and for the sake of brevity will not be repeated. However, further discussion is necessary to define the progression of some of the components of the cars.

COUPLERS. The coupler types were listed in an earlier introduction but are described more fully and pictured in Figure 9.

TRUCKS. Over the years of Standard gauge production, numerous changes of the trucks design has occurred in each series, making trucks useful in dating cars. This must be tempered with the realization that trucks are easily removed and changed. Many of the trucks have been labeled for the car series on which they commonly occur. Because of the utility of this convention, it has been continued here.

- Small hole eyelet — 3/16″ diameter head, 0.099 diameter hole.
- Large hole eyelet — 9/32″ diameter head, 0.193 diameter hole.
- Hollow rivet — 3/8″ diameter head, 0.161 diameter hole.

All trucks have hollow two-piece steel wheels unless otherwise noted. On three-rivet trucks the axles revolve in the truck frames, on all others the wheels revolve on the axles. Trucks prior to 1925 were generally painted or plated, whereas those from 1925 on were blackened by several methods of oxidation. As can be readily seen, only the 200-, 500- and 6-Wh trucks series have journal boxes. These follow the dating guidelines noted in other sections except for the die-cast journals used on the 400 tender, Blue Comet cars and State cars from 1929-31, and brass journals instead of copper on the State cars and Stephen Girard cars from 1931 to late 1934. See figure 10. The construction of the passenger cars is also very useful in dating. The presence of three knobs soldered on the roof indicates a car made prior to 1912. The early series passenger cars (18, 31, 180, 418) all had arch (A) windows, while

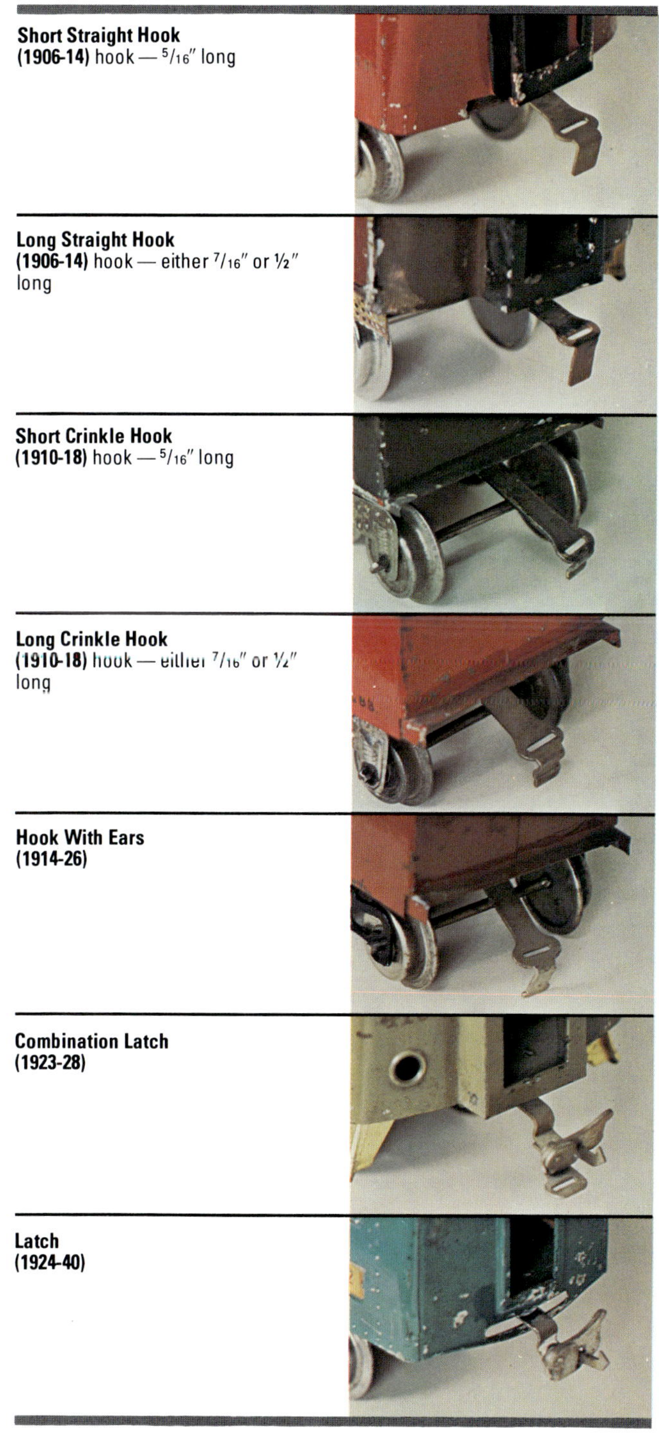

FIGURE 9

Short Straight Hook
(1906-14) hook — 5/16″ long

Long Straight Hook
(1906-14) hook — either 7/16″ or 1/2″ long

Short Crinkle Hook
(1910-18) hook — 5/16″ long

Long Crinkle Hook
(1910-18) hook — either 7/16″ or 1/2″ long

Hook With Ears
(1914-26)

Combination Latch
(1923-28)

Latch
(1924-40)

FIGURE 10

10 Series — Type I (1906-10)
plain solid side frame, three rivets, straight bolster.

10 Series — Type II (1909-12)
open side frame, three rivets, cut out bolster, embossed springs only.

10 Series — Type III (1911)
open side frame, cutout bolster, embossed springs only, large hole eyelet.

10 Series — Type IV (1912-14)
open side frame, embossed rivets and springs, cut out bolster, large hole eyelet or hollow rivet.

10 Series — Type V (1914-27)
open side frame, embossed rivets and springs, single hollow rivet, thick or thin rim wheels, straight bolster, commonly referred to as 10 SERIES TRUCK. Later trucks have slots punched in bolster for pickup roller support.

100 Series — Type I (1910-12)
solid side frame, embossed rivets and springs, small hole eyelet, pointed bolster, occasionally with cast iron wheels.

100 Series — Type II (1912-14)
solid side frame, embossed rivets and springs, small hole eyelet, round end bolster.

100— Type III (1912-24)
solid side frame, embossed rivets and springs, hollow rivet, round end bolster, ⅛″ taller than type II.

100 Series — Type IV (1912-13)
plain open side frames, no embossing, nickel plated, used on 35 and 36 passenger cars only.

100 Series — Type V (1912-26)
same as type IV but painted black, commonly referred to as 100 SERIES TRUCK.

180 Series — Type I (1911)
like 100 series type III but high (1/16″ higher) bolster, solid side frame, embossed rivets and springs, hollow rivet.

180 Series — Type II (1912-14)
open side frame, embossed rivets and springs, large eyelet.

180 Series — Type III (1912-21)
same as type II but hollow rivet.

200 Series (1926-40)
embossed side frame, attached journal boxes, two rectangular cutouts, with or without pickup for lights.

500 Series (1924-40)
embossed springs on side frames, attached journal boxes, early — cutout slots in side frame, later — reinforcing bar on side frame.

6-Wh trucks — Type I (1925-32)
used on 418 series, attached journal boxes, high or low bolster bar.

6-Wh trucks — Type II (1929-40)
used on State cars, Blue Comet and Stephen Girard cars, and 400 tender, attached journal boxes.

6-Wh trucks — Type III (1934-40)
used on 1700 series and 392 tender, attached journal boxes.

10 SERIES — TYPE I

10 SERIES — TYPE II

10 SERIES — TYPE IV

10 SERIES — TYPE V

100 SERIES — TYPE I

100 SERIES — TYPE II

100 SERIES — TYPE III

100 SERIES — TYPE IV

100 SERIES — TYPE V

180 SERIES — TYPE I

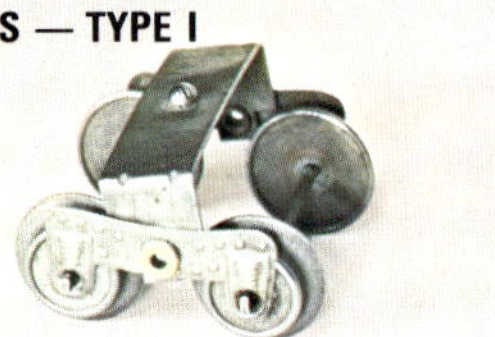

180 SERIES — TYPE II

180 SERIES — TYPE III

200 SERIES

500 SERIES

6-WH TRUCKS — TYPE I

6-WH TRUCKS — TYPE II

6-WH TRUCKS — TYPE III

10 SERIES — TYPE III

all passenger cars that started life after 1925 had rectangular windows. Open clerestory stampings were made after 1911 on each series of early passenger cars except the 31-series which always had unpunched clerestory stampings. Early cars of these series had red celluloid material above the windows, whereas later ones and the cars during the "brass plate" era had blue-green celluloid. The actual window material is clear celluloid except on very late cars, where frosted celluloid is found.

Observation cars made prior to 1926 (and including the 36 observation in 1926) had railings without space for a celluloid drumhead, and had neither dome lights nor marker lights. The "brass plate" era observation cars such as the early 338, 322, and 490 had a plain brass platform railing plate and no rear marker lights while those made from 1926 on had celluloid drumheads and marker lights. These drumheads were lettered LIONEL LIMITED on all the smaller series and on the Blue Comet observation. However, the Stephen Girard observation had a red keystone insert lettered PENNSYLVANIA LIMITED, and the State car observation drumhead is lettered TRANSCONTINENTAL LIMITED or occasionally LIONEL LINES. The only exceptions to this were the occasional department store specials (DSS) with specially lettered drumheads. Variations of platform design and length appeared in the 18-, 31-, and 180-series observations, and the variations are described fully under each car. The general rule is long platforms were early, short platforms were later.

Additional Brief Notes

1. Freight cars prior to the mid-1920's are completely soldered together and only the 15 tank car has embossed rivet detail, but thereafter many had embossed rivet detail and only tabs that were soldered.

2. Passenger cars were equipped with interior lights from 1923 on.

3. All car lengths are actual measurements and may not agree with lengths stated in the catalogs.

4. Freight cars in the "brass plate" period can have red or black lettering on the plates, except on the 500-series cars where the lettering is always black.

5. Handrails were soldered to early passenger cars and attached with stanchions on "brass plate" era cars.

6. Paint colors on early cars varied from batch to batch and do not necessarily match the colors in the color chart.

7. Some early 418-419-490 cars have PULLMAN block lettering instead of road name or LIONEL LINES lettering.

8. Abbreviations:

Br brass nameplates
DSS department store special
N nickel nameplates
NM never made
RS rubber stamped lettering
Wh wheel

EARLY LARGE SERIES PASSENGER CARS

1906-27

The large series passenger cars were constructed of sheet steel parts which were soldered together, enameled, and then striped and lettered in gold. The passenger doors were hinged except on the 1910, where they did not open. All the cars had platforms with vestibules and colored celluloid inserted in the window transoms and clerestories, and have 10-series trucks. Except on the early cars, roofs were removable so that miniature figures could be placed on the seats inside. The seats often had prongs on which to position the figures; these prongs are found on some early cars but not on the 1910 pullman. Provision was made for placing electric bulbs inside the cars. An accessory lamp outfit was first shown in the 1911 catalog and consisted of lights strung back through the cars from the engine. Interior lights self contained in each car, with pick-up shoes on the trucks, were introduced in this series in 1923.

Earlier cars have a flat red primer paint visible on the underside of the car. These cars also have the numbers on the car sides, while later cars have the numbers stamped on the ends — except for the 29 day coach on which the numbers are always on the sides. Very early cars were not embossed on the floor, but later cars until about 1918 were embossed "Lionel Mfg. Co, N.Y." From 1918 on, cars were rubber-stamped "The Lionel Corporation" on the underside.

Over the years, the observation cars came with four different styles of platform railings, and yet all the cars remained the same length. The three early variations had a longer platform and no rear lavatory window, while cars made after 1918 had a shorter observation platform and the additional window. Progressive changes in the long platform railings were (1) straight vertical slats, (2) a round scroll style with scalloped top edge, and finally (3) a plainer scroll style with flat top edge. On the combine, the baggage doors are always maroon or cream while the passenger doors can be maroon, wood-grained, or cream. The colored celluloid window material also changed colors over the years — from mottled red to mottled green to white. These cars are generally marked NEW YORK CENTRAL LINES, though some cars occur with NYNH&H or PENNSYLVANIA LINES.

1910 PULLMAN, first closed vestibule car made, three knobs on the roof, car body and roof all one piece, floor was either soldered or secured to the body with small rectangular pins or screws, dark olive green/dark olive green/maroon, uncat., 16¼". Circa 1909-10.

18 PULLMAN, early cars had no openings in the clerestory, three knobs soldered on roof, floor attached by screws through the side of the car, perforated step risers, later cars were soldered construction with removable roofs, 16¼". 1906-27.
dark olive green/dark olive green/maroon
yellow-orange/yellow-orange/cream
orange/orange/red

Note: Although the 18 and 19 were cataloged from 1906 on, the first cars were probably not made before 1910.

19 COMBINE, matches 18, 16¼". 1906-25.

29 DAY COACH, 13⅞" (early) or 15¼" (later). 1908-27.
early — same body as No. 3 trolley but numbered 29, open or closed platform railing, solid steps, dark olive green (circa 1908-09)
middle — no openings in clerestory, three knobs soldered on roof, perforated or three hole steps, roof soldered on, two chains on each platform, prongs in seats for figures, maroon or dark olive green (circa 1910)
later — openings in clerestory, roof removable, three hole steps, one chain on each platform railing, *dark olive green* with or *without* maroon window stripe and ends (circa 1911-27)

183 PULLMAN, same as 18 but brass, cataloged 1911 but NM.

184 COMBINE, same as 19 but brass, cataloged 1911 but NM.

185 OBSERVATION, same as 190 but brass, cataloged 1911 but NM.

190 OBSERVATION, matches 18, 15¾". 1910-27.
first series — no openings in clerestory, perforated steps, three knobs soldered on roof, long observation platform with vertical slats (circa 1910-11)
second — no openings in clerestory, with or without knobs on roof, perforated steps, long platform with scroll railing and scalloped top edge (circa 1911-12)
third — openings in clerestory, no knobs on roof, three hole steps, long observation platform with plainer scroll railing and flat top edge (circa 1913-18)
fourth — openings in clerestory, three hole steps, short observation platform (circa 1918-27)

1910 dark olive green

18 (early) dark olive green

19 (later) yellow-orange

29 (early) dark olive green, closed railing

29 (early) dark olive green, open railing

29 (middle) maroon

29 (later) dark olive green/maroon window stripe

29 (later) dark olive green, PENNSYLVANIA LINES

190 (first) dark olive green

190 (second) dark olive green

190 (third) yellow-orange

190 (fourth) orange

EARLY MIDDLE SIZE PASSENGER CAR SERIES
1911-21

The introductory comments for the 18-series passenger cars also apply to this series. In addition, early cars in this series have no openings in the clerestory, while later cars have clerestory openings with celluloid inserts. All cars have 100 or 180 series trucks. The cars are rubber stamped — NEW YORK CENTRAL LINES. The maroon and brown cars have dark olive green doors while the yellow-orange cars have orange doors.

180 PULLMAN, 12½". 1911-21.
maroon; brown
Note: No pullmans have been found in yellow-orange.

181 COMBINE, 12½". 1911-21.
maroon; brown; yellow-orange

182 OBSERVATION, matches 181, 12½". 1911-21.
first series — closed clerestory, long platform
second — open clerestory, long platform
third — open clerestory, short platform

Note: One set of maroon cars found lettered CANADIAN PACIFIC RAILWAY.

180 (early) maroon

181 (late) yellow-orange

182 (first) maroon

182 (second) yellow-orange

182 (third) brown

EARLY SMALL SERIES PASSENGER CARS
1912-26

The introductory notes for the 18-series passenger cars also apply to this series except that the 31-series occurs only with 100- or 500-series trucks. Lettering is generally NEW YORK CENTRAL LINES but have been found lettered CHESAPEAKE and OHIO, or NYNH&H. Last production of 31-series are with 500-series trucks, combination latch couplers, rollers and interior lights.

31 COMBINE, can occur with or without passenger doors on the baggage compartment end of car, 10¾". 1921-25.
dark olive green
orange
maroon
brown
Note: On all colors of these cars the window trim is red except on maroon cars where it is green.

32 MAIL (four door baggage), can occur with or without passenger doors at either end of the car, matches 31, 10¾". 1921-25.

35 PULLMAN, matches 31, 10½". 1912-26.
early — two embossed ribs under windows, RS lettering on sides between the ribs, oval shaped lavatory windows, embossed handrails
later — no ribs, empire type lavatory windows, no handrails

36 OBSERVATION, matches 31, 10½". 1912-26.
early — two embossed ribs under windows, RS lettering on sides between the ribs, oval shaped lavatory windows, embossed handrails, long observation platform
later — no ribs, empire type lavatory windows, no handrails, short observation platform
Note: Both 35 and 36 can also be found in midnight blue. (SPECIALS)

31 maroon, passenger doors at baggage end

32 brown, no passenger doors

35 dark olive green, RS — C&O

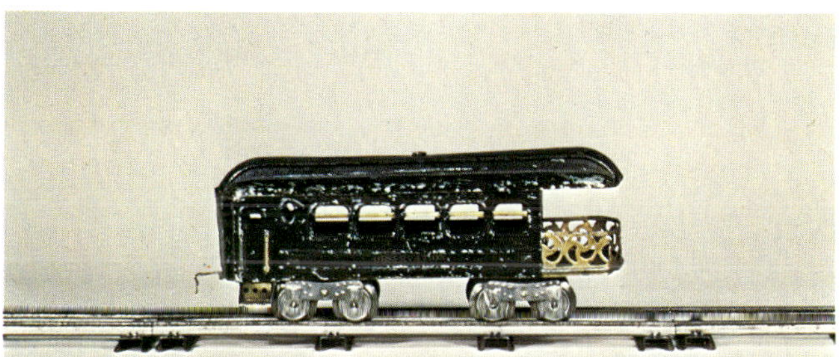

36 (early) midnight blue

36 (later) orange

LATER LARGE SERIES PASSENGER CARS
1923-32

All cars in this series have interior lights. The 418-19-90 cars had 10-series trucks in 1923-24; from 1925 on these cars came with 6-Wh trucks, and the 431 always used 6-Wh trucks. The 428-29-30 were equipped with 200-series freight trucks. All of the trucks had a roller pickup for the wiring of the interior lights. The early 418-19-90 cars have wood-grained doors, while the others have maroon doors except the orange 428 series which have apple green doors.

418 PULLMAN, RS — NEW YORK CENTRAL LINES, LIONEL LINES, or ILLINOIS CENTRAL, 18⅛". 1923-32.
mojave/mojave/maroon
mojave/mojave/orange
apple green/apple green/red

419 COMBINE, matches 418. 1923-32.

427 DINER, catalog number for diner in orange or dark green to match 428-29-30, NM numbered 427. 1930. (See 431)

428 PULLMAN, RS — LIONEL LINES, 18⅛". 1926-30.
dark green/dark green/maroon
dark green/dark green/orange
orange/orange/Stephen Girard green

429 COMBINE, matches 428. 1926-30.

430 OBSERVATION, matches 428, 17⅝". 1926-30.

431 DINER, interior has tables, matches 418. 1927-32.
- mojave/mojave/maroon — 6-Wh trucks
- mojave/mojave/orange — 6-Wh trucks
- dark green/dark green/orange — 200-series trucks (SPECIAL)
- orange/orange/Stephen Girard green — 6-Wh trucks (SPECIAL)
- *apple green/apple green/red — 6-Wh trucks*

Note: A 431 diner with 4-Wh trucks to match 428-29-30 is actually a 427 but is numbered 431. Some 431 diners have a hinged roof, but the majority have removable roofs.

490 OBSERVATION, matches 418, 17⅝". 1923-32.

418 mojave/mojave/orange

419 mojave/mojave/maroon

LATER MIDDLE SIZE PASSENGER CAR SERIES
1926-40

All cars in this series are 13¼". Early mojave/maroon cars have wood-grained doors; on some later cars windows and doors match, while on others they do not. Trucks are 500-series unless otherwise noted. Cars are RS — LIONEL LINES except when noted differently. The RS numbers are on enameled inserts not brass plates. Only the light blue/alum cars have nickel trim and frosted windows.

309 PULLMAN. 1926-40.
mojave/mojave/maroon
pea green/pea green/orange
maroon/terra-cotta/cream — RS — LIONEL LINES or NEW YORK CENTRAL LINES
State brown/dark brown/cream
medium blue/dark blue/cream
Stephen Girard green/dark green/cream
light blue/alum/alum
red-orange/alum/alum (SPECIAL)

310 BAGGAGE, matches 309, except no maroon/terra-cotta. 1926-40.
Note: Pea green cars may have orange or dark green doors and mojave cars have dark green doors.

312 OBSERVATION, matches 309. 1926-40.

319 PULLMAN, comes with 100-, 200-, and 500-series trucks, RS — NEW YORK CENTRAL LINES or LIONEL LINES, maroon/maroon/mojave. 1924-27.

320 BAGGAGE, matches 319, comes only with 200- or 500-series trucks, RS — LIONEL ELECTRIC RAILROAD, ILLINOIS CENTRAL or NEW YORK CENTRAL LINES. 1925-27.

322 OBSERVATION, matches 319, RS — NEW YORK CENTRAL LINES or LIONEL LINES. 1924-27.

427 dark green/dark green/orange

428 dark green/dark green/orange

429 orange/orange/Stephen Girard green

430 dark green/dark green/maroon

431 apple green/apple green/red

490 mcjave/mojave/maroon

309 maroon/terra-cotta/cream

309 Stephen Girard green/dark green/cream

LATER SMALL SERIES PASSENGER CARS
1925-33

All cars in this series are 12" long and have 500-series trucks. All cars are RS — THE LIONEL LINES or NEW YORK CENTRAL LINES. The lettering and RS numbers are on enameled inserts, and the car itself, not on brass plates.

332 **BAGGAGE**. 1926-33.
gray/gray/maroon
peacock/peacock/orange — orange or red doors
olive green/olive green/red
red/red/cream
peacock/dark green/orange
State brown/dark brown/cream (DSS)

337 **PULLMAN**. 1925-32.
mojave/mojave/maroon
olive green/olive green/maroon
olive green/olive green/red
red/red/cream
pea green/pea green/cream (DSS)

338 **OBSERVATION,** matches 337. 1925-32.

339 **PULLMAN**. 1925-33.
gray/gray/maroon
peacock/peacock/orange
peacock/dark green/orange
State brown/dark brown/cream (DSS)

341 **OBSERVATION,** matches 339. 1925-33.

310 pea green/pea green/orange

310 light blue/alum/alum

312 blue/dark blue/cream

319 maroon/maroon/mojave

320 maroon/maroon/mojave — ILLINOIS CENTRAL

322 maroon/maroon/mojave

332 olive green/olive green/red

337 mojave/mojave/maroon

338 red/red/cream

338 pea green/pea green/cream

339 gray/gray/maroon

339 peacock/peacock/orange

341 peacock/dark green/orange

LAST LARGE SERIES PASSENGER CARS
1929-35

These cars are the largest of the line. All cars in this series have complete interior trim — seats and washroom compartments with sinks and toilets. Roof ventilators on these cars can be found in either the roof or the body color; the roof is hinged on this series. These cars are always found with brass plates and trim, even though they were made overlapping the nickel trim and plates period.

412 PULLMAN, CALIFORNIA, 21½″. 1929-35.
State green/dark green/apple green
State green/dark green/cream
State brown/dark brown/cream

413 PULLMAN, COLORADO, same as 412. 1929-35.

414 PULLMAN, ILLINOIS, same as 412. 1929-35.

416 OBSERVATION, NEW YORK, matches 412, celluloid drumhead lettered — TRANS-CONTINENTAL LIMITED or LIONEL LINES, 21″. 1929-35.

412 State green/dark green/apple green

413 State brown/dark brown/cream — State brown ventilators

414 State brown/dark brown/cream — dark brown ventilators

416 State green/dark green/cream

LAST MIDDLE SERIES PASSENGER CARS
1930-40

The "Blue Comet" cars (420-22) and the "Stephen Girard" cars (424-26) have identical windows but vary in length and interior fittings. The Blue Comet set has full interior trim similar to the State cars but with fewer seats; the Stephen Girard set, however, has only a longitudinal bench on each side as found on the smaller passenger cars. Over the years of production the Blue Comet cars changed from brass trim, to mixed, to all nickel including the plates; late cars have frosted windows. The only important variation in the Stephen Girard set is the change from brass to nickel trim, though even on the latter the name and number plates are brass. All cars in this series have 6-Wh State car trucks. Finally, mention should be made of several variations of these cars that were never made: the 1930 advance catalog shows the 420 as a combine, but none of these have ever been found; and the 1931 catalog shows the 424 pullman lettered IRVINGTON and the 426 observation lettered HILLSIDE but neither of these have been seen.

420 PULLMAN, FAYE, 18¾". 1930-40.
medium blue/dark blue/cream
light blue/dark blue/cream
dark blue/black/cream (SPECIAL)

Note: The simulated diaphragms on early cars were either medium blue or dark blue.

421 PULLMAN, WESTPHAL, same as 420. 1930-40.

422 OBSERVATION, TEMPEL, matches 420, celluloid drumhead on platform lettered LIONEL LIMITED, 18½". 1930-40.

Note: One set of the above cars has been found lettered THE BLUE COMET over the windows, however the cars are usually not lettered.

424 PULLMAN, LIBERTY BELL, Stephen Girard green/dark green/cream. 16". 1931-40.

425 PULLMAN, STEPHEN GIRARD, same as 424. 1932-40.

426 OBSERVATION, CORAL ISLE, matches 424, celluloid drumhead on platform lettered PENNSYLVANIA LIMITED in red keystone, 15¾". 1931-40.

420 light blue/dark blue/cream-mixed trim

421 light blue/dark blue/cream-nickel trim

421 medium blue/dark blue/cream-brass trim

422 medium blue/dark blue/cream-brass trim

424 Stephen Girard green/dark green/cream — nickel trim

425 Stephen Girard green/dark green/cream — brass trim

426 Stephen Girard green/dark green/cream — nickel trim

LAST SMALL SERIES PASSENGER CARS
1934-40

The cars in this series first appeared in the "Ives" line of 1932, but in reality they were made entirely from Lionel dies manufactured at Lionel's Irvington plant. In 1934 the Ives name disappeared and the cars assumed the LIONEL LINES herald. All cars are 15" long, have interior lights, and have 6-Wh trucks (type III). Earlier cars have brass trim, later cars have nickel trim.

1766 PULLMAN, 1934-40.
terra-cotta/maroon/cream
red/maroon/alum

1767 BAGGAGE, matches 1766, some terra-cotta cars are RS in red lettering — BAGGAGE and MAIL on the doors. 1934-40.

1768 OBSERVATION, matches 1766. 1934-40.

1766 terra-cotta/maroon/cream

1767 red/maroon/alum

1767 terra-cotta/maroon/cream

1768 red/maroon/alum

EARLY LARGE SERIES FREIGHT CARS
1906-26

This is the earliest freight car series. The bodies were punched from sheet steel and soldered to the floor. On the earliest cars a cream or flat red primer coat of paint is visible on the underside of the floor, while on later cars the underside and interior is painted the same color as the car body. Lettering is RS in either gold or black on these cars. Some very early cars had no name embossed in the floor while most had "LIONEL MFG. CO, NY." embossed in the floor until about 1918; after this the cars were RS — "THE LIONEL CORPORATION NEW YORK" on the bottom. Over the years of production type I to VI trucks appeared on these cars. In the last years of production, Lionel pictured and described heralds of prominent railroads on the sides of some of these cars; however, as far as known, no cars were ever made with these heralds.

11 FLAT, no lettering or lettered PENNSYLVANIA, 11¼". 1906-26.
orange (SPECIAL)
red
brown
maroon
gray (SPECIAL)

12 GONDOLA, 11¼". 1906-26.
(early) — top edge flanged out at 90 degrees, no embossed rivet detail, brake wheel shaft through flange and soldered to outside of car (circa 1906-10)
(later) — rolled top edge, brake wheel shaft soldered on inside of car
red without (early) or with (later) dark olive green trim, RS — LAKE SHORE 65784
brown without or with dark green trim, RS — LAKE SHORE 65784
dark gray with or without top edge and bottom skirt trimmed in pea green or dark green, RS — LAKE SHORE 65784
gray with or without pea green or dark green skirt, RS — ROCK ISLAND LINES or LAKE SHORE 65784

13 CATTLE, no lettering, various shades of green, 11¼". 1906-26.
(early) — flat slats, 5 slots in side, 5 slots in door, with brake wheel
(middle) — embossed slats, 5 slots in side, 5 or 4 slots in door, with brake wheel
(late middle) — embossed slats, 6 slots in side, 5 slots in door, with brake wheel
(late) — embossed slats, 5 slots in side, 5 or 4 slots in door, no brake wheel

Note: Early roof is two pieces (separate roofwalk) while later roof is one piece bent to form roofwalk.

14 BOX, 11¼". 1906-26.
(early) — smooth sides, vertical striping with black paint, brake wheel originally on right, later switched to left end of car, 2 piece roof
(later) — embossed vertical striping on sides, with or without brake wheel, 1 piece roof.

- red with smooth sides, RS — CM&StP 19050
- red with embossed sides, RS — CM&StP 54087, 19050 or 9050, or NYC&HRRR 5906
- yellow-orange with embossed sides, RS — CM&StP 54087, 98237, or NYC&HRRR 4351
- *orange with embossed sides,* RS — CM&StP 98237
- dark olive green with embossed sides, decal — 898 (SPECIAL)

Note: Red box cars with embossed sides may be found with or without black painted vertical stripes on the embossing.

15 OIL, RS — PENNSYLVANIA, with or without RS — 416 on some early cars, 10¾". 1906-26.
(early) — wood ends on tank, U-shape wire step
(middle) — wood or metal ends on tank, three piece steps
(late) — metal ends on tank, one piece step
red/red domes and ends/red frame
red/black dome and ends/black frame
maroon/black dome and ends/black frame
brown/black domes and ends/black frame

16 BALLAST, RS — PENNSYLVANIA 65784 or 76399, end levers open sides, 10¾". 1906-26.
red
brown
maroon
dark green

Note: Ballast cars can be trimmed in black, pea green, or dark green on the red, maroon, or brown cars, and trimmed in maroon on the dark green cars.

17 CABOOSE, 11¼". 1906-26.
(early) — smooth sides, vertical striping with black paint, awnings over the windows, no awnings over cupola, steps formed from platform
(middle) — embossed vertical striping, awnings over the cupola windows only, steps formed from platform
(late) — embossed vertical striping, no awnings, steps formed from platform or three hole steps
red/black roof — plain sides, RS — NYC & HRRR 51906 or 5906
red/black roof — embossed sides, RS — NYC & HRRR 342715, 5906 or 4351
brown/black roof — embossed sides, RS — NYC & HRRR 5906, 342715 or 4351
maroon/black roof — embossed sides, RS — NYC & HRRR 4351

11 maroon — PENNSYLVANIA R.R.

12 (early) maroon

12 (late) gray/pea green

13 (early) green

13 (middle) green

14 (early) red

14 (late) yellow-orange

15 (early) red/red dome/red frame

15 (late) maroon/black dome/black frame

16 brown

16 dark green/maroon

17 (early) red/black roof

17 (middle) red/black roof

17 (late) maroon/black roof

EARLY SMALL SERIES FREIGHT CARS
1910-26

The notes in the introduction to the 10-series cars also apply here with the following exceptions: only the short gondola and ballast car had cream colored undersides, all others were always the color of the rest of the car; all of these cars are embossed "LIONEL MFG." or RS — "THE LIONEL CORPORATION" and all share the same trucks except the ballast car and short gondola. The earliest gondola in this series is a shorter (7") car than the standard 100 series cars.

112 GONDOLA,
(early) — dark olive green/red trim/red inside — some have cream underside, RS — LAKE SHORE or NYNH&H, 7". 1910-12.
(later) — 9½". 1913-26.
red/ RS — LAKE SHORE, PENNSYLVANIA, or NYC&HRR
maroon, RS — LAKE SHORE, PENNSYLVANIA, or NYC&HRR
brown, RS — PENNSYLVANIA, NYC&HRR or LAKE SHORE
dark gray, RS — LAKE SHORE or ROCK ISLAND
gray, RS — ROCK ISLAND or LAKE SHORE
Note: May be found RS 65784 or not numbered.

113 CATTLE, embossed sides, green, no lettering, 9½". 1912-26.

114 BOX, 9½". 1912-26.
red, RS — CM&StP 54087
yellow-orange, RS — CM&StP 54087 or 62926
orange, RS — CM&StP 62926 or 98237

116 BALLAST, RS — NYNH&HRR on all, 8¾". 1910-26.

dark olive green	brown	dark green
maroon	gray	

117 CABOOSE, RS — NYC&HRRR 4351, 9¾". 1912-26.
red/black roof
brown/black roof
maroon/black roof

Note: Cupola roof may be black or match car side.

117 maroon/black roof

112 (early) dark olive green

112 (late) maroon

113 green

114 red

116 maroon

LATE LARGE SERIES FREIGHT CARS
1926-40

These are the large freight cars in the "brass plate" line. All cars have black frames and are 12½" long. All cars have brass trim in early years and mixed or nickel-plated trim from 1934 on, except for the dark green railings on the orange 217 caboose with maroon roof. Lettering on the brass plates is red on some cars, black on others, and can be either on some cars. These cars always have 200 series trucks.

211 FLAT, RS — LIONEL LINES, black. 1926-40.

212 GONDOLA. 1926-40.
gray
maroon
green

213 CATTLE. 1926-40.
mojave/maroon
terra-cotta/maroon (SPECIAL)
terra-cotta/pea green
cream/maroon

214 BOX. 1926-40.
terra-cotta/dark green
cream/orange
yellow/brown

214R REFRIGERATOR. 1929-40.
ivory/peacock
white/light blue

215 TANK. 1926-40.
pea green
ivory with or without Sunoco decal
alum. with Sunoco decal
orange with Shell decal — cataloged 1939 but NM

216 HOPPER, dark green. 1926-38.

217 CABOOSE. 1926-40.
orange/maroon/dark green trim — maroon plates — RS
red/peacock/brass trim — cupola red or peacock
light red/light red/alum. trim
pea green/red/brass trim (SPECIAL)

218 **DUMP,** with one or two operating wheels. 1926-38.
pea green/maroon ends (SPECIAL)
mojave/plain brass or mojave ends
gray/brass ends (SPECIAL)

219 **DERRICK.** 1926-40.
peacock/dark green/red boom/ with or without red window trim
yellow/light red/light red boom/light red trim
yellow/light red/green boom/light red trim
ivory/light red/green boom/light red trim

220 **FLOODLIGHT,** RS — LIONEL LINES. 1931-40.
terra-cotta/brass lights
green/nickel-plated lights

211 black

212 green

213 mojave/maroon

214 yellow/brown

214 terra-cotta/dark green

214R ivory/peacock

215 ivory/no decal

216 dark green

217 orange/maroon

217 red/peacock/peacock cupola

218 gray

219 yellow/light red/green boom

220 terra-cotta/brass lights

LATE SMALL SERIES FREIGHT CARS
1927-40

All cars in this series are 11½″ long and have black frames unless otherwise noted. Early cars have brass trim, while later cars have mixed or nickel-plated trim except for the aluminum painted railings on the late caboose. All cars in this series have copper or nickel-plated journals and stamped steel bodies with embossed paneling.

511 **FLAT,** RS — LIONEL LINES. 1927-40.
dark green
medium green

Note: The load on early cars was a single wood block with scribed markings, while on later cars individual pieces of wood were used.

512 **GONDOLA.** 1927-39.
peacock; green

513 **CATTLE.** 1927-38.
olive green/orange
orange/pea green
cream/maroon

514 **BOX.** 1929-40.
cream/orange; yellow/brown

514 **REFRIGERATOR,** ivory/peacock. 1927-28.

514R **REFRIGERATOR.** 1929-40.
ivory/peacock; white/light blue

515 **TANK.** 1927-40.
terra-cotta/no decal
ivory/with or without Sunoco decal
alum/with Sunoco decal
Shell orange/Shell decal

516 **HOPPER,** with or without coal load, with or without RS lettering of capacity data, red. 1928-40.

517 **CABOOSE.** 1927-40.
pea green/red/Br; pea green/red/orange
red/black/orange — made for coal train with black 318E
light red/light red/alum
light red/light red/alum — no number plates and number RS on bottom

520 **FLOODLIGHT,** RS — LIONEL LINES. 1931-40.
terra-cotta/brass lights
green/nickel-plated lights

511 dark green

512 green

513 olive green/orange

514 yellow/brown

514 ivory/peacock

514R white/light blue

515 Shell orange/Shell decal

515 ivory/Sunoco decal

516 red

517 red/black/orange

520 green/nickel-plated lights

520 terra-cotta/brass lights

MACY CARS

These cars were regular productions made by Lionel for R.H. Macy and Company, New York with special lettering or paint. Circa 1930.
A more complete description of these sets can be found in the SPECIALS section.

332 BAGGAGE, peacock/peacock/orange, RS — MACY SPECIAL on the nameboards, 12″. Circa 1930.

337 PULLMAN, pea green/pea green/cream — no special lettering, 12″. Circa 1930.

338 OBSERVATION, matches 337 with MACY SPECIAL brass plate or celluloid drumhead on platform, 12″. Circa 1930.

339 PULLMAN, matches 332, 12″. Circa 1930.

341 OBSERVATION, matches 332, 12″. Circa 1930.

337 pea green

338 pea green

Trolleys

1906-1916

Lionel trolley cars were especially well proportioned, and a good representation of the actual cars used during the period. The cars followed prototype practice in that early cars had open platforms which were later closed with offset ends to protect the motorman. Even later the cars were built with the windows and platform ends in the same vertical plane (flush ends). Information has been compiled from the *T.C.A. Catalog Series IE-Standard Gauge Trolleys* published in 1961, a review of the catalogs, and examination of numerous trolleys still in existence. Dating of production has been attempted from these sources and by studying the changes made over the years of production in the components of each trolley.

Motors. These were battery, or house current powered. The early No. 1's had the New Departure motor which protruded through the car floor and was secured to the floor section. This early motor was a friction drive on two wheel flanges or a single gear drive. Later the standard motor was used, suspended from the axles and fitting under the floor. This necessitated an offset axle with one end of the motor suspended by a hook on the short framed four wheel and all eight wheel motor cars. The early motors had brass sides, while the later sides were nickel plated steel with bronze inserts for armature shaft bearings.

Wheels. Three types of wheels were used — an early, dished-type, stamped steel nickel-plated wheel, a later nickel-plated wheel with a definite ridge where the face meets the tread, and cast iron wheels. All were 1⁵⁄₁₆" diameter. Early motor unit wheels were all nickel-plated stamped-steel, followed by two cast iron driven wheels and two nickel-plated stamped-steel idler wheels, and, finally, all cast iron wheels on the power truck of eight wheel trolleys.

Reverse. Three types of reverse unit were employed — the ring and drum, the ring and disc, and the double disc. The first two were secured to the motor frame, while the double disc was attached to the truck frame. The reverse could be hand or track tripped.

Frames. The frames on early four wheel cars were 5⅝" long with a wheel base of 2⅝" (same centers as eight wheel trolley car trucks). The frames on later four wheel cars were 5⅞" with a wheel base of 3".

Trucks. Three different types of trucks were used on eight wheel cars — the solid side truck, the open three rivet truck, and the open single rivet truck. On the eight wheel open summer trolleys, taper cut solid side single rivet and solid side three rivet trucks were used. All the eight wheel car motor trucks were spring loaded with a spring on each side of the truck.

Headlights. Interurbans used either a slide on or a pedestal-type headlight. Early slide on lights were mounted to a bracket soldered on the roof; later, two tabs or wings were punched outward in the car roof for the light. Pedestal lights were mounted by a single screw. On the other trolleys, the early type headlight had a sleeve soldered into the platform end, with a socket inserted. Later there was no sleeve, only a socket inserted into a formed hole in the platform end. A binding post was used on the back end of later interurbans so that lights could be connected to trailer cars.

Fenders and Figures. Fenders were not listed after 1909. In 1909 a fender came with the Nos. 2, 3, 4, 8 and 9 trolleys or could be purchased separately. Fenders were secured to platform ends by wire brackets on the fenders inserted into holes in the platform ends. Seat pins for the figures on early models were escutcheon pins. After 1908 the pin was a tab punched up from the seat. The figures were ¹⁵⁄₁₆" high and made of a material similar to plaster of paris.

Additional Brief Notes:

1. All trolleys had a reverse except numbers 1, 100, and 101. Further, two-motor trolleys had a single reverse.

2. Four wheel cars were numbered 1, 2, 100, 101, 202. Their respective trailers were numbered 111, 200, 1000, 1100, 2200.

3. Eight wheel cars were numbered 3, 4, 8, 9, 10, 1011, 303, and 404. Their respective trailers were numbered 300, 40, (none for No. 8 or No. 9), 1010, 1012, 3300, and 4400.

4. Two-motored cars were numbered 4, 9, 1011 and 404.

5. THE LIONEL MFG. CO. embossing on the bottoms of the cars was used from 1908 through 1916. No embossing appears on the bottoms of trolleys made prior to 1908.

6. All motorized trolleys had headlights from 1910 through 1916 except No. 1.

7. From 1906 through 1909 trailer cars probably carried the number of the motor car. From 1910 through 1914, trailers could carry their own number as indicated in the catalogs. This was because trailers were not available for separate sale from 1910 on but available only as a set with a power car. No trailers were catalogued in 1915-16.

8. Four types of couplers were used: short straight hook (SSH), short crinkle hook (SCH), long straight hook (LSH), and long crinkle hook (LCH). The No. 8 and No. 9 trolleys have no couplers because no trailers were cataloged for them.

9. It is possible to have rounded roof ends on some of the open trolleys as indicated in the 1909 catalog.

10. Colors are given as body color/roof color/trim color for uniformity.

11. The abbreviation NM is used to indicate trolleys which are cataloged but *never made* as far as can be determined.

FIGURE 11

CHART OF LIONEL TROLLEYS BY NUMBER, YEAR AND PRICE FROM CATALOGS AND AVAILABLE INFORMATION

Number	1906	1907	1908	1909	1910	1911	1912	1913	1914	1915	1916
1	$	$	4.00	4.50	4.25	4.25	5.00	5.00	5.00		
With 1 or 111 Trailer			*1.25	*1.40	5.50	5.50	6.70	6.70			
2	$	$	5.50	6.25	6.25	6.25	7.50	7.50	7.50	7.50	9.50
With 2 or 200 Trailer			*1.75	*2.00	8.25	8.25	10.00	10.00			
3	$	$	8.50	9.50	9.00	9.00	11.00	11.00			
With 3 or 300 Trailer			*2.25	*2.50	11.50	11.50	14.00	14.00			
4 (Two Motors)	$	$	13.05	15.00	14.00	14.00	17.00				
With 4 or 40 Trailer			*2.25	*2.50	16.50	16.50	20.00				
8				@11.65	10.00	10.00	12.00	12.00	12.00	12.00	12.00
9 (Two Motors)				17.00	15.00	15.00	18.00				
10					10.00	10.00	12.00	12.00	12.00	12.00	12.00
With 1010 Trailer					13.75	13.75	14.50	16.50	16.50		
1011 (Two Motors)					5.00	15.00	18.00				
With 1012 Trailer					18.75	18.75	22.50				
100					5.00	5.00	6.00	6.00	6.00	6.00	8.00
With 1000 Trailer					6.50	6.50	8.00	8.00			
101					5.00	5.00	6.00	6.00			
With 1100 Trailer					6.50	6.50	8.00	8.00			
202					6.25	6.25	7.50	7.50			
With 2200 Trailer					8.25	8.25	9.90	9.90			
303					9.00	9.00	11.00	11.00			
With 3300 Trailer					11.50	11.50	14.00	14.00			
404 (Two Motors)					14.00	14.00	17.00				
With 4400 Trailer					16.50	16.50	20.00				
Figures by the dozen			.50	.60	.60	.60	.70	.70	.70	.70	

* Trailer only. After 1909 Trolley and Trailer listed by set price.
@ 9 window; 11 window starting 1910.
$ Indicates year made, price unknown.
Note: 1906 and 1907 had flat windows. Embossing starting 1908. Before 1913 closed cars had overhanging platform windows.

FIGURE 12
CONSTRUCTION DETAILS AND OPERATING EQUIPMENT

Interurban Roofs and Headlights

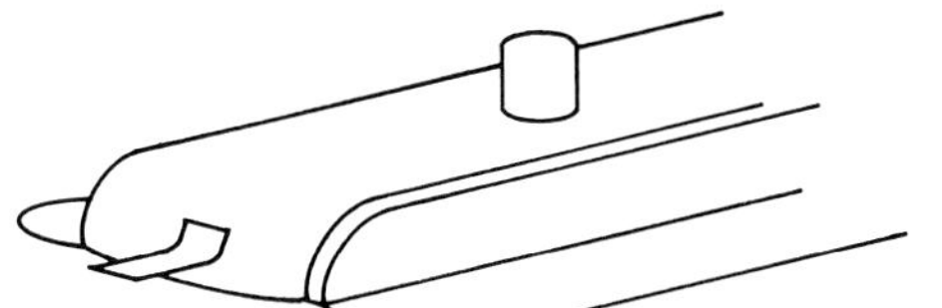

Bracket Mount For Slide On Headlight — Solid Clerestory — Roof Knobs

Slide On Headlight

Wing Mount — First Open Clerestory

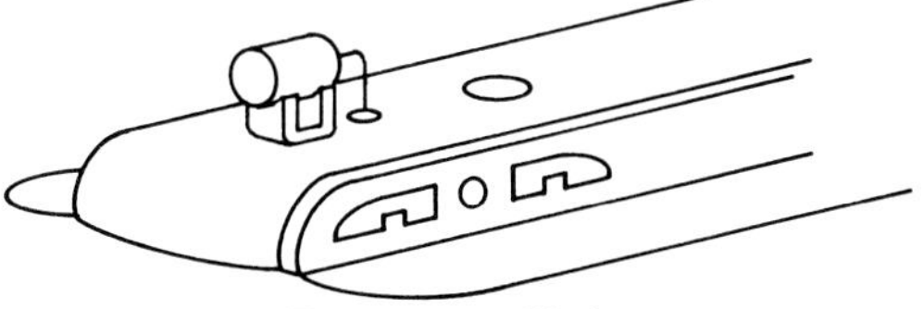

Pedestal Type Headlight Second Type Clerestory

Doors and Steps

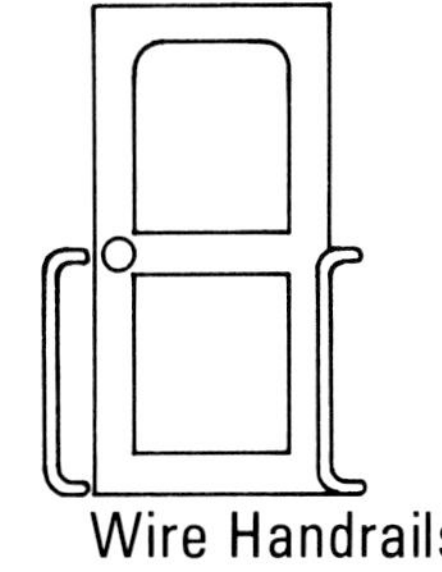

Wire Handrails Turned Door Pulls

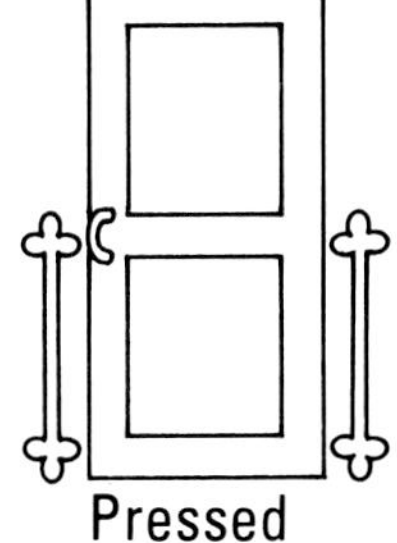

Pressed Handrails And Pulls

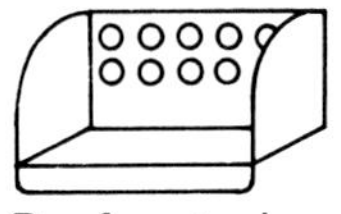

Perforated Step

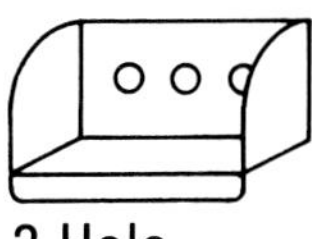

3 Hole Step

Strap or Stirrup Type

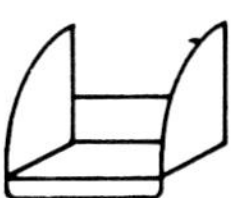

Similar With Short Back

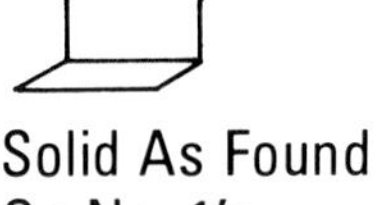

Solid As Found On No. 1's

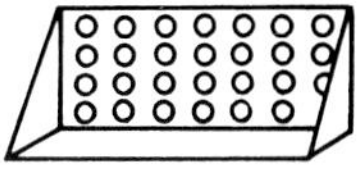

Perforated As Found On No. 8's

Reverses

Ring and Drum

Ring and Disc

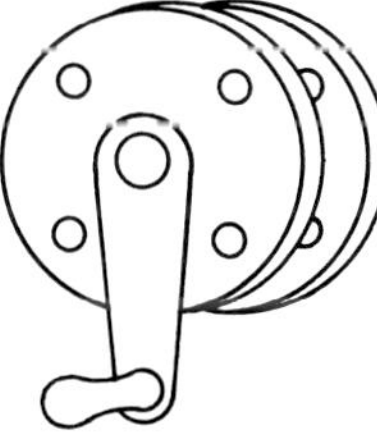

Double Disc

Couplers

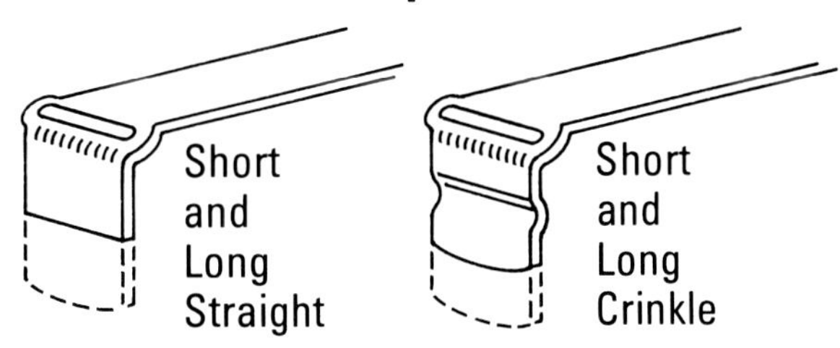

Short and Long Straight

Short and Long Crinkle

End Construction

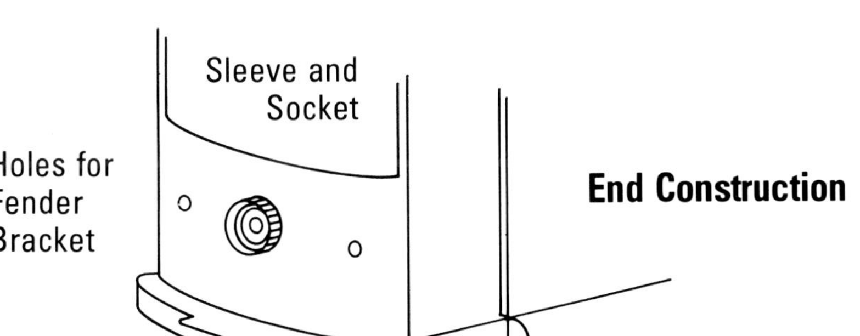

Sleeve and Socket

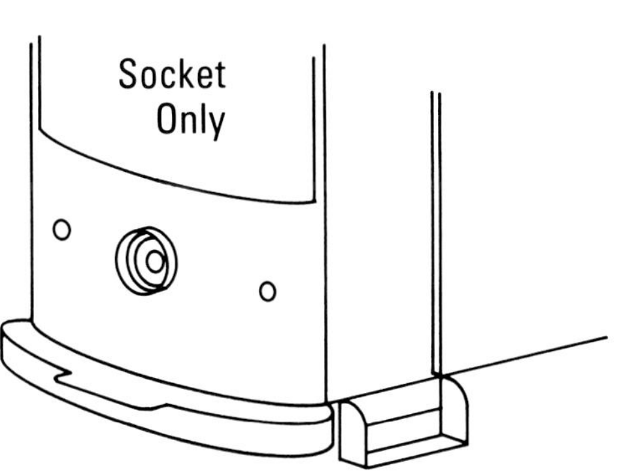

Socket Only

DIRECTIONS FOR THE USE AND CARE OF LIONEL TOYS.

PLEASE READ CAREFULLY

By devoting a few moments to the study of them, no difficulty will be experienced in setting up and operating the various outfits. In addition, useful knowledge will be derived and the maximum amount of pleasure obtained

THE TRACK. Insert the pin terminals of one section into the openings of the other. It is **MOST IMPORTANT** that track is clean at all times. Wipe rail with a clean cloth, and if very dirty moisten cloth with a little benzine and dry with clean cloth. The separate connecting ties supplied are for holding the sections of track together. They slide over the end ties of the track.

THE MECHANISM. The shoe which collects the current from the third rail must always be bright. If it is not, clean it with a cloth saturated in benzine and if this does not remove all the dirt, rub it with a piece of fine sandpaper. Also clean the tread and flange of the wheels with a little benzine. Lubricate all bearings with a little vaseline after removing the gummy substance which collects. Benzine will aid materially when parts are very dirty, but only a little.

THE MOTOR. Occasionally clean the commutator in the following manner: Place a clean cloth over the point of a small screwdriver or similar instrument and press it against the commutator, at the same time revolving the wheels to which the commutator is geared so that it is cleaned all over. If a dry cloth will not remove all the dirt, saturate it in benzine. After it is thoroughly cleaned put a little vaseline on the point of a toothpick and place it under the commutator, revolving the wheels as before. Use very little vaseline—too much is worse than none at all. Do not use Oil.

THE BATTERY. -The Battery is the life of the outfit. It is very important therefore that the following directions be strictly adhered to. On the other hand, read carefully what we say and you will find the cost of battery renewals very nominal and you will learn something about their care.

A battery is almost human. The less it does and the longer it rests naturally adds to its lasting powers Don't use it hour after hour, but give it a chance to recuperate. It is therefore not prudent to run car continually in a circle. Use as many straight sections of track as possible.

CONNECTING THE CELLS.—When connecting batteries use insulated wire, either No. 18 gauge or heavier. Thinner wire will not carry current properly.

Remove the insulation from ends of wire sufficient to go around battery terminals scrape wire to make good contact.

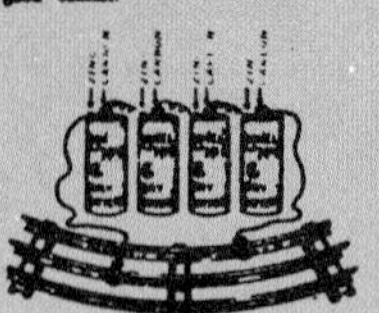

Connect cells as per illustration. Where two or more cells are used, the Carbon of one must be connected to the Zinc of the other. (If like poles are connected they work against each other and no current can be obtained to operate the car.) Keep the cells a little apart. It is a good idea to put them in a box with some newspapers packed between them. The wire connected to the Zinc must not touch the carbon pole of the same cell, but should be connected with the carbon pole of the next cell, and so on until all the cells are connected. If the same wires should touch both poles of the same cell it will exhaust it so that no use can be had from it. After connecting all the cells, the remaining Carbon and Zinc poles should be connected to the terminals which will be found on one section of track. Care should be taken that the same wire does not touch the outside rail of the track and also the middle insulated rail. Care should also be taken that metal of no kind is placed across the track. Do not allow a car to stand on the track when it is not running unless the controller is turned off. When disconnecting batteries, it is advisable to allow the long wires leading from the cells to the track to remain on the track so that the dangling wires do not come in contact with the poles of the batteries and ruin them. Metal of no kind should come in contact with the poles of the battery.

USING THE HOUSE CURRENT.—The most economical way to operate Lionel Toys is by using the house current either direct or alternating, with the aid of **LIONEL CURRENT REDUCERS**, fully described on page 3 of our catalogue. Full directions are given with each apparatus. Don't experiment with other makes of transformers. Lionel Current Reducers are specially constructed for Lionel Cars and will also operate all other makes of miniature trains.

INCANDESCENT BULBS.—The incandescent bulbs supplied with our outfits are not guaranteed by us. They are tested before being inserted in the cars and when burnt out will *not* be replaced without charge. Your dealer carries them in stock. All cars are equipped with 3½ volt bulbs and a resistance so that when the proper voltage is used to operate them they will not burn out, that is, when current is obtained from dry cells, storage batteries or direct current properly reduced, but when the alternating current is used our special No. 26 bulbs which are 14 volts must be substituted for the 3½ volt bulbs or they will burn out immediately.

IF CARS DO NOT RUN AFTER BEING PROPERLY SET UP

The preceding directions when carefully followed should result in the perfect performance of all our motor cars, as they are thoroughly tested before shipment; but as goods may be hurt in transit or by careless handling, the following suggestions should be followed to locate any trouble that may arise:

CAUTION.

Always make sure that the proper current is obtained before looking for trouble in the motor cars. Connect batteries or current reducer as directed then turn motor car upside down and connect one of the wires to any bright steel part of the car and the other wire to the shoe which collects the current from the third rail. If the controller of the car (those equipped with controllers) is placed forward or reverse the wheels should revolve, if the proper current is applied, but the voltage may not be sufficient to operate the motor car when it is on the track, for greater voltage is necessary to propel it than when the wheels revolve idly. To determine whether the current is ample a meter should be applied or another car substituted. The table in last column shows the proper voltages to be employed both on batteries or the house lighting circuit. Should the current be ample for operating the car and it doesn't run when on the track it may be due to the fact that the track is short-circuited. This happens very rarely and can be ascertained in the following manner:

Be sure that nothing is on the track, not even the car, also make sure that a nail or other piece of metal is not in contact with the outside and insulated rails. Then connect one wire to the outside rail and touch the other wire to the middle rail. If the track is perfect no spark will be visible when wire is brushed across third rail, but should there be a short-circuit in the track a spark will be visible where the wire touches. The next thing is to locate the short-circuited section. The best way is as follows: Disconnect one section of track at a time after which operation apply the wires to the remaining sections. As soon as the defective sections are removed the sparking will cease.

Be sure to lubricate cars as directed. When utilizing the reduced alternating current cars must be kept perfectly clean and lubricated frequently.

Our Current Reducers are the most perfect on the market and are made to operate all of our outfits, but some of them are ofttimes condemned for no structural fault, but because other makes of current reducers are used, which are not adapted to them. It is, therefore, to the interest of purchasers of our trains to use our current reducers exclusively, which are carried by all dealers. DO NOT EXCEPT ANY SUBSTITUTE.

NUMBER OF CELLS AND VOLTAGES TO BE USED ON THE VARIOUS CARS.

Outfit No.	Dry Batteries	Storage Batteries or Reduced Direct Current	Reduced Alternating Current
1	4 or 5	4½ volts	17 volts
100	4 or 5	5 "	17 "
101	4 or 5	5 "	17 "
2	4 or 5	5½ "	17 "
202	4 or 5	5½ "	17 "
3	5 or 6	5½ "	17 "
303	5 or 6	5½ "	17 "
8	6 or 7	6 "	17 to 20 "
10	6 or 7	6 "	17 to 20 "
1010	6 or 7	6½	20 "
5	5 or 6	6 "	15 to 18 "
51	5 or 6	6 "	15 to 18 "
6	6 or 7	6½ "	15 to 18 "
7	6 or 7	6½ "	15 to 18 "
33	4 or 5	5 "	15 "
38	5 or 6	6 "	15 to 17 "
53	6 or 7	6½ "	17 to 20 "
42	6 or 7	6 "	15 to 17 "
54	6 or 7	6 "	15 to 17 "
37	4 or 5	5½ "	15 "
34	5 or 6	6 "	15 "
39	5 or 6	6 "	15 to 17 "
40	6 or 7	7½	17 to 20 "
41	6 or 7	7½ "	17 to 20 "
50	6 or 7	7½ "	17 to 20 "
52	6 or 7	7½ "	17 to 20 "
43	6 or 7	7½ "	17 to 20 "

When trailers are added to locomotive use as many more cells or volts as will be found necessary to operate the outfit properly. On the average it requires about ½ of a volt extra for each additional trailer. Do not overload motor cars, as it hurts their efficiency.

By reference to the above table, it will be noted that very much higher voltage is necessary to operate the cars on the alternating current than on the direct, or from batteries. Cars so run are bound to get much warmer than when operated otherwise, therefore cars should be cleaned and lubricated frequently.

Instruction Sheet pasted in lid of Lionel Interurban set purchased in 1914.

Maryland Electrical Supply Company

JOSEPH A. BECKER, PROP.

EUTAW AND MULBERRY STREETS

We beg to call your attention to the fact that we have taken great pains to have the cars that are illustrated in this catalogue named after the popular cars lines in the city of Baltimore. The names are as follows:

No. 1 Curtis Bay	No. 2 Edmondson Ave.
No. 3 Bay Shore	No. 8 Gilmor St. *P-A-Y-E*
No. 100 Linden Ave.	No. 101 Wilkens Ave.
No. 202 Preston St.	No. 303 Madison Ave.

No. 1010 Washington, Baltimore and Annapolis

We carry a complete line of Batteries for Tree Lighting Outfits and House Current, Motors, Dynamos, Mechanical Attachments, Storage Batteries, Pocket Flashlights and many other useful novelties. Storage Batteries recharged and repaired. :: :: :: ::

If you want to please your children on Christmas Day, stop in to see our complete line of Christmas novelties. :: :: ::

Call early so you can select the choice of our Stock. ::

We install Trains and Electrical Toys in your Christmas Garden so that they will give you entire satisfaction. If your trains are not working properly, bring them to us, and we will repair them promptly and accurately. Bring them early to get them early. :: ::

We are showing this year many different imported Electroliers, Domes, Showers and Fancy Fictures. We do wiring and equip your home complete. :: :: :: :: :: ::

Reprint page is from a 1911 Lionel catalog for a dealer in Baltimore, Maryland.

1 **Motor Car** (A). Five window, open platform, 4-wh, New Departure motor, friction drive, RS — No. 1 ELECTRIC RAPID TRANSIT, cream/orange roof/orange letterboards, ends and steps, 5⅝″ frame, 8½″ roof. Circa 1906.

1 **Motor Car** (B). Five window, open platform, 4-wh, New Departure motor, gear drive SSH or no couplers, RS — No. 1 ELECTRIC RAPID TRANSIT, cream/blue roof/blue letterboards, ends and steps, 5⅝″ frame, 8½″ roof. Circa 1907.

1 **Trailer**. Five window, open platform, RS — No. 1 ELECTRIC RAPID TRANSIT, matches above motor car. Circa 1907.

1 **Motor Car** (C). Six window inset, open platform, 4-wh, standard motor in brass or nickel, SSH or LSH couplers, RS — No. 1 ELECTRIC RAPID TRANSIT, cream/blue roof/blue letterboards, ends and steps, 5⅞″ frame, 9 9/16″ roof. Circa 1908.

Note: Same trolley has been found lettered CURTIS BAY.

1 **Trailer** (D). Six window inset, open platform, RS — No. 1 ELECTRIC RAPID TRANSIT, matches above motor car. Circa 1908.

1 **Motor Car** (E). Six window inset, open platform with posts, 4-wh, standard motor, SSH couplers, RS — No. 1 ELECTRIC RAPID TRANSIT, blue/blue roof/cream windows and maroon steps and posts, 5⅞″ frame, 10 5/16″ roof. Circa 1910.

1 **Motor Car**. Six window inset, open platform with posts and rounded roof ends, 4-wh, standard motor, SSH couplers, RS — No. 1 ELECTRIC RAPID TRANSIT, blue/red and cream roof/cream windows and maroon steps and posts, 5⅞″ frame, 11⅝″ roof. Circa 1910.

Note: The last two cars are made with the No. 2 body of 1909.

1
111 **Trailer**. Six window inset, open platform with posts — to match above motor cars but NM.

2 **Motor Car** (F). Six window flat, open platform with posts, 4-wh, standard motor, SSH couplers, RS — No. 2 ELECTRIC RAPID TRANSIT, cream/red roof/red letterboards and cream platform ends, 5⅞″ frame, 10 5/16″ roof. Circa 1906.

2 **Trailer** (G). Six window flat, open platform with posts, matches above motor car. Circa 1906.

2 **Motor Car**. Six window inset, open platform with posts, 4-wh, standard motor, SSH or SCH couplers, RS — No. 2 ELECTRIC RAPID TRANSIT, 5⅞″ frame, 10 5/16″ roof. Circa 1908.
- cream/red roof/red letterboards and cream ends
- blue/blue roof/cream windows and blue letterboards

2 **Trailer**. Six window inset, open platform with posts — to match above motor car but NM.

2 **Motor Car**. Six window, closed offset platform ends, 4-wh, standard motor, SCH couplers, RS — No. 2 ELECTRIC RAPID TRANSIT, red/red roof/cream windows and doors, 5⅞″ frame, 11⅝″ roof. Circa 1910.

2
200 **Trailer**. Six window, closed offset platform ends, RS — No. 200 ELECTRIC RAPID TRANSIT, matches above motor car. Circa 1910.

2 **Motor Car** (H). Six window inset, closed flush platform ends, 4-wh, standard motor, LSH or LCH couplers, RS — No. 2 ELECTRIC RAPID TRANSIT, 5⅞″ frame, 11⅝″ roof. Circa 1913.
- red/red roof/cream windows and doors
- dark olive green/dark olive green roof/orange windows and doors
- cream/cream roof/red lettering

2
200 **Trailer**. Six window inset, close flush platform ends — to match above motor car but NM.

2 **Motor Car** (I). Six window inset, closed flush platform ends, 4-wh, standard motor, LCH couplers, headlights on each end, RS — No. 2 ELECTRIC RAPID TRANSIT, red/red roof/cream windows and doors, 5⅞″ frame, 11⅝″ roof. Circa 1914-16.

200 **Trailer**. Six window inset, closed flush platform ends — to match above motor car but NM.

3 **Motor Car**. Nine window flat, open platform with posts, 8-wh, standard motor, SSH couplers, RS — No. 3 ELECTRIC RAPID TRANSIT, cream/orange roof and letterboards/cream ends, 13⅞″ roof. Circa 1906.

3 **Trailer**. Nine window flat, open platform with posts — to match above motor car but NM.

3 **Motor Car** (J). Nine window inset, open platform with posts, 8-wh, standard motor, SSH couplers, RS — No. 3 ELECTRIC RAPID TRANSIT, 13⅞″ roof. Circa 1908.
- cream/dark olive green roof/dark olive green letterboards and ends
- cream/orange roof and letterboards/cream platform ends
- orange/orange roof and letterboards/cream windows and platform ends

3 **Trailer** (K). Nine window inset, open platform with posts, RS — No. 3 ELECTRIC RAPID

TRANSIT, matches above motor car. Circa 1908.

3 **Motor Car.** Nine window inset, closed offset platform ends, 8-wh, standard motor, SCH couplers, RS — No. 3 ELECTRIC RAPID TRANSIT, dark olive green/dark olive green roof/cream windows and doors, 15¼″ roof. Circa 1910.

3
300 **Trailer.** Nine window inset, closed offset platform ends — to match above motor car but NM.

3 **Motor Car** (L). Nine window inset, closed flush platform ends, 8-wh, standard motor, LSH couplers, RS — No. 3 ELECTRIC RAPID TRANSIT, dark olive green/dark olive green roof/cream windows, doors and clerestory roof, 15¼″ roof. Circa 1913.

Note: Same trolley has been found lettered BAY SHORE.

3
300 **Trailer.** Nine window inset, closed flush platform ends — to match above motor car but NM.

4 **Motor Car.** Nine window flat, open platform with posts, two motors, to match similar No. 3 but NM.

4 **Motor Car** (M). Nine window inset, open platform with posts, 8-wh, two motors, SSH couplers, RS — No. 4 ELECTRIC RAPID TRANSIT, cream/dark olive green roof/dark olive green letterboards and ends, 13⅞″ roof. Circa 1908.

4 **Trailer.** Nine window inset, open platform with posts — to match above motor car but NM.

4 **Motor Car.** Nine window inset, closed offset platform ends, two motors, to match similar No. 3 but NM.

4 **Motor Car** (N). Nine window inset, flush platform ends, 8-wh, two motors, LSH couplers, RS — No. 4 ELECTRIC RAPID TRANSIT, dark olive green/dark olive green roof/cream windows and doors, 15¼″ roof. Circa 1913.

4
40 **Trailer.** Nine window inset, flush platform ends — to match above motor car but NM.

8 **Motor Car.** Nine window inset, long vestibule, closed offset platform ends, 8-wh, standard motor, no couplers, RS — No. 8 PAY AS YOU ENTER, cream/orange roof and letterboards/cream doors and platform ends, 17¾″ roof. Circa 1909.

8 **Motor Car** (O). Eleven window inset, long vestibule, closed offset platform ends, 8-wh, standard motor, no couplers, RS — No. 8 PAY AS YOU ENTER, dark olive green/dark olive green roof/cream windows and doors, 20¼″ roof. Circa 1910-16.

Note: A single factory refinished No. 8 trolley as above exists in dark olive green/dark olive green roof/orange windows, doors and platform ends.

9 **Motor Car** (P). Nine window inset, long vestibule, closed offset platform ends, 8-wh, two motors, no couplers, RS — No. 9 PAY AS YOU ENTER, cream/orange roof and letterboards/cream platform ends, 17¾″ roof. Circa 1909.

9 **Motor Car.** Eleven window inset, long vestibule, closed offset platform ends, 8-wh, two motors, no couplers, RS — No. 9 PAY AS YOU ENTER, dark olive green/dark olive green roof/cream windows and doors, 20¼″ roof. Circa 1910-12.

10 **Interurban** (Q). Seven window, closed vestibule, solid clerestory, three knobs soldered on roof, 8-wh, standard motor, SCH couplers, RS — 10 INTERURBAN, 15 5/16″ roof. Circa 1910.

- maroon/black knobs/gold window trim-no vestibule doors
- dark olive green/black knobs/maroon window trim and vestibule doors

1010 **Trailer** (R) (S). Seven window, closed vestibule, solid clerestory, three knobs soldered on roof, RS — 1010 INTERURBAN, matches above 10 motor cars, 15 5/16″ roof. Circa 1910.

Note: One maroon 1010 trailer with 3 knobs known to exist lettered 1910 INTERURBAN.

10 **Interurban** (T). Seven window, closed vestibule, open clerestory, no knobs on roof — roof removable, 8-wh, standard motor, LSH couplers, RS — 10 INTERURBAN, dark olive green/maroon windows and doors, 15 5/16″ roof. Circa 1913.

Note: At least one No. 10 Interurban known to exist RS — 10 W.B. & A.

1010 **Trailer.** (U). Seven window, closed vestibule, open clerestory, no knobs on roof — roof removable, RS — 1010 INTERURBAN, matches above 10 motor car, 15 5/16″ roof. Circa 1913.

Note: At least one No. 1010 Interurban known to exist RS — 1010 W.B. & A.

10 **Interurban** (V). Seven window, closed vestibule, open clerestory, no knobs on roof — roof removable, three hole step risers, 8-wh, standard motor, LSH or LCH couplers, RS — 10 INTERURBAN, dark olive green/maroon doors/gold and maroon window trim, 15 5/16″ roof. Circa 1913-14.

1010 **Trailer.** Seven window, closed vestibule, open clerestory, no knobs on roof — roof removable, three hole step risers, RS — 1010 INTERURBAN, matches above 10 motor car, 15 5/16″ roof. Circa 1913-14.

10 **Interurban** (W). Seven window, closed vestibule, open clerestory, no knobs on roof, three hole step risers, 8-wh, terminal post on rear vestibule, standard motor, LSH or LCH couplers, RS — 10 INTERURBAN, dark olive green/maroon doors/gold and maroon window trim, 15 5/16" roof. Circa 1914-16.

1010 **Trailer** (X). Seven window, closed vestibule, open clerestory, no knobs on roof, three hole step risers, terminal post on one end, RS — 1010 INTERURBAN, matches above 10 motor car, 15 5/16" roof. Circa 1914-15.

1011 **Interurban.** Seven window, closed vestibule, solid clerestory, three knobs soldered on roof, 8-wh, two standard motors, 15 5/16" roof, NM. Circa 1910-12.

1012 **Trailer.** Seven window, closed vestibule, solid clerestory, three knobs soldered on roof, to match above motor car but NM.

100 **Motor Car** (Y). Five window inset, closed platform, offset vestibule, 4-wh, standard motor, SCH couplers, RS — 100 ELECTRIC RAPID TRANSIT, blue sides and platform ends/blue main roof/cream windows, doors and clerestory roof, 5 7/8" frame, 10 7/16" roof. Circa 1910.

1000 **Trailer.** Five window inset, closed platform, offset vestibule, RS — 1000 ELECTRIC RAPID TRANSIT, matches above motor car. Circa 1910.

100 **Motor Car** (Z). Five window inset, closed platform, flush vestibule, 4-wh, standard motor, LSH couplers, RS — 100 ELECTRIC RAPID TRANSIT, 5 7/8" frame, 10 7/16" roof. Circa 1913-14.

- blue sides and platform ends/blue main roof/cream windows, doors, and clerestory roof
- red sides and platform ends/red main roof/cream windows doors and clerestory roof

Note: Same trolley has been found lettered LINDEN AVE.

1000 **Trailer.** Five window inset, closed platform, flush vestibule, to match above motor car but never found numbered 1000.

Note: Has been found RS — 100.

100 **Motor Car.** Six window inset, closed platform, flush vestibule, 4-wh, standard motor, LSH couplers, RS — 100 ELECTRIC RAPID TRANSIT, red sides and platform ends/red main roof/cream windows, doors and clerestory roof, 5 7/8" frame, 11 1/2" roof. Circa 1914-15.

1000 **Trailer.** Six window inset, closed platform, flush vestibule, to match above motor car but NM.

100 **Motor Car.** Six window inset, closed platform, flush vestibule, 4-wh, standard motor, LCH couplers, two headlights, RS — 100 ELECTRIC RAPID TRANSIT, blue sides and platform ends/blue main roof/cream windows, doors and clerestory roof, 5 7/8" frame, 11 1/2" roof. Circa 1915-16.

101 **Motor Car** (AA). Five bench open summer trolley, 4-wh, standard motor, LCH couplers, RS — 101 ELECTRIC RAPID TRANSIT, blue main roof, platform and seat ends/cream clerestory roof and interior/maroon letterboards and footboards, 5 5/8" frame, 10 3/8" roof. Circa 1910.

101 **Motor Car.** Five bench open summer trolley, 4-wh, standard motor, LSH or LCH couplers, RS — 101 ELECTRIC RAPID TRANSIT, blue main roof, platform and seat ends/cream clerestory roof and interior/blue letterboards and footboards, 5 7/8" frame, 10 3/8" roof. Circa 1911-12.

1100 **Trailer** (BB). Five bench open summer trolley, RS — 1100 ELECTRIC RAPID TRANSIT, matches above motor car. Circa 1911-12.

101 **Motor Car** (CC). Five bench open summer trolley, 4-wh, standard motor, SCH couplers, RS — 101 ELECTRIC RAPID TRANSIT, red main roof, platform and seat ends/cream clerestory roof and interior/black letterboards and footboards, 5 7/8" frame, 10 3/8" roof. Circa 1913-14.

1100 **Trailer.** Five bench open summer trolley, to match above motor car but NM.

202 **Motor Car** (DD). Six bench open summer trolley, 4-wh, standard motor, SCH or LCH couplers, RS — 202 ELECTRIC RAPID TRANSIT, red main roof, platform and seat ends/cream clerestory roof and interior/black letterboards and footboards, 5 7/8" frame, 11 1/2" roof. Circa 1910-14.

Note: This trolley has been found incorrectly lettered No. 1.

2200 **Trailer.** Six bench open summer trolley, RS-2200 ELECTRIC RAPID TRANSIT, matches above motor car. Circa 1910-14.

303 **Motor Car** (EE). Eight bench open summer trolley, 8-wh, standard motor, LSH or SCH couplers, RS — 303 ELECTRIC RAPID TRANSIT or 303 THE LIONEL LINES, dark olive green main roof, platform and seat ends/cream clerestory roof and interior/maroon letterboards and footboards, 15" roof. Circa 1910-14.

3300 **Trailer** (FF). Eight bench open summer trolley, RS — 3300 ELECTRIC RAPID TRANSIT or 3300 THE LIONEL LINES, matches above motor cars. Circa 1910-14.

404 **Motor Car.** Eight bench open summer trolley, 8-wh, two motors, 15" roof, NM. Circa 1910-12.

4400 **Trailer.** Eight bench open summer trolley, to match above motor car but NM.

1 **Motor** (A)

1 **Motor** (B)

1 **Motor** (C)

1 **Motor** (C) CURTIS BAY

1 **Trailer** (D)

1 **Motor** (E)

2 **Motor** (F)

2 Trailer (G)

2 Motor (H)

2 Motor (I)

3 Motor (J)

3 Trailer (K)

3 Motor (L) BAY SHORE

4 Motor (M)

4 Motor (N)

8 Motor (O)

9 Motor (P)

10 Interurban (Q)

1910 Trailer (R)

1010 Trailer (S)

10 Interurban (T)

1010 Trailer (U) W.B. & A.

10 Interurban (V)

10 Interurban (W)

1010 Trailer (X)

100 Motor (Y)

100 Motor (Z)

101 Motor (AA)

1100 Trailer (BB)

101 Motor (CC)

202 Motor (DD)

303 Motor (EE)

100 in box

Streamliners 1934-1941

Contained in this section are the O gauge passenger sets which were made to resemble the "streamlined" trains that appeared on several American railroads around 1934. The prototype trains were light weight, either steam or diesel powered, and had cars with full width vestibules and unbroken roof lines which gave the impression of a single continuous car body. Some of these trains were articulated, i.e. constructed with adjacent cars sharing a single truck. These features were incorporated to a varying degree in the sets listed here, but only on the "City of Portland", which is a 17/64 scale version of the Union Pacific M10000, are all of these features found.

The STREAMLINERS section is subdivided according to the radius of the track with which the set was sold — 072, 0, or 027. In each section set components are listed first, and then the set combinations. Streamliner specials are listed in the SPECIALS section. Since many of these trains were named after prototypes, these names are included in quotes in the description.

The steam type locomotives that head some of these sets have all been described in the O GAUGE LOCOMOTIVES section, so only the loco number and color are included here. Most of the tenders used have a rear drawbar and carry the "X" designation. Exceptions are the 700 TW with scale coupler, and tenders used with the 027 streamlined cars which have a hook coupler. Certain terms are used in this section which are not defined elsewhere in the book. Articulated was defined above. The smaller series cars are not truly articulated as each car has two four wheel trucks. Vestibules are the connections between car bodies. On the 027 series these are stamped sheet metal. However, on the 0 and 072 series the vestibule is the four wheel truck, electrical pickup and lighting for the car, and the latches to hold the cars together. Skirts refer to the sheet metal that partially conceals the wheels. On the 027 streamliners this is just an extension of the bottom of the car body sides, whereas on the O gauge series it is a piece attached to the truck side frames.

Abbreviations used in this section are:

- **Al** dull aluminum finish
- **Ch** chrome plated
- **Fl** fluted sides, similar to prototypes
- **NM** never made as far as known
- **RS** rubber stamped lettering
- **W** Whistle

072 STREAMLINERS

The three 072 streamline sets are composed of mechanically identical cars headed by either a diesel type power car or steam type locomotive. Adjoining cars have open ends which couple to a vestibule mounted on a four wheel truck. This one truck supports both cars. Construction is all sheet metal except for the underbody of each car, the closed end of the front coach or combine, and the tapered end of the observation — all of which are die cast. All windows have frosted celluloid material illuminated by lamps located in the vestibules and above the front and rear trucks. There is no externally applied trim (journals, railings, skirts) other than the handrails on the 752 power car. All lettering is RS on these cars.

COMPONENTS

752E DIESEL TYPE POWER CAR, for "City of
752W Portland", with or without W, 16⅛".

753 COACH, 13¼".
754 OBSERVATION, 15¾".

782 FRONT COACH OR COMBINE, 15½".
783 COACH, 13¼".
784 OBSERVATION, 15¾".

792 FRONT COACH OR COMBINE, scale coupler, 15½".
793 COACH, 13¼".
794 OBSERVATION, 15¾".

SETS BY LOCOMOTIVE NUMBER

"Hiawatha"

250E and 250WX — Hiawatha orange/ Hiawatha gray and black; 782, 783, 784 — Hiawatha orange sides and ends/Hiawatha gray roof/maroon underbody, RS — THE MILWAUKEE ROAD above windows and LIONEL LINES below windows, W. 1935-41.

"Rail Chief"

700E and 700TW-black; 792, 793, 793, 794 — red sides/maroon roof/red underbody, RS — LIONEL LINES below windows, W. 1937-41.

"City of Portland"

752E/752W,753, 754; RS — UNION PACIFIC above windows and LIONEL LINES below windows, W in 1935 only. 1934-36.
yellow sides/brown roof and ends/brown underbody
all aluminum

752W, 753, 753, 754; RS — UNION PACIFIC above windows and LIONEL LINES below windows, W. 1936-41.
yellow sides/brown roof & ends/brown underbody
all aluminum (1936 only)

Note: "City of Portland" set shown in 1934 catalog with LIONEL LINES lettering above windows and car type lettering, i.e. COACH, below windows. None ever found and presumed NM.

Rail Chief

Hiawatha

City of Portland aluminum

City of Portland yellow/brown

O STREAMLINERS

These sets are composed with several different locomotives but with only three basic cars, each of which are found in several color and number variations. The cars are articulated, i.e. they couple to four wheel vestibules in the manner described for the 072 streamliners. They have frosted celluloid window material, and are illuminated from the vestibules with an additional lamp in the rear of observation cars. Trim is nickel and all lettering is found on nickel plates except for RS — LIONEL LINES on some 636W power cars. The trucks have side skirts, which are normally all the same color in any one set, but are occasionally found mixed. Skirt color is black unless noted otherwise.

Construction is all sheet metal except for the die-cast body of the 636 diesel power car and the die cast top section of the 616 power car. Fluting, when specified, is found on the roof, underbody, and side panels below the windows for all or part of the length of the unit. If fluting (Fl) is not noted, these areas are smooth.

COMPONENTS

616E **DIESEL TYPE POWER CAR,** for "Flying
616W Yankee", with or without W, 11¾".

617 **COACH,** early models have four doors while later have only two doors, 8".

618 **OBSERVATION,** round end, 11½".

619 **COMBINE,** 11¼".

636W **DIESEL TYPE POWER CAR,** for "City of Denver", 11¾".

637 **COACH,** 8".

638 **OBSERVATION,** 11½".

SETS BY LOCOMOTIVE NUMBER

265E and 261TX black/nickel trim; 619, 618-all Ch, Ch skirts, Fl. 1935.

"Blue Streak"
265E and 265TX or 265TWX — light blue/nickel trim; 619, 617, 618 — light blue/white window stripe, with or without W, Fl. 1936-38.

Note: Shown in 1938 catalog with blue skirts, but none ever found, and presume NM.

"Flying Yankee"
616E/616W — Ch/black top; 617, 617, 618 — all Ch, Ch skirts, with or without W, Fl. 1935
616E/616W — Ch/gunmetal top and nose; 617, 617, 618 — Ch/gunmetal tail, gunmetal skirts, with or without W, Fl. 1936-41.

"City of Denver"
636W, 637, 637, 638-yellow sides/brown roof and ends/brown underbody, W, Fl. 1936-39

Note: Some sets have reddish brown rather than brown roofs.

265E with 619, 618

Blue Streak

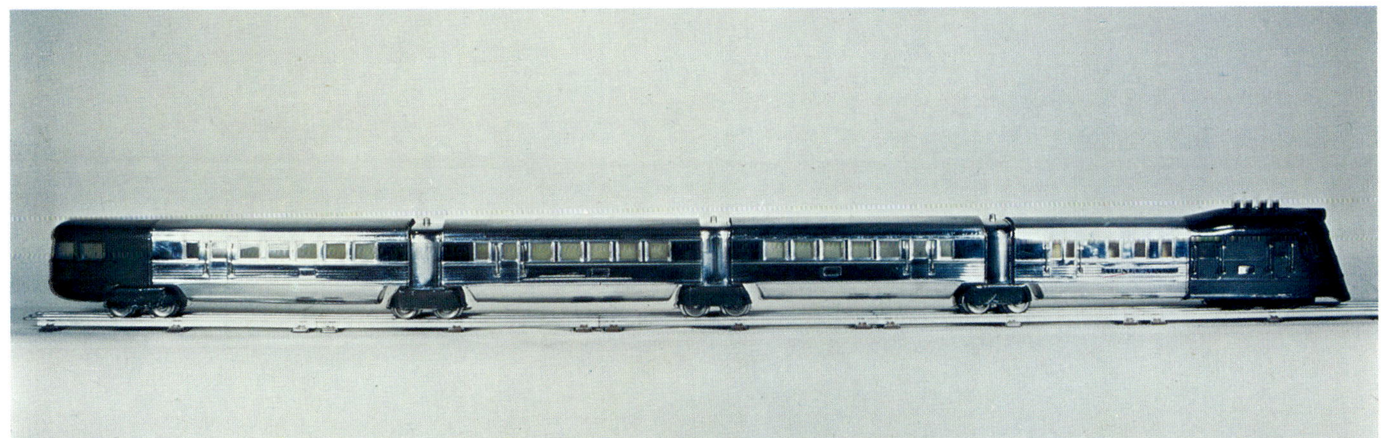
Flying Yankee chrome/gunmetal

Flying Yankee chrome/black

City of Denver yellow/brown

027 AND WINDUP STREAMLINERS

This group of streamliners consists of two sets of cars which were actually manufactured and a third set with two wheel vestibules which were described in the 1935 catalog but were never made. Unlike the cars in the larger series, these cars are not truly articulated as each car has two type IV O gauge trucks. The vestibule is a simple sheet metal stamping which closes the gap between adjacent cars and serves as a coupler. These cars are completely formed from sheet metal with no celluloid window material, interior illumination, or external trim. All cars have brass or nickel plates etched LIONEL LINES. No number designation is visibly applied to any component though the corrugated cardboard boxes are appropriately numbered. Fluting, when specified, is found only on the roof and sides below the windows. The 1700 series have an extension of the car body which partially conceals the wheels called the skirt for purposes of color description. The sequence of colors listed for each set is body color/skirt/nose, tail and vestibules.

COMPONENTS

1542 **COACH,** cataloged 1935 but NM

1543 **OBSERVATION,** cataloged 1935 but NM

1673 **COACH,** no journal boxes, 9¼″.

1674 **PULLMAN,** No journal boxes, 9⅛″.

1675 **OBSERVATION,** no vestibule, no journal boxes, 9¼″.

1700E **DIESEL TYPE POWER CAR,** 9⅝″.

1700 **DIESEL TYPE POWER CAR,** similar to 1700 E but no reverse, used in uncataloged sets, 9⅝″.

1701 **COACH,** 9″.

1702 **OBSERVATION,** 10¾″.

1703 **FRONT COACH,** no vestibule, uncataloged, 9⅜″.

1816
1816W **DIESEL TYPE POWER CAR,** similar to 1700 but with windup motor, with headlight, with or without W, 9⅝″.

1817 **COACH,** similar to 1701 but no journal boxes, 9″.

1818 **OBSERVATION,** similar to 1702 but no journal boxes, 10¾″.

SETS BY LOCOMOTIVE NUMBER

1508 and 1541T — light red, windup; 1542, 1542, 1543 — light red, cataloged 1935 but NM.

1508X and 1541T — black, windup; 1542, 1543 — orange, cataloged 1935 but NM.

1588 and 1588T — black, windup; 1673, 1674, 1675 — light red, W, Fl. 1936-37.

1700E, 1701, 1702 — alum/light red/light red, Fl. 1935.

1700E, 1701, 1702 — Ch/light red/light red, Fl. 1935.

Note: Cataloged in 1935 with smooth sides and chrome finish but presumed NM.

1700E, 1701, 1701, 1702 — Ch/light red/light red, Fl. 1936-37.

"Silver Streak"
1816, 1817, 1818 — Ch/orange/orange, Fl. 1935.
1816W, 1817, 1818 — Ch/orange/orange, W, Fl. 1936-37.

Note: Cataloged in 1935 with smooth sides and chrome finish but presume NM.

1588 with 1673, 1674, 1675

1700E, 1701, 1701, 1702 chrome/light red

1700E, 1701, 1702 chrome/light red

Silver Streak

Tender Lists

Standard, OO, and O gauge tenders are listed in numerical order along with the matching locomotive numbers in the following three subsections. Unlike most of the other rolling stock, tenders do not have number plates and are normally only identified by the number that is rubber stamped on the bottom of the frame. Unfortunately, this practice was not followed consistently. Early Standard gauge tenders and both O and Standard gauge tenders made in the period 1931-34 are generally not marked. Occasionally tenders from other years are not marked. In these cases catalogs and the packing boxes, where available, have been used as guides.

As an aid in identification, photographs of the major variations are shown along with the assigned numbers. Where several numbers are listed for one basic design or where production continued over a number of years, the type of truck, finish or trim, couplers, and other details may vary. No attempt has been made to completely catalog these variations. The general notes on dating found in the other sections apply and further there is almost always consistency of paint or finish and trim on both the locomotive and tender.

Additional Brief Notes:

1. Tenders have eight wheels unless noted otherwise.

2. O gauge tenders made in the period 1938-42 generally have electric couplers and the "2" prefix added to the number. Exceptions are the 700T, 701T, the 1588T found in special sets, and the 1689T cataloged with the 1664, 1668, some 1684's, and also used in special sets.

3. The "X" designation is mentioned only where its purpose is obvious.

4. Drawbar length is taken from the car frame to the end of the bar. This is shown in parentheses under description.

5. Length is given over the frame and does not include couplers, steps, footboards, etc.

6. Rubber stamping (RS) may include the number plus W, T, WT, TX, or WX.

7. Abbreviations are as used elsewhere.

O GAUGE TENDERS

Tender	Description	Length	Year	Locomotive
225W	gunmetal	6½″	1939	249E (uncat.)
250W, WX, 2250W	Hiawatha orange/ Hiawatha gray, 12-Wh	8⅜″	1935-42	250E
257T	black with orange stripe, 4-Wh	5¾″	1930	257, 258
			circa 1931	257 (uncat.)
	black, 4-Wh		1931	261
			circa 1932	257 (uncat.)
	crackle black, 4-Wh		circa 1932	257 (uncat.)

Tender	Description	Length	Year	Locomotive
258T	black with orange stripe	5¾″	1930	258
259T	black, 4-Wh	5½″	1932 circa 1932 1933	259 257 (uncat.) 259E
260T	black with cream stripe black with dark green frame black with dark green frame 12-Wh crackle black with dark green frame, 12-Wh	7¼″	1930 1931-33 1933	260E 260E 260E (uncat.)
261T	black light red	5½″	1935 1935	261E 264E
261TX (drawbar)	black	5½″	1935	265E
262T	black, die-cast	5¾″	1931-32 1933	262 262E
262T	black, stamped steel	5½″	1934	259E, 262E
263T,263W,263TWX, 2263W	dark gunmetal, 12-Wh gunmetal, 12-Wh blue/dark blue frame, 12-Wh	7⅜″	1934-35 1935-36 1935-39 1937-40 1936-39	260E 255E 263E 763E 263E
265T, 265W, 2265T, 2265W	black gunmetal light red	6½″	circa 1935-36 circa 1936 circa 1936-38 1935-36	265E, 249E 262E, 264E (uncat.) 225E, 238E, 249E 265E 264E
265TX, 265WX (drawbar)	light blue	6½″	1936-38 1936-38	265E 264E (uncat.)
700T, 700W	black, 12-Wh	10″	1937-42	700E
700K5	kit for building 700T, 12-Wh body finished in gray primer	10″	1939-42	700K
701T	black	6⅝″	1939-42	701 (708)
1016	black, orange trim "Winner" 4-Wh	5″	1931-32	1015, 1035
1502T	black, red trim, 4-Wh	4″	1933-34	1506L
1509T	light red "Mickey Mouse", 4-Wh	4″	1935	1506, 1508
1516T	black, 4-Wh light red, 4-Wh	5⅞″	1936 1937	1511 1511

Tender	Description	Length	Year	Locomotive
1588T, 1588TX, 1588W	black, 4-Wh	5⅞″	1936-37 circa 1937 circa 1936-40	1588 289E (uncat.) 259E (uncat.)
1661T	black, 4-Wh	5″	1933 1934-35	1661E 1681, 1681E
1689T,1689W,2689TX 2689T,2689W	gunmetal, black	5⅞″	1936-37 1937-41 1936 circa 1937 1938-42 1938-40 1938-40 1941 circa 1938-41	1689E 1668/1668E 1688/1688E 289E (uncat.) 1664/1664E 1666/1666E 259E 258 (uncat.) 204E (uncat.)
	black (only) gunmetal (only)		1942 1938 1939-40	1684 224E 229E
2201T, 2201B	black	5⅞″	1940-42	201, 1663
2203T, 2203B	black	5⅞″	1940-42	203, 1662
2224T, 2224W	gunmetal, black, die-cast	8″	1939-40	224/224E
2224T, 2224W	black, plastic	7½″	1941-42	224/224E
2225T, 2225W	gunmetal, black	6⅛″	1938 1938-40	225E 238E (uncat.) 265E
2226W, 2226WX (coupler height)	black, 12-Wh gunmetal, 12-Wh	8⅝″	1938-41 1940-42 circa 1940	226/226E 763E 763E
2227T, 2227B	black	6½″	1939-42	227
2228T, 2228B	black	6½″	1939-42	228
2230T, 2230B	black	6½″	1939	230
2231T, 2231B	black	6½″	1939	231
2232B	black	6½″	1940-42	232
2233B	black	6½″	1940-42	233
2235T, 2235W	gunmetal, black, die-cast	8″	1939-40	225/225E
2235W	black, plastic	7½″	1941-42	225/225E
2245W	black, die-cast	8″	1939-40	225/225E
2666T, 2666W	black, plastic	7½″	1941-42 1941-42 1942 circa 1942	1666/1666E 229/229E 1664/1664E 1684 (uncat.)

250W Hiawatha orange and gray

257T crackle black

258T black/orange stripe

259T black

260T black/dark green frame

260T black/dark green frame, 12 Wh

261T black (same as 261TX, 262 sheet-metal)

262T diecast, black

263T gunmetal

265T light red (same as 225, 2225, 265TX or WX)

700W black (same as 700K5)

2227T black (same body as 701T and 2228-2233 tenders)

1016 black/orange trim

1502T black/red trim

1509T light red

1516T light red

1588T black

1661T black/red trim

1689T black

2203T black (same as 2201)

2224T die-cast, gunmetal (same as 2235, 2245)

2224T plastic, black (same as 2235 or 2666)

2224T paper train, black

2226T gunmetal

STANDARD GAUGE TENDERS

Tender	Description	Length	Year	Locomotive
5	black, 4-Wh, (single 10 series truck)	5 13/16″	1906-09	5 Special
5	black	5 13/16″	1910-11 1912-23	5 Special 51
6	black nickel finish	9¾″	1906-23 1908-09	6 6 Special
7	nickel finish	9¾″	1910-23	7
384T	black with green stripe, (1 7/32″ drawbar)	8 3/16″	1930-32	384, 384E
	black with green stripe, (1 7/16″ drawbar)		circa 1932	392E
	crackle black		circa 1933	392E
	black		1932-34 1934	392E 1835E
	dark gunmetal		1933	385E
	crackle gunmetal		circa 1934	385E
	gunmetal		1934	385E
384TX	black with orange stripe		circa 1933	392E
385W	gunmetal	8 3/16″	1935-39	385E
390T	black with orange stripe	8 3/16″	1929 1929-31	390 390E
	medium blue/dark blue frame/ cream stripe		1930	390E
	dark green/orange stripe		circa 1930	390E
	dark green/Stephen Girard green stripe		circa 1930	390E
390TX	black with orange stripe	8 3/16″	1930	390E
392W	black, 12-Wh gunmetal, 12-Wh	10⅛″	1935 1935-39	392E 392E
400T	black, 12-Wh	12⅛″	1931-33	400E
	black, red stripe, 12-Wh		circa 1931	400E
	dark blue, red stripe, 12-Wh		circa 1931	400E
	medium blue/dark blue frame, 12-Wh		1931-34	400E
	crackle black, 12-Wh		circa 1933	400E
	dark gunmetal, 12-Wh		1933-34	400E
400W	gunmetal, 12-Wh light blue/dark blue frame, 12-Wh	12⅛″	1935-39 1935-39	400E 400E
1835W	black	8 3/16″	1935-39	1835E

Note: Early tenders through 1923 in reality do not have a drawbar but rather hook couplers on both ends of the tender. These extend 1¼″ and, 9/16″ on the 5 and 6 tenders respectively.

Note: The 384T is cataloged with the 390E in 1933 and pictured as having an orange stripe. This combination has not been verified, but, if it exists, probably includes the 384T without stripe.

5 black, B&O, 4-Wh

5 black, NYC & HRRR, 4-Wh

5 black, PENNSYLVANIA

6 black, NYC & HRRR

6 black, PENNSYLVANIA

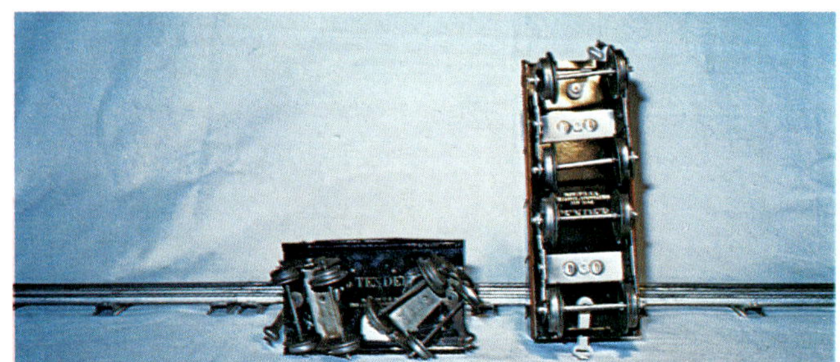

bottom lettering on 5 and 6 tenders

7 nickel plated

384T dark gunmetal

384T crackle

385W gunmetal

390TX black

390T medium blue

00 GAUGE TENDERS

Tender	Description	Length	Year	Locomotive
001T, 001W	black, 12-Wh, full scale, 3 rail	6½″	1938-42	001
002T, 002W	black, 12-Wh, modified scale, 3 rail	6½″	1939-42	002
003T, 003W	black, 12-Wh, full scale, 2 rail	6½″	1939-42	003
004T, 004W	black, 12-Wh, modified scale, 2 rail	6½″	1939-42	004

392W black

392W gunmetal

400W gunmetal

1835W black

384X box

003 black

384TX black

Special and Unique Items

In this section special items produced by Lionel are described in detail. All of these items are uncataloged and the indicated dates of production are approximate from available evidence. Several types of specials have been made by Lionel and the definition of these must be made clear before utilizing this section. A *department store special* (DSS) is a set made especially for one or a small group of department stores where either the set box, the locomotive, or the cars are marked with the name of the store. Using this rigorous definition many of the included sets in this list may well be department store specials but are not so designated as they do not meet these criteria. *General release specials* are uncataloged sets sold through a large number of stores where neither the cars, the locomotive, nor the boxes are specially marked for the store. However, both the box and/or the contents may be marked with an X-indicating only that the item is different from the cataloged current production. *Factory specials* were made for corporations, i.e. Quaker Oats electric locomotives or the Harmony Dairy box car, in small numbers. Though it is unclear why these were made, it may well be that they were used for corporate advertising. *Factory promotion specials* were often manufactured by Lionel and pictured in their executive catalogs. These specials usually were low cost sets especially boxed for promotional sales by Lionel dealers. At other times leftover items found in cleaning out the factory, such as during the early part of World War II, were put together into odd set combinations. These *odd sets* are noted here but are only considered special because of the mixed age of the items. Finally, Lionel produced a number of *unique items,* often one or only a small number, for display. These items were often hand painted or hand crafted and may represent preproduction designs that were never put into use.

Early special sets through the 1920's often were designated with Special #1 or #2, etc. for each store. Special sets manufactured in the 1930's, however, were given numbers in Lionel's chronologic number list between 5000 and 8000. The items described in this section are divided into three subgroupings — 0 gage, Standard gauge, and Streamliners for ease of use. Colors as in other sections are given in the following manner — body color/roof color/window color — plate color or type of lettering. All of the special items noted in this section can be found cross-referenced in their appropriate section except the unique items. The abbreviation DSS at the end of the set description indicates a set that the committee feels meets our criteria for a department store special. The presence of the store name without the DSS marking indicates where the set was purchased but does not imply that it is a DSS.

0 GAUGE

204 Black or gunmetal — E but not so RS; 1689W tender-black or gunmetal; 609-609-611 light blue/alum/alum, RS — THE LIONEL LINES. Circa 1941.

204 Black-E but not so RS; 2689T tender — black, RS lettering; 2717 — litho gondola, 2719 — litho box, 2722 — litho caboose. Set box marked #6629E. Circa 1940.

204 Black-E but not so RS; 2689W tender — black; 654 tank — alum Sunoco, 655 box — cream/tuscan, 657 caboose — light red/light red/white. Circa 1940.

204 Black-E but not so RS; 0-2689TX tender — black; 2620 floodlight — red, 2652 gondola — burnt orange, 2654 tank — orange/Shell decal, 2757 caboose. Circa 1941.

204 Black-E but not so RS; 1689W tender — black (no number on tender); 607-607-608 Stephen Girard green/dark green/cream — nickel journals. Circa 1940.

204 Black-E but not so RS; 0-2689WX tender — black; 654 tank — light gray/Sunoco decal, 655 box — cream/tuscan — RS, 657 caboose — light red/tuscan/white — RS. Box marked Lionel #8100W and SEARS #05973. Circa 1941. DSS

204 Black-E but not so RS; 2689 tender — black; 2659 dump — red, 2652 gondola — burnt orange, 2657 caboose — light red/tuscan/white. Circa 1941.

204 Black-E but not so RS; 0-2689WX tender — black (box labeled bronze gunmetal); 2620 floodlight — light red, 2652 gondola — burnt orange, 2654 tank — orange/Shell decal, 2757 caboose — light red/tuscan/white. Circa 1940-41.

204 Black-E but not so RS; 1689T tender — black, black journals, RS — LIONEL LINES; 804 tank — orange/Shell decal — black journals, 809 dump — medium green — nickel journals, 807 caboose — light red/light red/cream — black journals. Circa 1940.

229E Gunmetal; 2689W tender — gunmetal; 2655 box — cream/tuscan — RS, 2654 tank — orange/Shell decal, 2659 dump — medium green, 2657 caboose — light red/tuscan/white — RS. Circa 1939.

238 Black; 2265W tender — black; 2600-2601-2602 light red/red/ivory — black journals. Box marked — SPECIAL #186WX O-Gauge Passenger Train Outfit, SEARS-ROEBUCK No. 59-79P. Circa 1939.

238 Black; 2225T tender — black; 2653 hopper — black — RS, 2654 tank — orange/Shell decal, 2655 box — cream/tuscan — RS, 2657 caboose — light red/tuscan/white — RS. Circa 1941.

249E Gunmetal; 2225WX tender — gunmetal; 1717 — litho gondola, 1719 — litho box, 1722 — litho caboose. Circa 1938-39.

249E Black or gunmetal — nickel trim; 261T sheet metal tender — LIONEL LINES plate; 610-610-612 light red/alum/alum — block lettering. Box marked set #6517E. Circa 1937.

249E Black — nickel trim; 265 tender — black; 1685-1686-1687 vermillion/maroon/cream — black lettering. Set box marked #6709. Circa 1937.

249E Black or gunmetal — nickel trim; 265 tender — black or gunmetal; 1685-1686-1687 light blue/alum/alum — black lettering. Circa 1936.

252 **Elec., —** maroon/black/cream with cream stripe around cab bottom; 607-607-608 maroon/maroon/cream with MACY SPECIAL brass plate on observation platform, no interior lights. R.H. MACY CO., New York. Circa 1931. DSS

252 **Elec., —** maroon/black/cream same as above with 607-607-608 maroon/maroon/cream but no Macy markings or plates. All car boxes marked WINE and set box marked SPECIAL #1H. Circa 1931.

252 **Elec., —** maroon/black/cream same as above with 603-603-604 maroon/maroon/cream, with MACY SPECIAL brass plate on observation platform. R.H. MACY CO., New York. Circa 1931. DSS

252 **Elec., —** olive green/black/Br with strap headlight, spoked wheels; 603-603-604 orange/orange/maroon — combination latch couplers. Box marked 296T-SNELLENBERG SPECIAL No. 1. Circa 1927. DSS

252 **Elec., —** olive green/black/Br with strap headlight, spoked wheels and combination latch couplers; 603-603-604 orange/orange/maroon — combination latch couplers. ROSENBAUM SPECIAL #1. Circa 1927. DSS

253 **Elec., —** Stephen Girard green/dark green/cream; 603-603-604 Stephen Girard green/dark green/cream — copper journals, no interior lights. All car boxes marked 603X or 604X APPLE, loco box marked 253X APPLE, and set box marked Special #22. Circa 1931.

253 **Elec., —** dark green/black/Br; 610-612 dark green/dark green/maroon (cataloged set had 3 cars). K.&B. #2. KAUFMANN AND BAER, Pittsburgh or also GIMBELS SPECIAL #1. Circa 1925. DSS

253E **Elec., —** gray/black/Br; 610-610-612 red/red/cream with RS — MACY SPECIAL in script lettering above the window. R.H. MACY CO., New York. Circa 1931. DSS

254 **Elec., —** olive green/black/Br — with red stripe along bottom of cab and red celluloid on inside of ventilators; 605-605-606 olive green/olive green/red — no special lettering or plates. Circa 1933.

254 **Elec., —** olive green/Br — cast headlights, combination latch couplers; 610-610-612 — olive green/olive green/red — THE LIONEL LINES decals over Ives decals above windows, Lionel paper label on bottom, over

Ives paper label, copper journals on 612, nickel journals on 610. Circa 1933-34. Note: Factory alteration to use up remaining Ives lettered cars.

254E **Elec., —** orange/black/Br; 605-605-606 orange/orange/cream windows and pea green doors — MACY SPECIAL brass plate on observation platform. R.H. MACY CO., New York. Circa 1930-32. DSS

257 Black/no stripe; 259T — black/no stripe; 607-607-608 Stephen Girard green/dark green/cream with air tanks and copper journals. Carton stamped Set #97. SPECIAL #1, AMC. Circa 1932.

257 Black/no stripe; 257T with orange stripe; 607-608 Stephen Girard green/dark green/cream with air tanks. Box marked — SPECIAL #2. Circa 1931-32.

257 Black/no stripe with L.L. on plates and motor; 4-Wh Ives tender-copper journals; Ives lithographed cars — 1708 cattle, 1709 box, 1712 caboose. (Lionel label on Ives box) HORNES #5004. Circa 1932. DSS

258 Black/orange stripe; 258T tender/no stripe, nickel journals; 629-630 light red/light red/cream — 8-Wh cars. Circa 1935.

258 Black/orange stripe; 259T black/no stripe; 603-604 red/black/cream — copper journals. Circa 1933.

258 Black/no stripe; 262T — black/no stripe; 629-629-630 red/red/cream, 4-Wh, brass plate on observation platform — MACY SPECIAL. R.H. MACY CO., New York. Circa 1931. DSS

258 Late Black; 1689T — black, RS; 1679 litho box—yellow/maroon, 1680 litho tank — alum SUNX, 1682 litho caboose — light red/light red/cream. Set box marked #7003. Circa 1940.

Note: Set numbers 7000 to 7008 represent factory promotional specials.

258 Late Black; 1689W — back, RS; 1679 litho box—yellow/maroon, 1680 litho tank — orange SHELL, 657 caboose — light red/tuscan/white. Set box marked #7005WX. Circa 1941.

258 Late Gunmetal; 1689T — gunmetal; 1679 litho box—yellow/maroon, 1680 litho tank — orange SHELL, 1682 litho caboose — light red/light red/cream, black journals on all cars. Circa 1940.

258 Late Black; 2689TX tender; 1679 litho box—yellow/maroon, 1680 litho tank — alum SUNX, 1682 litho caboose — brown/brown — NYC. Circa 1941.

Note: All cars have non-automatic box couplers and are marked X on cartons because of absent journals.

259 Black-nickel trim, not E; 259T — black; 529-529-530 terra-cotta/terra-cotta/cream — maroon frame, copper journals. Set box marked OUTFIT No. 5015. Circa 1933.

259 E but not so marked, black; 1588 tender — no journals; 629-629-630 red/red/cream 8-Wh cars — nickel journals, nickel observation platform. MONTGOMERY WARD. Circa 1934.

259E Black — copper and brass trim; 261T — black/no stripe; 1685-1687 light red/maroon/cream — 4-Wh trucks. SEARS. Circa 1934.

259E Black — copper and brass trim; 261T — black/no stripe; 1685-1686-1687 light red/maroon/cream — 4-Wh trucks. SEARS. Circa 1934.

259E Black-E but not so marked; 1689 tender — black; 654 tank — Shell orange — RS, 652 gondola — burnt orange — RS, 657 caboose — light red/tuscan/white — RS, all cars with latch couplers and black journals. Circa 1940.

259E Black — nickel trim; 259T — black; 629-629-630 red/red/cream, 8-Wh, nickel journals, brass observation platform. Set box marked Set #150 and car boxes marked 629 or 630 O GAUGE. Circa 1935.

259E Gunmetal; 2689TX — gunmetal, black journals; 1717 litho gondola, 1719 litho box, 1722 litho caboose — orange-red, all cars with black journals and latch couplers. Circa 1940.

259E Black — copper and brass trim; 259T — black; 1717 litho gondola, 1719 litho box, 1722 litho caboose — copper journals on cars. Circa 1933.

259E Black — nickel trim; 1689 tender with black journals; 609-609-611 light blue/alum/alum. Circa 1937.

259E Black; 1588 TX — black; 831 lumber—green, 804 tank — alum Sunoco or Shell orange, 807 caboose — light red/light red/cream. Circa 1940.

Note: Some of these sets also contain 809 dump — orange. Cars have RS lettering, not plates and either black or nickel journals.

259E Black; 1689W tender — black; 1717 litho gondola, 1719 litho box, 1722 litho caboose — nickel journals on cars, latch couplers. Circa 1936.

259E Gunmetal — 2689WX — gunmetal, automatic box coupler with special leaf spring, no hook to keep it shut; 652 gondola — yellow, 654 tank — alum Sunoco, 657 caboose — red/red/cream. SEARS. Circa 1939.

262 Black, not an E; 262T — black; 831 lumber — dark green, 809 dump — orange, 807 caboose — red/peacock. Set box marked #1139. MACY. Circa 1932.

262E Black — nickel trim; 262T sheet metal— black; 1685-1686-1687 light blue/ alum/alum — 4-Wh trucks. Circa 1935.

262E Black — copper and brass trim; 262T sheet metal — black; 1685X-1685X-1687X red/maroon/cream. X marked on individual boxes and 5016E stamped on outside box. Circa 1934.

262E Black; 262T sheet metal — black; 1685 (nickel journals), 1686 (copper journals), 1687 (nickel journals) red/maroon/ cream — latch couplers. Car boxes marked 1685XR-1686X-1687XR with the R stamping different from the rest. HUDSON'S (Detroit). Circa 1936-37.

262E Black; 261T — black; 1717 litho gondola, 1719 litho box car, 1719 litho box car, 1722 litho caboose. Circa 1936.

262E Black — N or Br plates, nickel trim; 265T-black; 610-610-612 light blue/alum/alum — scroll lettering. Circa 1935-36.

262E Black — nickel trim; 262T — black, copper and brass trim; 600-601-602 light blue/ alum/alum — latch couplers. Circa 1935.

262E Black; 262T sheet metal — black; 610-610-612 light red/alum/alum. MAY STERN, Pittsburgh. Circa 1935.

262E Black; 265T — black; 610-610-612 light red/alum/alum. Circa 1936.

262E Black — brass and copper trim; 262T — black; 610-610-612 light red/alum/alum — block lettering. Set box marked M-1 and 5000E. MAY COMPANY, Cleveland. Circa 1935.

262E Black — copper trim; 262T — black; 610-610-612 light red/alum/alum — block lettering. Circa 1935.

262E Black — nickel trim, with 249 boiler front; 262T — black; 610-610-612 light red/alum/ alum — block lettering. Set #6517EX. GIMBELS, Pittsburgh. Circa 1935.

262E Black — nickel trim; 265T — black; 1685-1686-1687 vermillion/maroon/cream — black lettering. Circa 1936-37.

263E Gunmetal; 263T — gunmetal; 1686-red/ maroon/cream — gold lettering and 1685-1685-1687 vermillion/maroon/cream — black lettering.WANAMAKER, Philadelphia. Circa 1937.

264E Black — nickel trim; 265T — black; 609-609-611 light blue/alum/alum, SEARS. Circa 1936-37.

264E Black — nickel trim; 262T — black; 609-609-611 light blue/alum/alum/no air tanks, no journals, RS — THE LIONEL LINES. Circa 1935-37.

264E Light red — nickel trim; 265T — light red; 1685-1686-1687 vermillion/maroon/cream — black lettering. Circa 1936-37.

264E Light red — nickel trim; 265T — light red; 1685-1685-1687 vermillion/maroon/cream — black lettering, set box marked 6511E. Circa 1936-37.

264E Light red — nickel trim; 261T — light red; 1717 litho gondola, 1719 litho box, 1722 litho caboose — nickel journals, latch couplers. Set #5236E, Circa 1935-36.

265E Black; 265T — black; 1685-1686-1687 vermillion/maroon/cream — black lettering. Circa 1936-37.

265E Black; 265T — black; 1685-1686-1687 light blue/alum/alum — black lettering. Circa 1936.

265E Gunmetal; 265T — gunmetal, nickel trim; 609-609-611 light blue/alum/alum — RS — THE LIONEL LINES. Set box marked #6500E and SEARS #5974. Circa 1937.

265E Gunmetal; 2225W — gunmetal; 2652 gondola — orange, 3651 operating lumber, 2654 tank — Shell orange, 2657 caboose — light red/light red. SEARS. Circa 1940.

289E Black; 1588W — black; 804 tank — alum Sunoco, 831 flat — green, 807 caboose — light red. Circa 1937.

450 Elec — red/black/Br, same as 253 but R.H. Macy plate on third rail pickup and script letters Br plate on side MACY SPECIAL; 610-610-612 red/red/cream — RS — MACY SPECIAL in script lettering above windows. R.H. MACY CO., New York. Circa 1930. DSS

450 Elec — apple green/dark green/Br, same as 253 but etched Br plate-script letters MACY SPECIAL. R.H. MACY CO., New York. Circa 1930. DSS

728 Elec — dark green, same as 700 but RS — QUAKER 728; 600-600 pullmans — dark green. Factory special for QUAKER OATS COMPANY. Circa 1915-16.

732 Elec — dark green, same as 701 but RS — QUAKER 732; 601-601 pullmans — dark green. Factory special for QUAKER OATS COMPANY. Circa 1915-16.

1684 Black; 1689W —black; 1679 litho box-yellow/maroon, 1680 litho tank — orange Shell, 1682 litho caboose — light red/light red/cream, all cars with black journals and non-automatic box couplers. Set box marked #7008, factory promotional special shown in 1940 executive catalog. Circa 1940-41.

1688 Black; 1689T — black; 1679 litho box, 1680 litho tank — alum Sunoco, 1682 litho caboose — light red/light red/cream/yellow clerestory stripe. Factory special promotion in 1939 executive catalog. 1939.

Note: Set boxes numbered 6401-6402-6403 depending on amount of track and manual or electric switches. All cars and tenders are pictured without journals and therefore boxes could be found marked "X".

1688E Black; 1689T — black; 1679 litho box — yellow/maroon, 1680 litho tank — gray SUNX, 1682 litho caboose — dark brown NYC, all cars have black journals and non-automatic box couplers. Set box marked No. 8063. Circa 1942.

1689E Black — no marker light holes (box marked 1689EX); 1689W — black, with power pickup in center of body; 1692-1692-1693 litho peacock/peacock/cream. Box marked #6206W — Lionel Jr. passenger train. Circa 1936.

1689E Gunmetal — with marker lights; 1689W-gunmetal; 1692-1692-1693 litho peacock/peacock/cream. Circa 1937-38.

1689E Gunmetal; 1588TX — black; 655 box — cream/maroon-nickel, 659 dump — dark green-nickel, 657 caboose — red/red/cream. Circa 1943.

Note: Purchased 1943, may be a factory clean out and not a true special.

249E Gunmetal with 1717, 1719, 1722

249E Gunmetal with 610, 610, 612 — light red/alum

252 Maroon with 607-607 maroon/cream

253 Gray with MACY 607-607-608 maroon/cream

254 Olive green with 605-605-606 olive green

258 (late) black with 1679, 1680, 1682

259E Black with 629-629-630 red/cream

259E Black with 609-609-611 light blue/alum

259E Black with 809, 804, 807

262E Black with 1685-1686-1687 light blue/alum

262E Black with 610-610-612 light blue/alum

450 Red-MACY

728 QUAKER — dark green with 600-600 dark green

1689E Black with 1692-1692-1693 peacock/cream

8 **Elec.** — red/no stripe/cream window trim; 337-337-338 red/red/cream. Set box marked SPECIAL #2. Circa 1931-32.

8 **Elec.** — red/cream stripe/cream window trim; 337-337-338 red/red/cream. SPECIAL #3. Circa 1931-32.

8 **Elec.** — red; 114 box-orange, 114 box-orange, 117 caboose-brown/black. ELDER-JOHNSTON, Dayton. Circa 1925-26.
Note: The cataloged set had 112-114-117 cars.

8E **Elec.** — peacock/orange windows and stripe; 332-339-341 peacock/peacock/orange — RS — MACY SPECIAL in place of BAGGAGE, PULLMAN, and OBSERVATION, celluloid drumhead in observation platform — MACY SPECIAL. Boxes marked as follows: 8E-P. BLUE, 332-P. BLUE MS, 339-P. BLUE, 341-P. BLUE MS. SPECIAL #2. R.H. MACY CO., New York. Circa 1928-30. DSS

8E **Elec.** — peacock/orange stripe; 332-339-341 peacock/peacock/orange. No Macy lettering, no special drumhead, no special markings on individual boxes. Set box marked SPECIAL. KAUFMANN's, Pittsburgh. Circa 1928.

8E **Elec.** — pea green/cream windows; 337-337-338 pea green/pea green/cream — usual RS lettering on sides but with celluloid drumhead in observation platform — MACY SPECIAL. Set box has MACY label and marked SPECIAL #2. R.H. MACY CO., New York. Circa 1932. DSS

9 **Elec.** — dark green; 418-431-490 mojave/mojave/maroon. Set box marked P-091. Circa 1928.

9E **Elec.** — gunmetal; 309-309-312 State brown/dark brown/cream. Individual boxes marked No. 9E-GM, 309 and 312 BROWN and set box marked 6900E. Circa 1936.

9E **Elec.** — orange; 418-419-490 mojave/mojave/orange. Circa 1928-30.

9U **Elec.** — orange; 428-429-430 orange/orange/apple green. Set box marked P050. Circa 1929.

10 **Elec.** — peacock/dark green frame — Super motor; 332-339-341 peacock/peacock/orange. Box marked SPECIAL #2. KAUFMANN's, Pittsburgh. Circa 1931.

10 **Elec.** — red/cream stripe — marked MACY SPECIAL on motor plate; 332-337-338 red/red/cream. R.H. MACY CO., New York. Circa 1931. DSS

10E **Elec.** — red/cream stripe; 332-337-338 red/red/cream — usual RS lettering on sides but with celluloid drumhead in observation platform — MACY SPECIAL. R.H. MACY CO., New York. Circa 1931-32. DSS

10E **Elec.** — State brown/green stripe/dark cream frame; 332-339-341 State brown/dark brown/cream. Individual boxes all marked MS and set box marked Set No. 352E BROWN. R.H. MACY CO., New York. Circa 1932. DSS

10E **Elec.** — peacock/dark green frame/orange stripe — Bild-A-Loco motor; 332-339-339-341 peacock/dark green/orange — MACY SPECIAL celluloid drumhead observation platform. R.H. MACY CO., New York. Circa 1935. DSS

10E **Elec.** — peacock/black/Br; 332-339-341 peacock/peacock/orange, RS — THE LIONEL LINES and also MACY SPECIAL on baggage, MACY SPECIAL celluloid drumhead in observation platform. R.H. MACY CO., New York. Circa 1928-30. DSS

14 **Box** — dark olive green, with or without decal lettering — #898 HARMONY CREAMERY CO. (Pittsburgh). Factory special for dairy promotion. Circa 1920.

33 **Elec.** — midnight blue, 4 cast iron wheels; 35-36 midnight blue — with or without horizontal embossed rib sides. MONTGOMERY-WARD. Circa 1913. DSS
Note: Photostats of 1913 Montgomery Ward catalog show this set; it may have been for mail order only.

60 **Elec.** — 0-4-0, same as 33, black, RS-FAOS 60. F.A.O. SCHWARZ, New York. Circa 1915. DSS

61 **Elec.** — 0-4-4-0, same as 42, black RS-FAOS 61. F.A.O. SCHWARZ, New York. Circa 1915. DSS

62 **Elec.** — 0-4-0, same as 38, black, RS-FAOS 62. F.A.O. SCHWARZ, New York. Circa 1915. DSS

318 **Elec.** — pea green; 309-310-312 pea green/pea green/orange-dark green doors on baggage car. Set box marked either SPECIAL #2 or PO-51. Circa 1928-30.

381 E **Elec.** — State green/apple green sub-frame; 428 dark green/dark green/orange, 429 dark green/dark green/maroon, 430 dark green/dark green/orange. Circa 1931.

381-S **Elec.** — Preproduction 381, two motors, dark green/Br windows — no lettering. Handmade preproduction model. Circa 1927.

381-SS **Elec.** — Preproduction 381, non-powered, dark green/Br windows — no lettering, longer than 381-S. Circa 1927.

384E Black; 384T — black; 332-337-338 red/red/cream. Regular production items but set box has MACY label and marked SPECIAL #2. R.H. MACY CO., New York. Circa 1930-32. DSS

390E Black/orange stripe; 390T — black/orange stripe; 319-319-320-322 maroon/maroon/mojave — early 500 series trucks. Car boxes marked WINE 309-310-312 on ends. Circa 1930.

Note: These cars dropped from catalog after 1927.

390E Black/orange stripe; 390T — black/orange stripe; 319-320-322 maroon/maroon/mojave, some are RS — ILLINOIS CENTRAL on baggage car. Car boxes are marked WINE 309-310-312, and set box marked #394E. Circa 1929.

402E **Elec.** — mustard brown/red windows/Br trim; 418-419-431-490 mustard brown/mustard brown/red windows and doors — 6-Wh trucks. Circa 1931-32. UNIQUE

408E **Elec.** — cream/red windows/Br trim; 418-419-431-490 cream/cream/red windows and green doors — 6-Wh trucks. Circa 1931-32. UNIQUE

408E **Elec.** — pink/Br windows; 418-419-431-490 pink/pink/apple green windows and doors — 6-Wh trucks. Circa 1931-32. UNIQUE

408E **Elec.** — gray/Br windows; 418-419-431-490 gray/gray/red windows and doors — 6-Wh trucks. Circa 1931-32. UNIQUE

705 Hudson tube electric locomotive with 706 and 707 trail cars. Made for Hudson & Manhattan Railroad display. Circa 1916.

1835E Black; 384TX — black; 337-337-338 red/red/cream. Set box marked Set No. 5301E. Circa 1934.

8E peacock/orange stripe — KAUFMANN's

10E peacock/dark green frame — MACY'S

10E State brown/dark green frame — MACY

14 HARMONY DAIRY box car — dark olive green

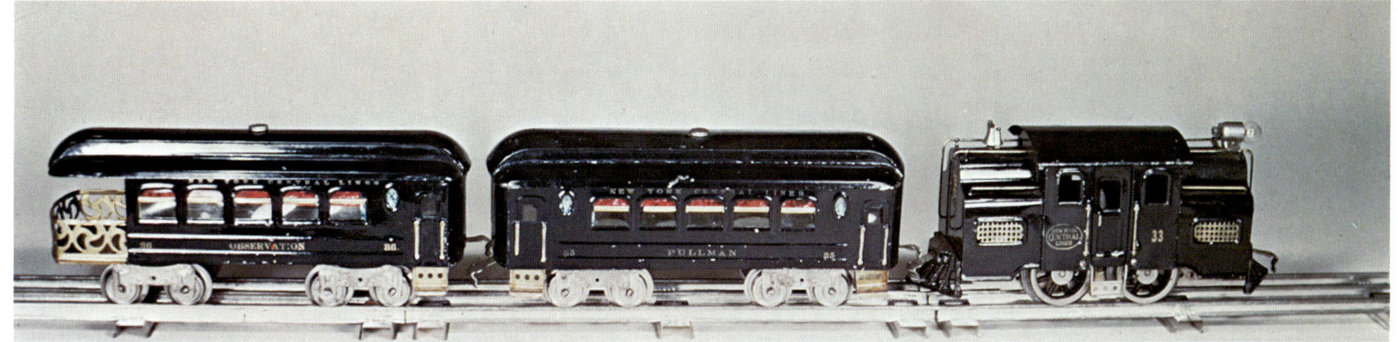

33 midnight blue with 35 and 36 — MONTGOMERY-WARD

33 midnight blue

217 Red/peacock-peacock cupola

218 pea green/maroon

310 red-orange/aluminum

408E pink/Br

419 pink/apple green

431 pink/apple green

490 pink/apple green

381 S Dark green/Br

408E gray/Br

420 medium blue lettered THE BLUE COMET

419 gray/red

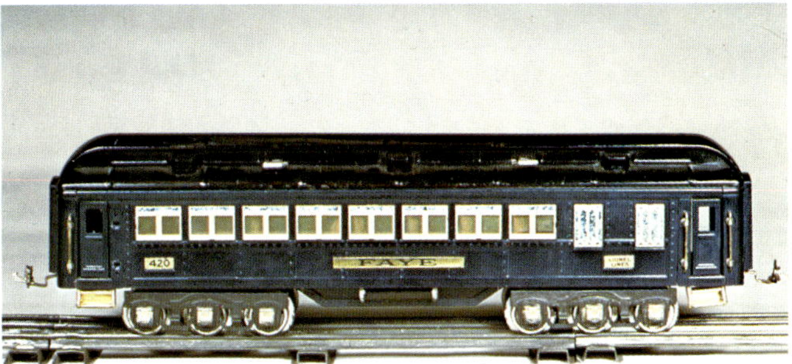

420 dark blue/black

705 Hudson tube train

STREAMLINED SPECIALS

In the period 1935 to 1939, Lionel manufactured a diverse line of 027 and 0 gauge special streamline passenger sets. Some differ significantly from the cataloged sets in that they include the 1700 power unit or the 1703 car which were themselves uncataloged. Others are distinguished from the cataloged sets only by differing in train consist or finish. They are listed in the same format as the other streamliners, with reference to the appropriate subsection of streamliners noted in parentheses.

259E and 1689T — black; 1703, 1701, 1702 — light red/maroon/maroon, Fl, (027). Circa 1936.

259E and 1689T — black; 1703, 1701, 1701, 1701, 1702 — alum/light red/light red, Fl, (027). Circa 1936.

264E and 265T — black; 619, 617, 618 — Ch except gunmetal end on 618, Fl, (0). Circa 1936.

265E and 265T — black; 619, 617, 618 — all medium blue/no stripe, Fl, (0), set box marked No. 6510E. Circa 1937.

289E and 1689T — black; 1703, 1701, 1702 — alum/light red/light red, Fl, (027). Circa 1936.

289E and 1689T — black; 1673, 1674, 1675 — all light red, Fl, (027). Circa 1936.

"Flying Yankee"

616E — alum with light red top; 617, 618 — alum, alum skirts, (0). Circa 1935.

616E — alum with light red top; 617, 618 — alum, some have alum skirts, Fl, (0). Circa 1936.

616E — alum with black top; 617, 618 — alum, (0), set box marked No. 5224E. Circa 1935.

"City of Denver"

636W, 637, 638 — Stephen Girard green/dark green roof and underbody, Fl, W, (0), set box marked No. 6531W. Circa 1937.

636W, 638 — Stephen Girard green/dark green roof and underbody, Fl, W, (0). Circa 1937.

1668E and 1689T — black; 1703, 1701, 1701, 1701, 1701, 1702 — alum/light red/light red, Fl, (027), set box marked No. 8059. Circa 1937.

1688E and 1689T or W — black or gunmetal; 1673, 1674, 1675 — all light red, Fl, set box marked No. 6208, (027). Circa 1936.

1689E and 1689T — black; 1703, 1701, 1702 — alum/light red/light red, Fl, (027). Circa 1936.

1700, 1701, 1702 — Hiawatha orange/Hiawatha gray/Hiawatha orange, (027). Circa 1936.

1700, 1701, 1702 — alum/light red/light red, Fl, (027). Circa 1937.

1700, 1701, 1702 — alum/light red/alum nose and tail but light red vestibules, (027). Circa 1935.

1700, 1701, 1701, 1702 — yellow/brown/yellow, (027). Circa 1936.

1700, 1701, 1701, 1702 — Hiawatha orange/ Hiawatha gray/Hiawatha orange, (027). Circa 1936.

265E with 619, 617, 618 medium blue

Flying Yankee alum/light red — Fl

Flying Yankee alum/light red — smooth

City of Denver Stephen Girard green/dark green

1700, 1701, 1702 alum/light red/light red

1700, 1701, 1702 alum/light red/alum

1700,1701,1702 Hiawatha orange/Hiawatha gray/Hiawatha orange

2 7/8 Inch Gauge 1901-1905

Though we have tried to be consistent in our presentation of each section, the 2 7/8" gauge presents some problems. In other sections the dating denotes the years that the item was cataloged, but no catalogs have been located before the 1902 catalog — so the dates used in this section refer to the years of manufacture. In addition several other sections were divided into series of locomotives and rolling stock but here all are discussed together.

The 2 7/8" gauge trains were Joshua Lionel Cowen's first venture into trains. All contained the same electric motor, and utilized either dry cell battery power or direct current from acid jars and plates. Track was assembled from 3/8" steel rail and grooved wood ties. The earliest gondolas were wood on a cast iron frame but all later motor units and cars had sheet steel bodies japanned and lettered in color. All pieces powered or not are 4 wheeled with LIONEL MFG. CO. N.Y. stamped in the floor of most. Early production (1901-02) items have a cast controller lever, wood stand with cast control stand top, Lionel metal tag on bottom of gondolas, round cast journals, and stamped brass wheels. In 1903 all items were all metal construction, even the gondolas, with a control lever made of bent wire, stamped metal control stand top, square cast journals, generally cast wheels on trailers, stamped brass wheels on powered units, and are painted in apple green enamel. In the final years (1904-05) of production all powered and non-powered units have square cast journals, cast wheels, and are finished in a maroon enamel. Cast link and pin coupler swings from side to side on triangular draft gear.

100 ELECTRIC LOCOMOTIVE, open-sided, patterned after 1800 horsepower B&O electric, gold RS lettering - B&O, No. 5, 12". 1903-05.
apple green/black frame/apple green roof
maroon/black frame and roof

Note: May be found lettered C. & St.L.

200 ELECTRIC EXPRESS, 12". 1901-05.
- wooden car body, no steps, no handrails, no corner braces, natural wood or red painted finish, lettered ELECTRIC EXPRESS (1901)
- wooden car body, brass steps, brass handrails, brass corner braces, natural wood or painted red, lettered ELECTRIC EXPRESS (1902)
- sheet metal car body with vertical simulated angle iron side braces, apple green/black frame, gold RS lettering B. & O. on sides, No. 2425 on end (1903)
- sheet metal car body with flat sides, no side braces, apple green/black frame, gold RS lettering LAKE SHORE, CAPACITY 80,000 LBS., and WEIGHT 35,000 LBS. on sides (1903)
- sheet metal car body with flat sides, no side braces, maroon/black frame, gold RS or decal lettering LAKE SHORE, CAPACITY 80,000 LBS., and WEIGHT 35,000 LBS. on sides (1904-05)

300 ELECTRIC TROLLEY CAR, summer car, 6 reversible seats, destination board lettered UNION DEPOT on one side and CITY HALL PARK on reverse side, wooden base with Lionel tag attached, maroon sides and roof/black frame/apple green posts and seats, 16½". 1902-05.

Note: Uses Morton E. Converse and Co. trolley body. Converse trolley bodies were blue/yellow — except for the maroon/apple green color combination made for Lionel.

309 TROLLEY TRAILER, summer trolley, same as 300 but without motor. 1904-05.

400 EXPRESS TRAILER CAR, same as 200 but without motor, made in wood (1902) or sheet metal (1903-05). 1902-05.

500 ELECTRIC DERRICK CAR, 8½" high cast iron derrick, brass chain with tackle attached, no lettering, 12". 1903-04.
- apple green floor and controller stand/black frame and derrick
- maroon/black

600 DERRICK TRAILER, same as 500 but without motor. 1903-04.

700 STORE DISPLAY SET — 100 Electric locomotive and 400 Express trailer with track. 1904-05.

800 ELECTRIC BOX CAR, closed sides, maroon/black frame and roof, gold RS lettering — METROPOLITAN EXPRESS, 12". 1904-05.

900 BOX CAR TRAILER, same as 800 but without motor. 1904-05.

1000 ELECTRIC PASSENGER CAR, closed sides, 8 windows per side, maroon/black frame and roof, gold RS lettering — METROPOLITAN ST. R.R. CO., MARYLAND ST. RY. CO., or PHILADELPHIA R.T. CO., 14". 1905.

Note: A single 1000 passenger car lettered METROPOLITAN EXPRESS exists.

1050 PASSENGER CAR TRAILER, same as 1000 but without motor. 1905.

100 maroon/black

200 wood, ELECTRIC EXPRESS

200 wood, red

200 maroon, LAKE SHORE

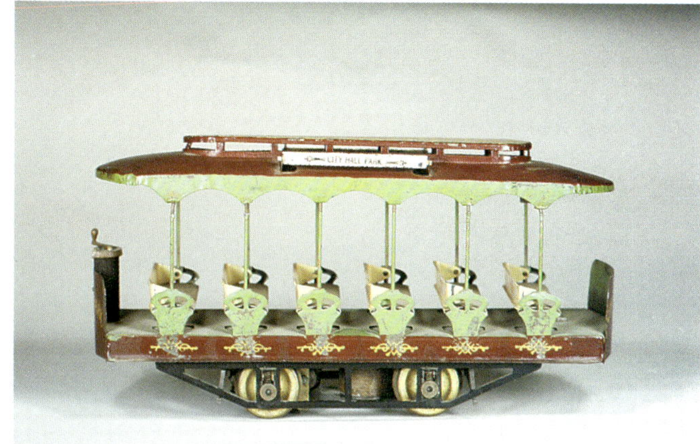

300 maroon/light green

300 end view

400 apple green, B&O

400 maroon, LAKE SHORE

500 maroon/black

600 apple green/black

800 maroon/black

1000 maroon/black MARYLAND ST. RY. CO.

1050 maroon/black, PHILADELPHIA R.T. CO.

Early and later motors

OO Gauge

1938-1942

In 1938 Lionel introduced their OO gauge line of scale model trains headed by the 5342 Hudson steam locomotive. These trains were 4 mm scale, and a perfect miniature of the 5344 scale Hudson introduced in O gauge a year earlier. Though available only in sets for three rail track the first year, in 1939 Lionel introduced two rail track and both super-detailed and semi-detailed (modified) locomotives for either track. Semi-detailed versions of some of the cars (box car, tank, caboose) were also made and differed only in the absence of brake cylinders and the caboose smokejack. Unlike the O gauge scale cars all of the OO cars are made of die-cast metal. Unfortunately, production of these fine scale trains ended with the start of World War II and they did not reappear after the War. As in other sections the abbreviation NM means never made as far as known.

OO LOCOMOTIVES & TENDERS

001 Hudson 4-6-4, superdetailed, three rail, RS — 5342, 9″. 1938-42.

001T Superdetailed coal tender, three rail, no whistle, RS — NEW YORK CENTRAL, 6½″. 1938-42.

001W Superdetailed coal tender, three rail, with whistle, RS — NEW YORK CENTRAL, 6½″. 1938-42.

002 Hudson 4-6-4, modified (same as 001 but less detail) three rail, RS — 5342, 9″. 1939-42.

002T Modified coal tender, three rail, no whistle, RS — NEW YORK CENTRAL, 6½″. 1939-42.

002W Modified coal tender, three rail, with whistle, RS — NEW YORK CENTRAL, 6½″. 1939-42.

003 Hudson 4-6-4, superdetailed, two rail, RS — 5342, 9″. 1939-42.

003T Superdetailed coal tender, two rail, no whistle, RS — NEW YORK CENTRAL, 6½″.1939-42.

003W Superdetailed coal tender, two rail, with whistle, RS — NEW YORK CENTRAL, 6½″. 1939-42.

004 Hudson 4-6-4, modified, two rail,RS — 5342, 9″. 1939-42.

004T Modified coal tender, two rail, no whistle, RS — NEW YORK CENTRAL, 6½″. 1939-42.

004W Modified coal tender, two rail, with whistle, RS — NEW YORK CENTRAL, 6½″. 1939-42.

0081 Catalog number for combination of 001 Hudson and 001T tender, three rail. 1938-42.

0081W Catalog number for combination of 001 Hudson and 001W tender, three rail. 1938-42.

0081K Catalog number for kit version of 0081. 1938.

0081KW Catalog number for kit version of 0081W. 1938.

0083 Catalog number for combination of 002 Hudson and 002T tender, three rail. 1939.

0083W Catalog number for combination of 002 Hudson and 002W tender, three rail. 1939.

0091 Catalog number for combination of 003 Hudson and 003T tender, two rail. 1939-42.

0091W Catalog number for combination of 003 Hudson and 003W tender, two rail. 1939-42.

0093 Catalog number for combination of 004

Hudson and 004T tender, two rail. 1939-42.

0093W Catalog number for combination of 004 Hudson and 004W tender, two rail. 1939-42.

00 CARS

0014 **Box car,** detailed, three rail, 6⅞". 1938-42.
- orange/decal — LIONEL LINES (1938)
- yellow/maroon roofwalk/decal — LIONEL LINES, black lettering (1938)
- *tuscan/decal – PENNSYLVANIA, white lettering (1939-42)*

0015 **Tank,** detailed, three rail, 5¾". 1938-42.
- silver/decal — LIONEL LINES, SUNOCO herald — cataloged 1938 but NM
- silver/decal — SUNOCO herald, black lettering (uncat. circa 1938)
- *black/decal – SHELL herald, white lettering (1939-40 and 42)*
- gray/decal — SHELL herald, white lettering (1939-40 and 42)
- black/decal — SUNOCO herald, white lettering (1941)

0016 **Hopper,** detailed, three rail, 5½". 1938-42.
- gray/decal — LIONEL LINES, black lettering, cataloged 1938 but NM
- gray/decal — SP and herald, black lettering (uncataloged circa 1938)
- *black/decal – SP and herald, white lettering (1939-42)*
- black/decal — READING, white lettering — cataloged 1941 but NM

0017 **Caboose,** detailed, three rail, 4⅝". 1938-42.
- red/decal — LIONEL LINES, white lettering — cataloged 1938 but NM
- *red/decal – NYC, white lettering (1938-42)*
- red/maroon roofwalk/decal — PRR, white lettering (1940)

0024 **Box,** semi-detailed, three rail, tuscan/decal — PENNSYLVANIA, white lettering, 6⅞". 1939-42.

0025 **Tank,** semi-detailed, three rail, 5¾". 1939-42.
- black/decal — SHELL herald, white lettering (1939-42)
- black/decal — SUNOCO herald, white lettering (1941)

0027 **Caboose,** semi-detailed, three rail, 4⅝". 1939-42.
- *red/decal – NYC, white lettering (1939-42)*
- red/maroon roofwalk/decal — PRR, white lettering (1940)

0044 **Box,** detailed, two rail, tuscan/decal — PENNSYLVANIA, white lettering, 6⅞". 1939-42.

0044K **Box,** kit, semi-detailed, two or three rail, tuscan/decal — PENNSYLVANIA, white lettering, 6⅞". 1939-42.

0045 **Tank,** detailed, two rail, 5¾". 1939-42.
black/decal – SHELL herald, white lettering (1939-40 and 42)
black/decal — SUNOCO herald, white lettering (1941)

0045K **Tank,** kit, semi-detailed, two or three rail, 5¾". 1939-42.
black/decal – SHELL herald, white lettering (1939-40 and 42)
black/decal — SUNOCO herald, white lettering (1941)

0046 **Hopper,** detailed, two rail, 5½". 1939-42.
black/decal — SP and herald, white lettering (1939-42)
black/decal — READING, white lettering — cataloged 1941 but NM

0046K **Hopper,** kit, detailed, two or three rail, 5½". 1939-42.
black/decal — SP and herald, white lettering (1939-42)
black/decal — READING, white lettering — cataloged 1941 but NM

0047 **Caboose,** detailed, two rail, 4⅝". 1939-42.
red/decal — NYC, white lettering (1939-42)
red/maroon roofwalk/decal — PRR, white lettering (1940)

0047K **Caboose,** kit, semi-detailed, two or three rail, 4⅝". 1939-42.
red/decal – NYC, white lettering (1939-42)
red/maroon roofwalk/decal — PRR, white lettering (1940)

0074 **Box,** semi-detailed, two rail, tuscan/decal — PENNSYLVANIA, white lettering, 6⅞". 1939-42.

0075 **Tank,** semi-detailed, two rail, 5¾". 1939-42.
silver/decal — SUNOCO herald, black lettering (uncat. circa 1939)
black/decal – SHELL herald, white lettering (1939-40 and 42)
black/decal — SUNOCO herald, white lettering (1941)

0077 **Caboose,** semi-detailed, two rail, 4⅝". 1939-42.
red/decal– NYC, white lettering (1939-42)
red/maroon roofwalk/decal — PRR, white lettering (1940)

003 Hudson and 003W tender

0014 Boxcar yellow/maroon

0046 Hopper black — SP

0016 Hopper gray — SP

0075 Tank silver — SUNOCO

0044 Boxcar tuscan — PENNSYLVANIA

0077 Caboose red — NYC

0045 Tank black — SHELL

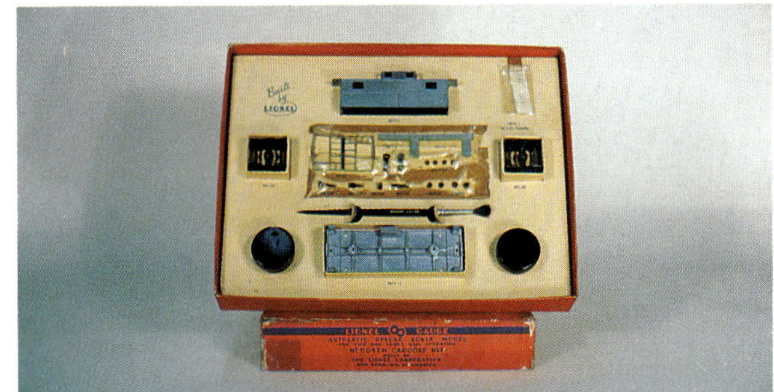
0047 caboose kit box

Catalogs 1902-1969

Though Lionel began train production in 1901, the earliest known catalog was published in 1902. One copy of that first catalog is known to exist and remained in the possession of Joshua Lionel Cowen until his death. Catalogs have been issued every year since 1902 except during World War II (1943-44). The early catalogs probably were intended primarily for the use of the dealers and distributors. They were black and white on matte paper. In the years 1910-12 covers in four colors were added but the orientation was still to the dealer. Finally in 1915 the catalogs became consumer oriented with sales pitches such as "Come on Boys! I'll Show You Why Lionel Trains Are Better". The 1919 printers strike resulted in a year of scarce catalogs but each year thereafter the catalogs grew bigger, more colorful, and more extravagant, peaking from 1927-29 with three page center foldouts of the top standard gauge sets. Through the depression and the early forties the catalogs remained in color but not the quality of the late twenties. The sounds of war brought an abrupt halt to toy trains and catalogs as Lionel changed over to the production of instruments for the Navy. With the post-war train boom Lionel catalogs again grew each year culminating in the gold cover "Golden Anniversary Issue" in 1950. But by the early sixties the toy train market began to disappear and the catalogs began to shrink. There is a return to monotone printing except for color covers, and in fact a year with no new catalog — the same catalog having been released in 1966 and 1967. Then along came MPC, a division of General Mills, and the cycle began again with expanding catalogs each year since 1970. This is a brief sketch of Lionel consumer catalogs which are released each year in early summer to bring Christmas train dreams to every boy. But what about the other types of Lionel paper? Well, there are the following:

(1) Advance catalogs have been issued from 1926 to the present. Their purpose is to introduce the new line of trains to the dealers attending the Toy Fair each February. In the early years these were crudely altered catalogs of the previous year with new items dubbed in. As the years went by these catalogs took the format of black and white issues resembling the color consumer catalog published later in the year. However, only with the advent of MPC did full color become a constant feature of advance catalogs.

(2) Dealers catalogs — unlike American Flyer, Lionel rarely ever issued a dealers catalog. The dealers received the advance and consumer catalogs, and supplementary price lists at irregular intervals.

(3) Pocket catalogs are miniature catalogs showing the current line of trains, publshed first in 1928 and 1929, and intermittently since the early fifties. These are not reductions of the consumer catalog pages but totally different page layout designs.

(4) Executive catalogs are known to exist from 1935 on. They apparently were the mock-ups on heavy cardstock for the consumer catalog each year. Several of these were made each year for the top executives and production supervisors to sell the current line of trains. With all the pages mounted on cardboard, these catalogs would often be four to five inches thick. Needless to say they are very rare.

(5) Accessory catalogs are usually small catalogs issued after the consumer catalog each year to introduce more new items or emphasize the line of accessories. They are often in full color and packed with the directions in train sets.

(6) Foreign edition catalogs should be self-explanatory. They have been issued irregularly since the depression years for Canada and parts of Europe. These catalogs are in full color.

The other promotional data issued by Lionel includes single sheet flyers, folders, brochures, banners, advertising displays, and price sheets. Each of these can take a variety of forms. Described and pictured below are the catalogs from 1902 through 1969, and in addition many advance catalogs and folders prior to World War II.

1902 6⅛x3½, 16 pages, 2⅞" gauge
p. 2 — "general public for the second year"
p. 3 — electric trolley car 300
p. 5 — electric express 200
c.f. — plunge battery 302

1903 6¼x3½, 20 pages, 2⅞" gauge
p. 2 — "goods offered for third year"
p. 3 — B. & O. 5
p. 5 — 200 car
c.f. — left — 500 derrick, right — 320 switch

1904 6x5½, 12 pages, 2⅞" gauge
p. 3 — "goods offered for the fourth year"
p. 5 — 300 electric trolley car
c.f. — left — 500 derrick, right — 800 box car

1905 6x6, 12 pages, 2⅞" gauge
p. 2 — "for the past five years . . ."
p. 3 — 400 and 800
p. 5 — 100 electric locomotive
c.f. — left — 200, 300, 309, right — 340 bridge

1906 4½x6½, 24 pages plus covers
First year for Standard, last of 2⅞" gauge
p. 2 — "Features of our goods . . ."
p. 3 — Electric car outfit No. 1
p. 5 — "The track supplied with our outfits"
p. 9 — Loco No. 5 — price boxed $5.50
p. 10 — Loco No. 6 — price boxed $7.50
c.f. — left — 13 ($1.55), 14 ($1.45), 15 ($1.55), right — 16 ($1.45), 17 ($1.50), 18 ($3.50)

1907 9x6, 28 pages

1908 9x6, 28 pages including covers
p.3 — "Standard of the World . . . for close on to 10 years"
p.5 — "Description of working parts."
p.7 — 1 electric passenger car, 1 trail car
p.9 — Loco No.5 — price boxed $6.50
p.10 — Loco No.6 — price boxed $10.00
p.13 — 16 ($1.95), 17 ($2.00), 29 day coach ($2.50)
c.f. — "A thing of beauty and joy forever"

1909 9x6, 32 pages plus covers
p. 1 — "Standard of the World . . . for close onto ten years"
p. 3 — "Description of working parts"
p. 5 — 1 electric passenger car
c.f. — left — track, right — switches

1902

1903 (Early) Ewing Merkle

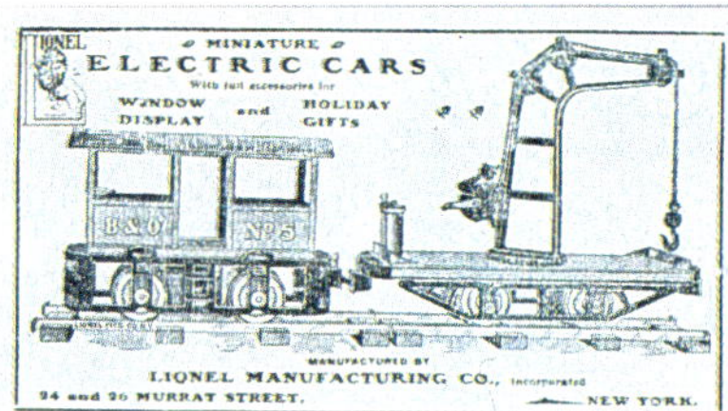

1903 (Later)

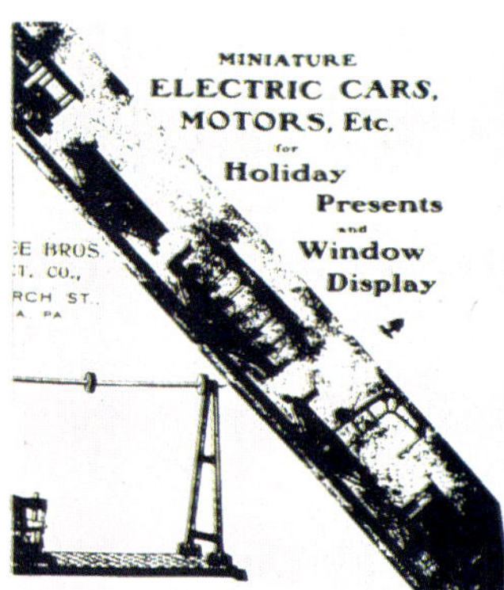

1904

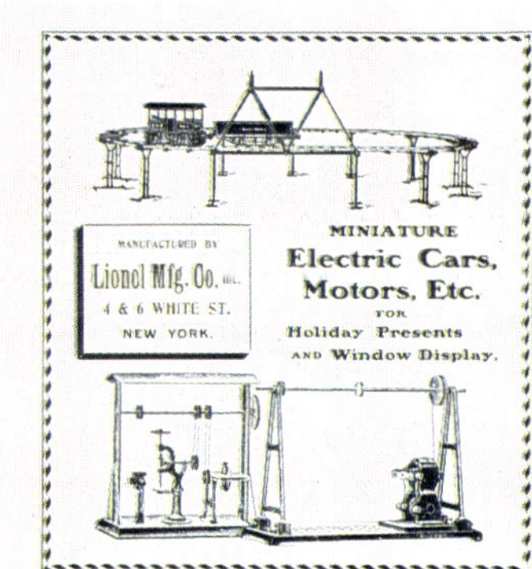

1905

1906

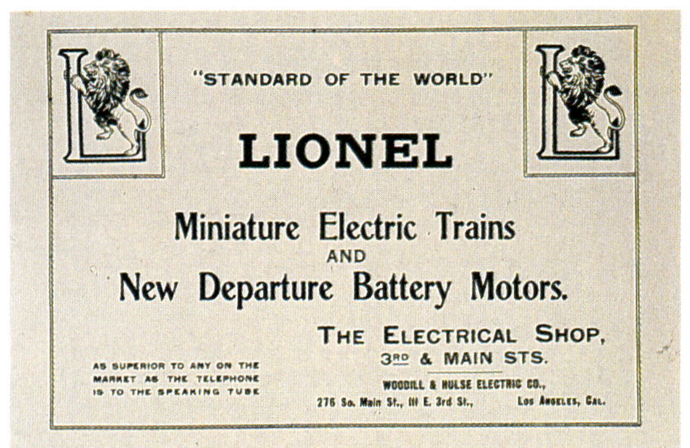

1908 and 1909

1910 Type I

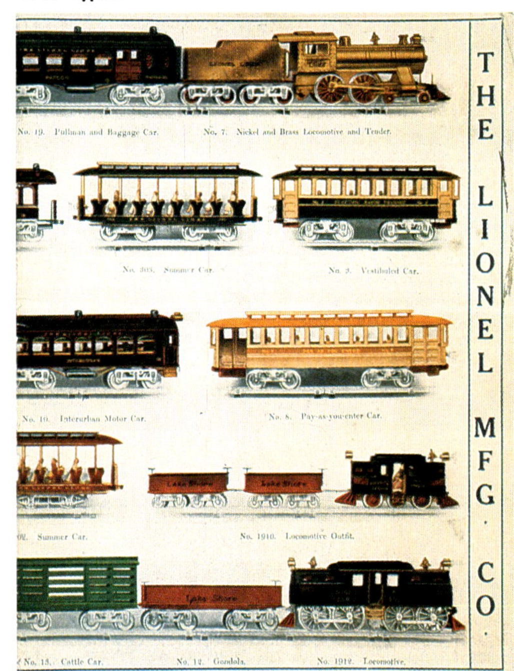

1910 Type II front

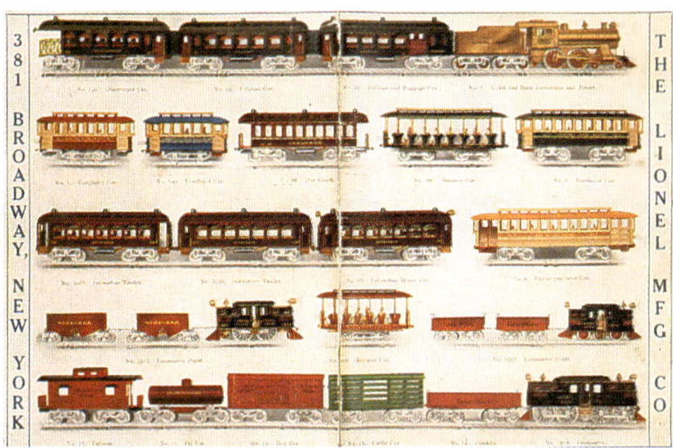

1910, 1911, 1912 Type II front and back

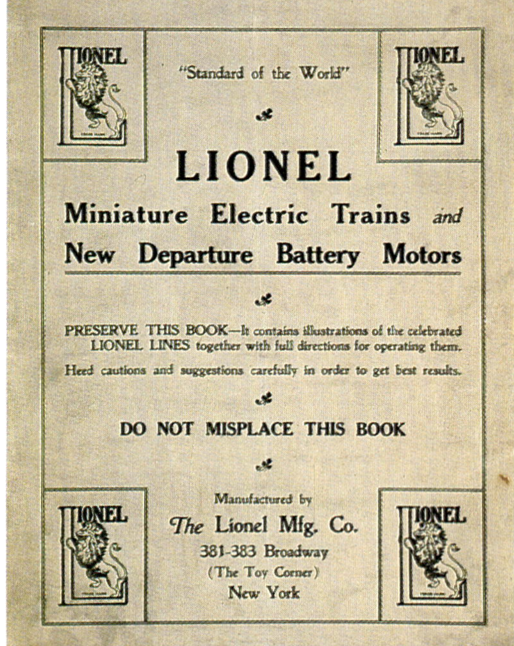

1911 Type I

1912 Type I

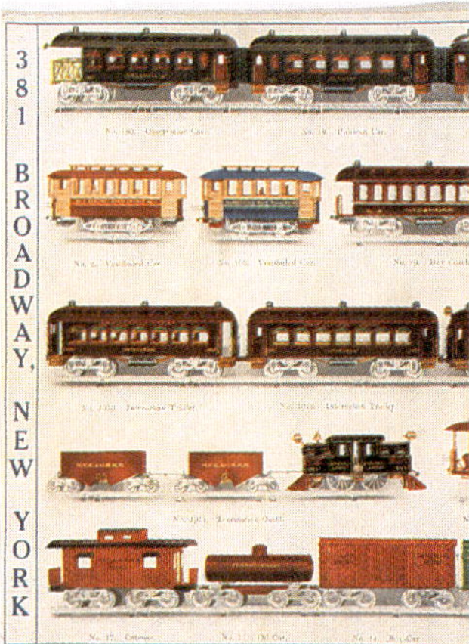

1912 Type II back

1913 front

1913 front and back

1913 Small

1910 8x10, 28 pages plus covers
Type I — matte paper cover in black and white, no date
Type II — glossy color cover, front and back form one large picture
Type III — matte paper cover in black and white, picture of factory bottom center of cover
p. 1 — "Introduction — please read this"
p. 2 — "Description of working parts"
p. 3 — "the flexible construction trucks"
c.f. — "For Show Window" — bottom of page

1911 8x10, 32 pages plus covers
Type I — matte paper cover in black and white
Type II — glossy color cover, front and back form one large picture, same picture as 1910
p. 1 — five pictures of Lionel Mfg.
p. 2 — "Introduction — please read this"
p. 3 — "Construction of car bodies"
c.f. — "For Show Window Attraction"

1912 8x10, 36 pages plus covers
Type I — matte paper cover in red and gray
Type II — glossy color cover, front and back form one large picture, same picture as 1910 and 1911
p.1 — five pictures of Lionel Mfg.
p.2 — "that twelve years ago . . . electric toys"
p.3 — "Construction of car bodies"
c.f. — left — outfit 34, right — outfit 33

1913 8x10, 36 pages plus covers,
p.1 — five pictures of Lionel Mfg.
p.2 — "thirteen years ago"
p.3 — "Construction of car bodies"
c.f. — left — outfit 34, right — outfit 33

1913 **SMALL**, 6x6¾, 16 pages
p.2 — "electric toys thirteen years ago"
p.3 — "Description of working parts"
p.5 — trolley cars
c.f. — left — electric locos, right — sets

1914 8x10, 32 pages plus covers
p.1 — same picture as cover
p.2 — "fourteen years ago"
p.3 — "Construction of car bodies"
c.f. — left side of 1913 Small cover

1914 **SMALL**, 6x6¾, 16 pages
p.2 — "electric toys fourteen years ago"
p.3 — "Description of working parts"
p.5 — trolley cars
c.f. — sets both left and right

1915 10x7, 38 pages with centerfold, O gauge first cataloged

p.2 — "for fifteen years I've been . . ."
p.3 — "A little trip through my factory-car construction"
p.5 — "A little trip-steel versus cast iron"
c.f. — outfit 420 on Meccano bridge at $31.50
All page headings read "250,000 boys"

1916 10x7, 40 pages
p.2 — "sixteen years"
p.3 — "A little trip-car construction"
p.5 — "A little trip-steel versus cast iron"
c.f. — outfit 420 on Meccano bridge at $33.50
All page headings read "over 260,000 boys . . ."

1916 **Folder,** 6x9, 16 page folds
Overall size 24x18, red and black on white paper
Main wording "Order from your dealer" and "Insist on Lionel"

1917 10x7, 40 pages
Type I — 40 pages and color cover sheet with plant pictures on inside and semaphores on back
Type II — 40 pages including B&W cover, no plant picture, back-"Lionel station, tunnel, etc."
p.2 — "Seventeen years ago I started to make"
p.3 — "The die making, raw material . . ."
p.5 — car construction pictures
c.f. — outfit 420 on Meccano bridge at $35.00
All page headings read "300,000 boys"

1917 **Folder,** 6x9, 16 page folds
Overall size 24x18, black and red on white paper
Main lettering "More than a toy" in red block lettering

1918 **Folder,** 6x9, 16 page folds
Overall size 24x17, red and black on white
Main lettering "More than a toy" and armored loco captioned "Play war"

1919 **Folder,** 6x9, 16 page folds
Overall size 24x17, red and black on white
Features armored loco with two box cars

1919 **Apology Folder,** 5½x8¼, 24 page folds
Overall size of each of three pages 11x17, red and black on white
c.f. — "An apology from the man . . . millions of boy friends"

1920-21 10x6¾, 46 pages
p.1 — "Standard of the world for twenty years"
p.3 — "Vault door. In this vault . . ."
p.5 — "Drill presses. For perforating material."

1914 Small

1915

1916

1917 Type I

1917 Type II

1917 Folder

1918 Folder

1919 Folder

1919 Apology Folder

1920-21

1920 Folder

1921 Folder

c.f. — 42, 53, 51
Includes supplement pp. 36a. to 36h.
All page headings read "500,000 boys"

1920 **Folder,** 5x7, 32 page folds
Overall size 40½x28, four color printing on white paper
Main lettering "Lionel electric trains are superior electrically and mechanically"

1921 **Folder,** 5x7, 32 page folds
Overall size 40½x28, four color printing on white paper
Main lettering "Lionel trains"

1922 10x6¾, 40 pages
p.2 — "Standard of the world for 22 years"
p.3 — "I jumped for joy"
p.5 — "Why Lionel trains are best"
c.f. — "Twin-motor" locomotives 42 and 54.
All page headings read "over two million"

1923 10x7, 48 pages
p.3 — "Writes one happy boy"
p.4 — "For nearly twenty-five years . . ."
p.5 — "Lionel leadership"
c.f. — 402, set 403 for $75.00
All page headings read "millions of happy users"

1924 10½x8, 44 pages, no numerical page headings
p.2 — "The fascinating sport of Lionel railroading"
p.3 — "For twenty-four years Lionel . . ."
p.5 — Lionel Standard motor specifications
c.f. — 402, set 403 for $62.50.

1925 10½x8, 44 pages
Type I — p.3 — lower left has patent dates for parts shown
Type II — no patent dates on p.3
p. 2 — "good fortune of Lionel for twenty-five years"
p.3 — "Lionel always leads"
p.5 — "O gauge single and twin-motor specifications"
c.f. — 402, set 403 for $60.75

1926 10½x8, 48 pages
p.2 — "good fortune of Lionel for twenty-six years"
p.3 — "The new Lionel 100% electrically controlled railroad"
p.5 — "O gauge single and twin-motor specifications"
c.f. — "Electrically controlled" — set 403E for $66.50

1927 11½x8½, 46 pages
Type I — no price sheet in back
Type II — with price sheet inside back cover
p.3 — "The new Lionel 100% electrically-controlled railroads . . . culmination of twenty-seven years devoted . . ."
p.5 — "Construction of Lionel standard super-motors"
c.f. — three page center foldout 408E, set 409E for $82.50

1928 11½x8½, 46 pages
p.3 — "The electrical brain of your Lionel"
p.5 — "Construction of Lionel standard super-motors"
c.f. — three page center foldout, set 409E for $85.00
back cover — copyrighted 1928

1929 11½x8½, 46 pages
p.2 — "Lionel railroading . . . for 29 years"
p.3 — "The Lionel distant-control system"
p.5 — "Construction of Lionel standard super-motors"
c.f. — three page center foldout, sets 409E and 411E
p.45 — price list
back cover — copyrighted 1929

1930 11½x8½, 48 pages
p.3 — "Lionel distant control system"
p.5 — "Construction of Lionel standard super-motors"
c.f. — "The big three — aristocrats . . . 381, 390E, 408E"
b.c. — copyrighted 1930

1930 **Winner folder** — 11½x8½, 4 pages
inside spread — Winner passenger train with 1000 electric loco — retail price $3.95

1931 11½x8½, 52 pages
p.3 — "Famous engineers who have chosen . . ."
p.5 — "Sterling silver for sterling quality . . ."
c.f. — "A prize possession . . . 400E Blue Comet, 408E, 400E"
b.c. — The Lionel Magazine

1931 **Winner folder** — 11½x8½, 4 pages, flap at top, inside — sets 1000, 1001, 1002, and 1003

1932 11½x8½, 52 pages
Type I — without Winner Railroad four page insert
Type II — with Winner Railroad insert
p.2 — letterhead "May 3, 1932"
p.3 — "Take your dad into partnership . . ."
p.5 — "Speedy and graceful locomotives at new low prices"
c.f. — "The aristocrats of model railroad-ing . . . 400E, 408E, 400E"
b.c. — "Lionel Engineers Club"

1932 **Winner folder** — 8½x11½, 4 pages, flap at top, sets 1000-1006

1922

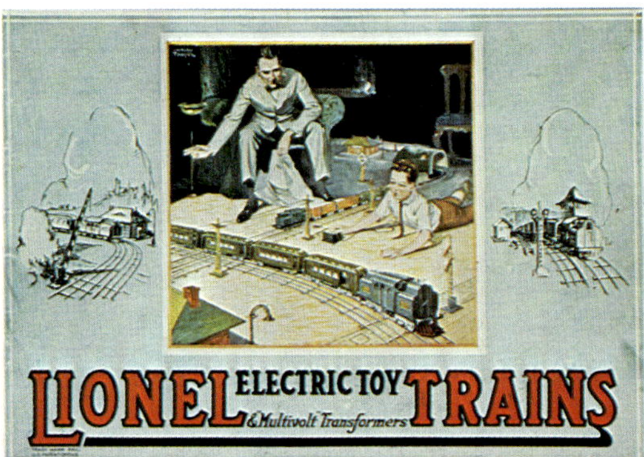

1923

1924

1925

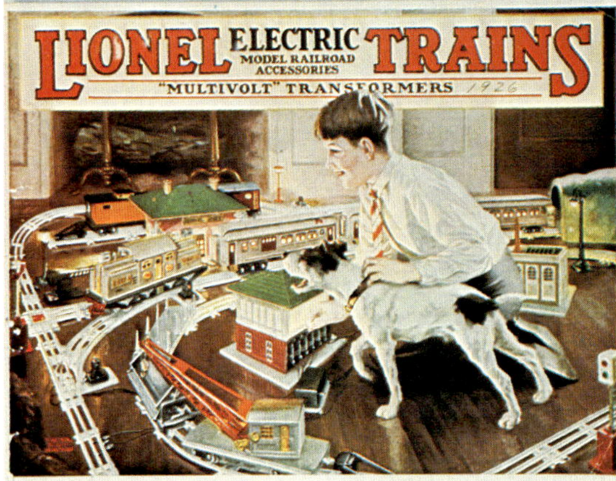

1926

1927

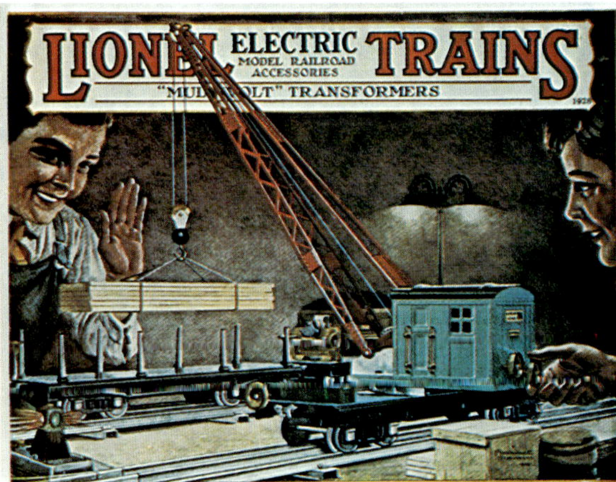

1928

1929

1933 11¼x8⅜, 52 pages

Type I — no price increase page inserted, no Pennsylvania Limited and keystone lettering on p. 24

Type II — NRA price increase page inserted at p. 11, with Pennsylvania Limited lettering and keystone on p. 24

p.3 — "Chug! Chug! Chug! Something . . ."

p.5 — "Will pull your railroad train with power to spare"

c.f. — "The greatest achievement . . . 400E, 408E, 400E"

b.c. — "The Lionel craft"

1934 11½x7½, 36 pages

Type I — "Lionel Trains" along bottom of cover

Type II — "Lionel Trains" along top of cover

p.2 — copyright 1934

p.3 — "Reasons why your railroad should be a Lionel"

p.5 — "Realism . . . power . . . speed . . . are built into these models"

c.f. — "Add freight cars to make your railroad complete . . ."

1935 11⅜x8½, 44 pages

Type I — one train on p. 41, no caption, and p. 4 — red stripe top and bottom

Type II — Same as type I but no stripe on page 4

Type III — one train on p. 41, caption "with brilliant chromium finish", and p. 4 — no red stripe

Type IV — three trains on p. 41, no red stripe on p. 4

p.2 — copyright 1935

p.3 — "Are the trains that give you . . ."

p.5 — 265E, 250E, 260E, 261E

c.f. — 439 panel board, switches, track

1936 11⅜x8½, 48 pages

Type I — "City of Denver" p. 14, outfit squares on p. 20 are blank, no prices

Type II — "City of Denver" p. 14, outfit squares on p. 20 with numbers in them, p.3 "this catalog effective . . . July 1, 1936 . . . and long-life features of Lionel motors"

Type III — no line bottom p. 3, otherwise same as II

Type IV — "Union Pacific Overland" p. 14, p. 33 — 46 automatic grade crossing

Type V — "Union Pacific Overland", no 46 automatic grade crossing on p.33

p.3 — "Watch them reverse!"

p.5 — "The Pennsylvania Torpedo"

c.f. — "Look inside — outside all transformers look alike"

b.c. — "Lionel airplane"

1937 11⁵⁄₁₆x8½, 48 pages

Type I — tan quadrants on p. 39, no cap-

1930

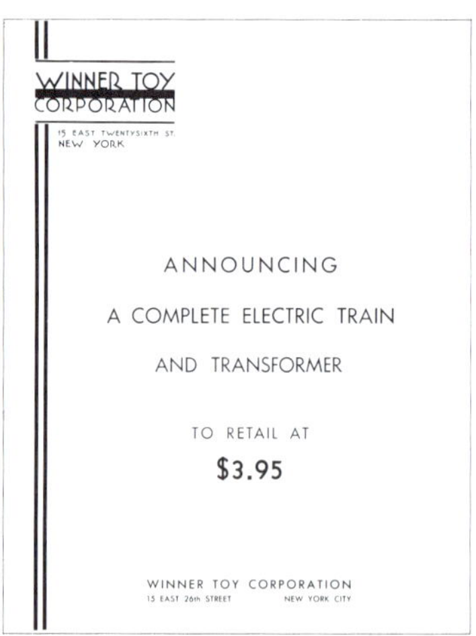
WINNER TOY CORPORATION
15 EAST TWENTYSIXTH ST
NEW YORK

ANNOUNCING

A COMPLETE ELECTRIC TRAIN

AND TRANSFORMER

TO RETAIL AT

$3.95

WINNER TOY CORPORATION
15 EAST 26th STREET NEW YORK CITY

1930 Winner folder

1931

1932

1932 Winner folder

1933

1934

1935

1936

1937

1937 Hudson brochure

1938

tion at bottom of p. 22, wrong colors on signal p. 38, early issue
Type II — same as type I except correct colors on signal p. 38
Type III — all white background p. 39, no caption bottom of p. 22
Type IV — all white background p. 39, misspelled caption "Worn Gear" bottom of p. 22
Type V — caption p. 22 corrected to "Worm Gear"
p.3 — "Dispatcher Control" and "This catalog effective August 1, 1937."
p.5 — "Hudson locomotive — 1/48 actual size"
c.f. — 1835E, 385E, Washington Special

1938 11⅜x8½, 52 pages
Type I — no revised price list
Type II — bound in revised price list between pp. 8-9
Type III — bound in small price list inside back cover
p.2 — "This catalog is effective August 1, 1938."
p.3 — "Watch what happens now when you press a button!"
p.5 — "Choice is Lionel"
c.f. — 763 sets, 700EW Rail Chief set

1939 10¾x8⅜, 52 pages
Type I — p. 49 — captions for street lights 56 and 57 are reversed
Type II — p. 49 — captions corrected
p.3 — "Excitement! Thrills! Happening every second!" and "This catalog is effective August 1, 1939."
p.5 — 1088W and 1087W sets
c.f. — Lionel OO — "Midget models that operate on 2-rail or 3-rail track."
b.c. — Model Builder magazine, "Locoscope"

1940 11¼x8, 64 pages
Type I — red "Lionel" on cover, mistake p. 20 — caption "Lumber car will unload"
Type II — red "Lionel" on cover, caption removed p. 20
Type III — "Lionel" outlined in white on cover, caption removed p. 20
p.2 — "This catalog effective August 1, 1940."
p.3 — "Yippee! Now I've got the whole works at my fingertips . . ."
p.5 — "a. Loading logs, b. Unloading 'em, c. . . ."
c.f. — 072 sets with 763, 701, 700EW
b.c. — "40 years of leadership"

1941 11¼x7⅜, 64 pages
Type I — borderless "Lionel" on front cover
Type II — black border around "Lionel" on front cover, Model Builder coupon inside front cover
p.2 — "This catalog is effective August 1, 1941."
p.3 — "Hobby on earth!"
p.5 — "Realism! Lionel trains are scale-detailed . . ."
c.f. — 072 sets with 763E — sets 748W, 749W, 787W

1942 11x8½, 32 pages
Type I — common type
Type II — revised layouts and more captions on p. 20
p.3 — "Train operations by electric remote control" and "this catalog is effective August 1, 1942."
p.5 — sets with 1684 — sets 1096W and 1094
c.f. — left — "Scale model engine of the century" and on right — "Lionel OO"

1945 **Folder,** 8½x11, 4 page folds
p.1 — "The Lionel line for Christmas 1945"
c.f. — "Only the beginning . . ."

1946 8⅜x11¼, 16 pages plus covers
Type I — with covers
Type II — no covers, 16 pages bound into the November 23, 1946 issue of Liberty magazine
p.1 — "Which Lionel do you want, son?"
p.3 — "Only Lionel trains have these scale-detailed . . ."
c.f. — "Masterpiece of scale detailing — Lionel 1946 . . ." and loose price sheet included between center pages

1947 11¼x8, 32 pages
Type I — no separate price sheet
Type II — with revised price sheet included
p.3 — "Boy! Oh, boy! Will this be fun!" and "This catalog is effective August 1, 1947."
p.5 — "Exclusive electronic control . . ."
c.f. — "Magnificent giants of the rails — Lionel O gauge trains."
b.c. — "Exciting adventures in chemistry land . . . with a Lionel Chem-Lab set"

1948 11¼x8, 36 pages
p.2 — "Copyright 1948 by the Lionel Corporation"
p.3 — "Only Lionel has features . . ."
p.5 — 027 sets — 1423W and 1425B
c.f. — "Magnificent Lionel giants of the rails" — GGI 2332 sets
b.c. — Lionel construction kits

1949 11¼x8, 40 pages
Type I — pp. 10-11 top loco is 622
Type II — pp. 10-11 top loco is 6220 and heading of "0-27" added
p.3 — "Lionel leads the world" and "copyrighted 1949 by Lionel Corporation"
p.5 — "Handsome 0-27 scout outfits" — 1115 and 1117

1939

1940 Type III

1941

1942

1943 Lionel Wonder Book

1945 Folder

1946 Type I

c.f. — "Swift — powerful — magnificent Lionel diesels" — 2333

1950 11¼x8, 44 pages (Gold cover issue is an advance catalog)
Type I — page 30 not numbered
Type II — page 30 is numbered
Type III — red and black reprint of Type II, not full color
p.3 — "Lionel first with the best and exclusive with most" and "copyrighted 1950"
p.5 — "this close-up of a box car end . . ."
c.f. — "Emperors of the rails — Lionel O twin diesels with magne-traction"
b.c. — "Complete electronic control exclusive with Lionel"

1951 11⅛x7¾, 36 pages
Type I — lower right corner of p. 25 is green
Type II — lower right corner of p. 25 is brown
p.3 — "Any way you look at it — Lionel leads them all"
p.5 — "Lionel precision-built direct worm drive motor . . ."
c.f. — "A rip-roaring giant Lionel's famous steam turbine"

1952 11⅛x7¾, 36 pages
p.2 — "copyrighted 1952, the Lionel Corporation"
p.3 — "Lionel scout train" — set 1119
p.5 — 0-27 sets 1465 and 1477S
c.f. — "Lionel triple unit diesels" — 2343 and 2344

1953 11¼x7⅝, 40 pages
Type I — p. 8 labeled "No. 2046 Lionel Steam Loco (above)" and "No. 2055 Steam Loco (right)" and p. 14 — "Lionel New No. 685 Steam Loco"
Type II — p. 8 — "No. 2046 Lionel Steam Loco and Tender (above)" and "No. 2055 Steam Loco and Tender (right)" and p. 14 — "Lionel New No. 685 Steam Loco"
Type III — p. 8 — "No. 2046 Lionel Steam Loco (above)" and "No. 2055 Steam Loco (right)" and p. 14 — "Lionel New No. 685 Steam Loco and Tender"
Type IV — p. 8 — "No. 2046 Lionel Steam Loco and Tender (above)" and "No. 2055 Steam Loco and Tender (right)" and p. 14 — "Lionel New 685 Steam Loco and Tender"
p.3 — "There's everything every boy wants in Lionel trains . . ." and "copyright 1953"
p.5 — "No. 1043, 50 watt transformer"
c.f. — "High powered triple diesel freights" — sets 2207W and 2209W
b.c. — "Airex spin fishing tackle"

1954 11¼x7⅝, 44 pages
p.3 — "Lionel trains with magne-traction" and "copyright 1954, the Lionel Corporation"

1946 Type II

1947

1948

1949

1950 Type I

1950 Type III

1951

1952

1953

1954

1955

1956

p.5 — "Lionel No. 1513S 0-27 4-car freight"
c.f. — "The thrill of power, beauty, speed" and sets 2222WS and 2225WS

1955 11¼x7⅝, 44 pages
p.3 — "The world's finest trains . . ." and "copyright 1955, the Lionel Corporation"
p.5 — "Here are some of the authentic freight cars . . ."
c.f. — "Coming or going . . . These diesels are the sweetest sight on rails!"

1956 11¼x7⅝, 40 pages
Type I — "Remember: Lionel train sets start as low as . . ." on back cover
Type II — blank space, no caption on back cover
p.2 — "Copyright 1956, the Lionel Corporation"
p.3 — No. 520 — $12.95 if bought separately
p.5 — "No. 627 Lehigh Valley in red and white."
c.f. — "Power — and then some! Three huge . . ." — Locos 646, 665, 736

1957 11¼x7⅝, 52 pages
Type I — with "Outfit Component and Retail Price List" included
Type II — without price list
p.2 — "Copyright 1957, the Lionel Corporation"
p.3 — "No. 202 — if bought separately, $14.95"
p.5 — "Now in the new Lehigh Valley markings"
c.f. — "First to make the run on Super O track" — loco no. 736LTS

1958 11¼x7⅝, 56 pages
p.3 — "Model railroading . . . from Super O . . . to 027 . . . to HO" and "Copyright 1958"
p.5 — sets 1595 and 1591
c.f. — "Past gates and banjo signals streaks the New Haven . . ."

1959 56 pages
Type I — 11x8½, 736, 1872 General and 44 U.S. Army on cover
Type II — 8½x11, 44 and 1872 General only on cover
p.2 — "copyright 1959, the Lionel Corporation"
p.3 — "Railroading! From Super O . . . to 027 . . . to HO" and "No. 1609 3-car steam freight"
p.5 — "No. 1611 4-car Alaskan freight $25.00"
c.f. — "Husky 14-wheelers! Hudson action freights roar by on Super O track"

1960 11x8½, 56 pages
p.2 — "Copyright 1960, the Lionel Corporation"
p.3 — "The Pacesetter at a thrifty $19.95"
p.5 — "With headlight and real smoke — outfit No. 1627S"
c.f. — "The majestic Berkshire with a caravan of operating cars"

1961 8½x11, 72 pages
p.2 — "copyright 1961, the Lionel Corporation"
p.3 — "It's Lionel . . . from Super O . . . to 027 . . . to HO . . . It's Lionel-Porter"
p.5 — "Recreate great moments in science"
c.f. — "A heavy duty Super O work train" — set 2570

1962 8½x11, 100 pages
p.2 — "Copyright 1962, the Lionel Corporation"
p.3 — "Means fun for the entire family"
p.5 — sets 11201 and 11212
c.f. — "Sturdy, realistic . . . HO cargo cars" and "Now an HO steamer with whistle . . ."

1963 8½x10⅞, 56 pages, color covers but inside pages monotone
p.2 — "Copyright 1963, the Lionel Corporation"
p.3 — sets 11311 and 11321
.5 — "Complete with circuit breaker transformers" and set 11331
c.f. — "Lionel exclusive . . . fun packed rolling stock

1964 8½x10⅞, 24 pages, monotone cover and pages
Type I — pulp paper, p. 13 — 6402 flat car — $2.50
Type II — slick paper, p. 13 — 6402 flat car — $2.50
Type III — pulp paper, p. 13 — 6402 flat car — $3.95 (errata)
Type IV — slick paper, p. 13 — 6402 flat car — $3.95 (errata)
p.2 — "Copyright 1964, the Lionel Toy Corporation"
p.3 — sets 11430 and 11440
p.5 — sets 11480, 11490, 11500, 11510
c.f. — "Lionel rolling stock . . . fun packed and exciting"

1965 8½x10⅞, 40 pages, color cover with inside pages monotone
Type I — pulp paper, p. 6 — 6130 and p. 14 — 6402
Type II — slick paper, p. 6 — 6130 and p. 14 — 6402
Type III — pulp paper, p. 6 — 6119 and p. 14 — 6401 (errata)
Type IV — slick paper, p. 6 — 6119 and p. 14 — 6401 (errata)
p.2 — "Copyright 1965, the Lionel Toy Corporation"
p.3 — "Sane toys for healthy kids"
p.5 — "1902: Lionel gondola" and "1912: early Lionel electric"
c.f. — "Lionel HO locomotives and rolling stock" and "Lionel HO accessories"

1966 11x8½, 40 pages, full color cover and pages
Type I — layouts pictured on pages 8 and 10
Type II — no layouts pictured on pages 8 and 10

1957

1958

1959 Type I

1960

1961

1962

1963

p.3 — "A great fast freight express — back by popular demand" and "Copyright 1966"
p.5 — sets 11520, 11530, 11560
c.f. — "Lionel HO locomotives" and "HO accessories"

1967 Reissue of 1966 catalog

1968 **Folder,** 8½x11, 8 page folds
p.1 — "Lionel proudly presents the greatest train of all times"
p.3 — "Copyright 1968, the Lionel Toy Corporation" and "Lionel locomotives and rolling stock"
p.5 — "Lionel track and accessories"

1969 11x8½, 8 pages
p.3 — "Copyright 1969, the Lionel Toy Corporation" and sets 11740, 11750, 11760
p. 5 — "Lionel rolling stock — a great way to get extra pleasure . . ."

1966 and 1967

1968

1969

1964

1965

Errata

First Edition

Following the page number is a number followed by an L or R in parentheses, this indicates the line of type in the Left or Right column that is in error.

Pg. 1 • (12L) available misspelled

Pg. 2 • (22R) 1935 not 1933

Pg. 4 • (1L) 1935 not 1933

• **253E** (chart) made 1931 not 1930

Pg. 6 • **152 Elec.** (47L) in gray not light gray.

Pg. 8 • (8R) All these locomotives have latch or combination couplers except the very early 250 which has only combination latch couplers.

• **4 Elec.** (16R) is body style CM&StP, not CMStP&P.

• **248 Elec.** (33R) in dark green/black/maroon, RS, made circa 1930, not 1927.

• **250 Elec.** (early) (41R) usually found without reverse slot in top of hood.

Pg. 9 • (29L) terra-cotta misspelled

• **254 Elec.** (44L) is body style CM&StP, not CMStP&P.

• (48L) red stripe not red strip

Pg. 11 • **257** (45R) last variation has 4-Wh 259 tender, not 2-Wh.

• **258** (late), (52R) black

Pg. 15 • (20L) uncat - should read uncat.

Pg. 31 • **605 and 606** (28L) olive green/olive green have red window trim not maroon.

• **610 PULLMAN** (50L) Note should read - Late pea green or olive green cars may be found with white window shades.

Pg. 32 • **603** (17L) series are generally type VI or VII.

Pg. 34 • **615** (29L) found lettered THE LIONEL LINES or LIONEL LINES.

Pg. 36 • **801** (23R) brown/black lettered NYNH&H - earliest.

• **820** (42R) dark olive green boxcar is only prewar Lionel car lettered ATSF.

Pg. 38 • (45L) Should read, from 1935-41 is unclear.

Pg. 39 • **655** (28R) in cream/tuscan - RS lettering, N or Black oxidized trim (uncat. - circa 1939-42).

Pg. 42 • **810** (19L) made 1930-42

Pg. 43 • **2814** (6L) in yellow/brown not tuscan

• **2814** (7L) in flat orange/tuscan not burnt orange

Pg. 45 • (19R) tuscan misspelled

Pg. 56 • **1911 Elec.** (chart) (38 body) made in 1913 not 1912.

Pg. 61 • **33 Elec.** (8L) found RS - NYC oval or C&O.

Pg. 65 • (9R) nickel misspelled

Pg. 67 • **10 Elec.** (41L) is body style CM&StP, not CMStP&P.

• **10 Elec.** (42L) colors stacked, should read -
mojave
gray
peacock

• **380 Elec.** (26R) is body style CM&StP, not CMStP&P.

• **381 Elec.** (34R) is body style CM&StP, not CMStP&P.

Pg. 73 • (4R) abbreviations misspelled

Pg. 74 • **190 OBSERVATION** (40R) (second series) made with or without openings in clerestory.

Pg. 82 • (6L) Change In 1934 to By 1934

Pg. 84 • **112 GONDOLA** (later) (26R)

Note: May be found RS - 65784, 76899, or not numbered.

• **116 BALLAST** (33R) - found RS - NYNH&HRR or PENNSYLVANIA

Pg. 93 • **2 TRAILER.** (3R) Six window inset, open platform with posts - to match above motor car found in cream/red roof/red letterboards/cream ends, RS - No. 2 ELECTRIC RAPID TRANSIT. Circa 1908.

Pg. 94 • **4 MOTOR CAR.** (20L) Nine window flat, open platform with posts, two motors, to match similar No. 3 found in cream/orange roof and letterboards/cream ends, RS - No. 4 ELECTRIC RAPID TRANSIT. Circa 1906.

• **10 INTERURBAN** (T). (34R)

Note: At least one No.10 Interurban known to exist RS - 1010 W.B.&A.

Pg. 95 • **1000 TRAILER.** (36L) Five window insert, closed platform, flush vestibules, found to match 100 Motor Car, numbered 1000 and lettered LINDEN AVENUE. Circa 1913-14.

Pg. 119 • **253 Elec.,** (42R) not 253E and circa 1926 rather than 1931.

Pg. 122 • **1688** Black set, (16L) 1682 caboose has yellow cupola stripe, not clerestory stripe.

4 Motor Car

2 Trailer with fender

1000 Trailer LINDEN AVENUE

Addenda

First Edition

152 pea green

156 maroon (glossy)

156X mojave

703 prototype, dark green

Pg. 6

- **Intro.** Early 700 series electric style locomotives have a small L stamped into rivets of motor pickup plate.
- **150 Elec.** Found in peacock, mojave and dark green with headlight and bell but numbered 158.
- **150 Elec.** (later), olive green
- **152 Elec.,** pea green/Br trim and headlight
- **153 Elec.,** dark gray; peacock; olive green, maroon (glossy)
- **156 Elec.,** (4-4-4), mojave, apple green
- **156X Elec.,** mojave
- **703 Elec.,** preproduction, dark green UNIQUE
- **706 Elec.,** dark green

Note: Known to exist lettered C.P.R.

Pg. 8

- **4 Elec.**

Note: 4 Elec. found with or without weights on frame.

- **248 Elec.**

Note: Late 248 cabs can be found with or without handrails.

- **251 Elec.**

Note: 251 and 251E in red/black frame usually have ivory windows but may be found with brass windows; 251 or 251E gray may be found with red or black lettering.

Pg. 9

- **253 Elec.,** gray/black/Br - Standard gauge flag stanchions (SPECIAL - circa 1923); red/black/cream (uncat. 1929)
- **253E Elec.,** RS "E" on cab dates to 1931-32
- **254 Elec.,** pea green/black/Br - orange stripe and orange hatches, HR. Circa 1931-32.

Note: Made for export with hand reverse slot, one headlight, no pantograph, RS - 254 on ends, underframe stamped Made in U.S. of America.

- **254 Elec.,** orange/black/Br
- **256 Elec.**

Note: First variation of 256 can be found with or without black rectangular RS border around RS lettering.

- **450 Elec.** in red/black may be found with Br or cream window trim.

Pg. 11 • **258 (early)**

Note: 257 and early 258 are found with Ives plates in 1931 and 1932.

• **258 (late),** gunmetal.

Pg. 12 • **260E**

Note: The 260 locos are found with brass or nickel plates with red lettering, whereas 255 and 263 have only nickel plates with black lettering.

• **261E**

Note: 261E and 261T found with or without red stripe on both loco and tender.

• **262E**

Note: 262 and 262T found with or without orange stripe on tender; 262E and 262T found with or without orange or red stripe on both loco and tender; 262 and 262T from 1931 are found with Ives plates and Ives 1663 number boards.

Pg. 15 • **238/238E**

Note: 1936 models of 238E and 250E had added weights inside, 1937 models had a heavier casting but no weights.

• **250E**

Note: The 250E pilot trucks were stamped metal in 1935 and 1936, diecast in 1937 and 1938, and stamped again thereafter.

• **264E** with light blue 265X tender.

• **265E**

Note: The inside of 265E cab plain in 1935 models, thereafter had firebox markings.

Pg. 18 • **224/224E**

Note: Same loco casting used for 224, 229, 1664, and 1666.

• **700EWX** 4-6-4, same as 700E but with tinplate flanges and blind drivers, tender coupler height for 800/2800 cars, 14⅛″, uncat. circa 1937-38.

• **708** Catalog number for 701 B6 switcher and slope-back 701 tender. 1939-42.

Pg. 19 • **1684** Gunmetal

Note: An 027 gauge "Hiawatha" prototype exists with 1684 motor, side rods, pilot and trailer truck, no tender has been found.

Pg. 23 • **1106 Santa Claus Handcar,** red base, no back pack, 8⅞″, made for export to Europe. Circa 1935.

• **1107 Donald Duck Rail Car** found with red or green roof.

Pg. 29 • **600 PULLMAN,** orange

Note: Dark green 600 pullmans are found with or without gilt window sill, no gilt window sill on cars of other colors.

• **603 PULLMAN (later)**

Note: 1920 models of 603 (later) and 604 (later) found with mottled blue-green or white celluloid in upper windows, and hook couplers.

• **611 MAIL** prototype

Pg. 31 • **612 OBSERVATION**

Note: Light red and light blue 612 have aluminum painted steel observation platforms, all others have brass platforms.

• **710 PULLMAN**

Note: Some 710 and 712 have square windows in doors, others have larger rectangular windows in doors.

706 CPR lettering

027 Hiawatha preproduction

600 orange

604 (later) dark green

608 light red/light red/cream

611 preproduction - dark green

613 green/aluminum

613 long wheelbase, no steps

2601 long wheelbase, no steps

800 yellow-orange/brown

2620 flat black/N

1049X Wartime freight set

Pg. 32

• 603 PULLMAN

Note: Some light red cars have interior lights. One set of 603 and 604 cars found in orange/terra-cotta/cream, not lettered above windows.

• 608 OBSERVATION, light red/light red/cream

Pg. 34

• 600 PULLMAN, gray/red/ivory - N trim

• 613 PULLMAN

Note: Some terra-cotta cars are lettered THE LIONEL LINES.

• 613 PULLMAN, green/green and alum/alum UNIQUE

• 2600-2601-2602

Note: Can be found with long wheelbase frame and no steps.

• 2613 PULLMAN

Note: Both blue and State green series can be found with long wheelbase frame, no steps, and diaphragms on ends.

Pg. 36

• 800 BOX, yellow-orange/brown, RS - WABASH 6399

• 801 CABOOSE, brown/black, RS - WABASH RR 4390 or 4890

• 801 CABOOSE, maroon/black, RS - WABASH RR 4890, black or gold lettering

• 802 CATTLE

Note: Early production cars are darker green, later are green. Early cars are stamped on end—802, with or without LIONEL LINES, N.Y. Later cars are marked LIONEL CORPORATION.

• 901 GONDOLA, brown, dark gray, dark olive green

Note: Lettered PENNSYLVANIA (gray and dark gray cars only) or LAKE SHORE (all colors). Gray 901 lettered in black or gold.

• 822 CABOOSE, maroon/black, vertical ribs embossed inward

Note: Cars with vertical ribs embossed inward have black lettering; those with ribs embossed outward are lettered in black or gold.

Pg. 38

• 807 CABOOSE, red/pea green/pea green - Br; light red/light red/cream - Br, N, or RS

Pg. 39

• 656 CATTLE

Note: Two shades of gray found on 656 cars. The lighter gray cars have light red doors and door guides while the others have light red door guides but gray doors.

• 2620 FLOODLIGHT, single light, black/nickled light. Circa 1943. SPECIAL

• 2651 FLAT, black - 4 stakes. Circa 1943. SPECIAL.

Note: Various combinations of 2620 black, 2651 black, 2677 black, and 3659 black/red were sold circa 1943. Freight car set #1049X for 027 track is one such set.

Pg. 40

• 2657 CABOOSE, light red/light red/white - N or RS

• 2660 DERRICK

Note: Boom is occasionally black plastic unpainted or painted dark green.

Pg. 42

• 812 GONDOLA, green - Br or N

• **813 CATTLE,** orange/orange - Br; orange/maroon - Br, and cream/maroon - Br or N

Note: Door guides normally match roof color but can be found in pea green on orange/orange cars.

• **814 BOX,** yellow/brown - Br or N

• **816 HOPPER,** black - N or RS

Pg. 43 • **3814 MERCHANDISE**

Note: Long wheelbase cars always RS lettering, not decal.

Pg. 45 • **2672 CABOOSE**

Note: Number listed in 1941 catalog but 2672 not shown as described.

Pg. 47 • **1680 TANK,** alum - PETROLEUM PRODUCTS on top, no herald.

Note: Tank cars made in 1941-42 have no handrails.

Pg. 48 • **1691 OBSERVATION**

Note: Both 1691 and 1693 have been found lithographed with pullman numbers.

• **1718 CATTLE,** litho, green and white/ green/brown doors and door guides, attached Br ladders, 9½", NM except preproduction, uncat. Circa 1933.

• **2677 GONDOLA,** black - no lettering. Circa 1943. SPECIAL

• **2680 TANK**

Note: Late gray car bodies may have alum or black tank domes.

Pg. 53 • **51 DEALER'S PAPER TRAIN DISPLAY.** Circa 1943.

Pg. 58 • **6 LOCO**

Note 5: Cab roof on locomotive with thin rim drivers is 4⅝" long, whereas on locomotive with thick rim drivers, cab roof is 4⅜".

Note 6: Binding posts first appeared in 1911 on both 5 and 6.

Pg. 61 • **33 Elec.,** 0-6-0, dark olive green with red stripe along bottom

• **33 Elec.,** 0-4-0, brown, mojave, and pea green

Note: Midnight blue 33 has black pilots, all other colors of 33 have red pilots.

• **34 Elec.,** 0-6-0, lettered NYC oval.

• **38 Elec.,** 0-4-0, dark olive green, RS - block PENN RR. Circa 1914.

• **42 Elec.,** 0-4-4-0, pea green

• **53 Elec.,** 38 body, brown

• **1910 Elec.,** 33 body

Note: A factory repaint 1910 is known in maroon, numbered 53.

• **1912 Elec.,** 0-4-4-0, maroon/dark olive green trim/gilt ventilators - script NYNH&H; black with gilt ventilators - NYC oval.

Pg. 64 • **INTRO.** Steam locomotives (385, 392, 400, 1835) have red lights under cab to simulate firebox glow.

1680 PETROLEUM PRODUCTS, no herald

1718 preproduction

10E mojave/cream stripe

42 mojave set

18 mojave

19 yellow orange, CM&St.P

29 (early) dark olive green PENNSYLVANIA

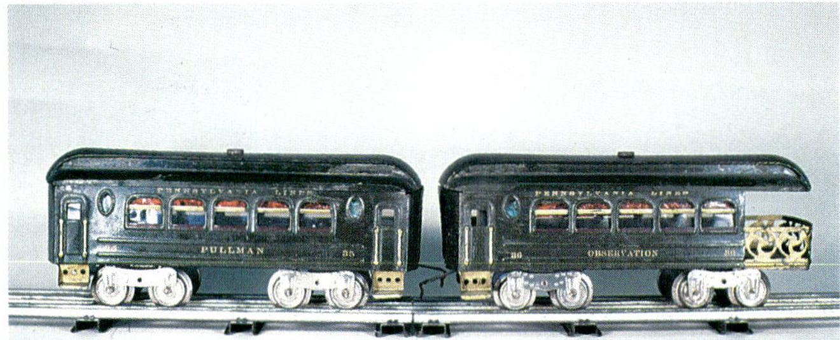

35&36 (early) PENNSYLVANIA LINES

36 (early) no embossed door frames

418 mustard brown/red

312 misnumbered 309

421 State green/dark State green/cream

• 384

Note: Cab window trim may be green or brass.

• 390, 2-4-2, medium blue/dark blue frame—no stripe/red pilot - Br

Pg. 65 **• 400E,** 4-4-4, all dark blue/no stripe SPECIAL

Pg. 67 **• 8E Elec.,** peacock/cream stripe/cream window trim SPECIAL

• 10E Elec., State brown/dark green frame—Bild-A-Loco or Super Motor

• 10E Elec., mojave/cream stripe

Pg. 68 **• 402 Elec.,** 0-4-4-0, dark olive green

Note: Early 402 can be found with hook couplers and terminal post.

• 402E Elec., 0-4-4-0, crackle red UNIQUE

Pg. 70 **• 8E Elec.,** peacock/cream stripe/cream window trim, MACY

Pg. 74 **• 18 PULLMAN,** dark olive green/dark olive green/gold; mojave/mojave/maroon

Note: Early cars had grooved diaphragms and two sizes of roof knobs - early ½" tall and later ⅜". Found lettered DINING CAR

• 19 COMBINE, lettered 18 COMBINE, also found lettered block RS - CHICAGO MILWAUKEE, and ST. PAUL RAILWAY

• 29 DAY COACH, early - lettered PENNSYLVANIA or NYC&HRRR

• 29 DAY COACH, middle - lettered NYC & HRRR

• 29 DAY COACH, later - lettered CANADIAN PACIFIC RAILWAY or NYC&HRRR

Pg. 76 **• 180 PULLMAN,** maroon

Note: Have been found lettered CANADIAN PACIFIC RAILWAY. Also have been found lettered DINING CAR.

• 36 OBSERVATION, early - no embossed door frames.

Note: 35 and 36 lettered PENNSYLVANIA LINES

Pg. 77 **• 418 PULLMAN**
peacock/peacock/orange windows and doors SPECIAL
gray/gray/red windows and doors SPECIAL
cream/cream/green doors/red windows SPECIAL
pink/pink/apple green doors/cream windows SPECIAL
dark green/dark green/cream windows and doors SPECIAL
mustard brown/mustard brown/red doors/red windows SPECIAL

Note: 418-419-431-490 cars have been found in odd colors as possible paint samples and designs for State car sets.

Pg. 78 • **312 OBSERVATION**

Note: Light blue/alum/alum cars have painted aluminum observation platforms. Early 309 and 312 have large rectangular windows in vestibule doors, later models have small square windows in doors. Cars in pea green, two-tone brown, and light blue can be found with both types of windows in vestibule doors. The 312 observation can be found marked 309 PULLMAN

Pg. 79 • **LATE SMALL SERIES PASSENGER CARS.** Have been found lettered ILLINOIS CENTRAL.

• **339 PULLMAN,** Ives 1694 gray/maroon/cream

Note: 339 and 341 peacock/dark green/orange can be found lettered THE LIONEL RAILWAY LINES or THE IVES RAILWAY LINES. The Ives lettered cars have a white paper sticker on the underside.

Pg. 81 • **420 PULLMAN,** State green/dark green/cream - Br trim SPECIAL

Note: Some 420-421-422 cars are lettered THE BLUE COMET above the windows. Light blue/dark blue/cream cars found with either dark blue or light blue roof ventilators. Can be found with "LIONEL LINES" 500 series plates instead of number plates.

Pg. 82 • **1767 BAGGAGE**

Note: Early series (cream) baggage doors are not embossed but may be found lettered whereas later series (aluminum) baggage doors are embossed but never lettered.

• **1768 OBSERVATION**

Note: The red/maroon/aluminum 1768 have aluminum painted observation platforms.

• **11 FLAT,** dark olive green

Note: A few of the early 11 flat cars have handrails.

• **12 GONDOLA,** lettered CM&StP 28277

Pg. 83 • **14 BOX,** dark olive green with embossed sides, no lettering

• **15 OIL (early),** maroon/maroon frame/cream primer, U-shape wire step

Note: Early type of 15 OIL made 1906-1913.

• **16 BALLAST,** RS - NYC&HRRR 342715

Note: Earliest 15 OIL and 16 BALLAST can have girder painted cream primer on bottom, all later variations have maroon or black girder.

• **17 CABOOSE,** smooth sides, RS - NYC&HRR

Note: In 1926 Lionel 10 series unlettered car bodies (gondola, cattle, boxcar, caboose) were sold to American Flyer who mounted their trucks on the cars and marked them with their numbers, not Lionel numbers.

Pg. 84 • **112 GONDOLA (early)** - gray **(later)** - maroon, RS - NYNH&H, or NYC&HRRR

Note: Early (1910-11) 112 GONDOLA may be found with one or two brakewheels.

• **113 CATTLE,** early cars darker green, later are lighter green

• **114 BOX,** dark olive green with embossed sides, decal—898 SPECIAL

• **114 BOX,** yellow-orange, lettered CM&StP 62976

• **115 OIL,** wood tank, dark gray/black frame, RS - STD. OIL CO. 12898 or

11 with handrails

217 olive green/dark olive green/red

218 peacock/Br ends

219 reversed door position

1 MOTOR (A) - cream/dark olive green

1 MOTOR (B) and 1 TRAILER - cream/blue

8 MOTOR - nine windows - cream/orange

8 MOTOR (O) eleven windows - brown

9 MOTOR, eleven windows - dark olive green/cream

29 MOTOR - dark olive green

CALIF. OIL CO. 12863, two pre-production cars only. Circa 1913.

• **116 BALLAST**

Note: May be found with or without RS 116 on sides. Lettering may be gold or black. Occasionally found lettered PENNSYLVANIA.

Pg. 85 • **117 CABOOSE**

Note: Early 117 with brown/black roof may be found stamped on ends LIONEL LINES, N.Y.

• **LATE LARGE SERIES FREIGHT CARS.** Early cars had 2-piece brakewheels, later production had 1-piece brakewheel. In 1930 Lionel 200 series unmarked freight car bodies were sold to Ives who painted and added plates with Ives numbers, being Ives they are not included here.

• **211 FLAT,** gray

Note: The stakes on 211 are always nickel, never brass.

• **212 GONDOLA,** apple green; terra-cotta

• **214 BOX,** maroon/olive green/black door guides SPECIAL

• **216 HOPPER,** ivory

• **217 CABOOSE,** olive green/dark olive green/maroon/peacock railings on ends UNIQUE

Note: Early orange 217 caboose had celluloid windows and no window frames. Pea green/red 217 has pea green painted railing on ends. Light red/light red 217 may have cream painted doors.

Pg. 86 • **218 DUMP,** peacock/Br ends.

• **219 DERRICK,** dark blue/dark green/red boom UNIQUE

Note: Cab door and window reversed in position on side of cab. Some early yellow/light red 219 have peacock base.

Pg. 87 • **514 BOX,** yellow/orange roof and door guides - N trim.

• **518 FLOODLIGHT,** cataloged in 1931 advance catalog but NM numbered 518. 1931.

Pg. 88 • **337 PULLMAN,** pea green, with or without MACY SPECIAL on side nameboards

Pg. 93 • **2 MOTOR CAR (H)** blue/blue roof/cream windows.

Pg. 94 • **29 MOTOR CAR.** Nine window flat, open platform with posts, 8-Wh, standard motor, SSH couplers, stirrup steps, seat pins, no underbody embossing, no headlight, cream primer, dark olive green/dark olive green/gold lettering, RS - No. 29 NYC&HRRR Co., $13\frac{7}{8}$" roof. Circa 1906.

Note: Appears to be the same as earliest 3 Motor Car but in 29 day coach colors and lettering.

Pg. 95 • **100 MOTOR CAR (Y)**

Note: Has been found No. 1 ELECTRIC RAPID TRANSIT.

• **1010 TRAILER (R),** dark olive green 1010 trailer known to exist lettered 1910 INTERURBAN.

• **1000 TRAILER.** Five window inset, closed platform, offset vestibule.

Note: Found RS 100 or 1000 ELECTRIC RAPID TRANSIT.

Pg. 105 • **"City of Portland"**

Note: 1934 motor units have GAUGE lettering on motor plates. One 752 set found lettered CITY OF SAN FRANCISCO.

Pg. 106 • **Set #257W "Victory Streamliner"** - 0(1942 advance) NM

Pg. 108 • **1674 PULLMAN,** Hiawatha orange/Hiawatha gray/Hiawatha orange, no journal boxes, 9⅛".

Pg. 111 • **260T TENDER,** crackle black/black frame

• **263T TENDER,** cream/red frame

Pg. 112 • **1588W** tender, came with 1689 loco, uncat. Circa 1937.

Pg. 115 • **384 TENDER,** crackle black with 385E, uncat. Circa 1933.

Note: Frequently found with gunmetal/copper trim 385E.

• **400W TENDER,** black/N trim

Note: Presumed to be replacement whistle tender.

Pg. 118 • **4U Elec.,** orange/black/Br; 605-605-606 orange/orange/cream with MACY SPECIAL brass plate on platform. R.H. MACY CO., New York. Circa 1930. DSS

• **204** Black - E but not so RS, non-spoked trailing wheels; 2689TX tender, 3659X dump - black/red hopper, 652 gondola - burnt orange -RS, 657 caboose - light red/light red/white - RS. Circa 1940-41.

• **204** Black - E but not so RS; 1689T tender - black, black journals; 610-610-612 light red/alum/alum - N journals. Box marked Set #8134, uncat. Circa 1940.

Pg. 119 • **229** Black - plate; 2224T tender - black/RS silver LIONEL LINES; 610-610-612 light red/alum/alum, RS - black lettering. Set box marked Outfit No. 7123 for O gauge track; uncat. Circa 1939.

• **229** Gunmetal; 02689WX tender - gunmetal; 2613-2614-2615 State green/dark green/cream, uncat. Circa 1939-40.

• **229** Black - RS; 2689W - black - RS; 2600-2601-2602 red/red/cream - no steps, aluminum observation platform. Sold by Sears with Lionel #8104W and Sears #59-52P. Circa 1940.

100 MOTOR - blue/cream, LINDEN AVENUE

1010 TRAILER (R) - high knobs

1674 Hiawatha orange and gray

260T crackle black

400W black/N

7 nickel plated

252 Macy Special, box top

252 Macy Special #1, boxes

902 gondola with Lionel Craft label

35 (early) maroon

- **229** Black - RS; 2666TS tender - black; 2812 gondola - green - N; 2815 tank - Shell orange - N; 3814 merchandise - tuscan/decal lettering; 2817 caboose - flat red/tuscan/white - RS; SR transformer. Set box marked #8125 SEARS ROEBUCK. Circa 1941.
- **238** Black - RS; 2225W or 2265W tender - black; 2653 hopper - black - RS; 2654 tank - orange/Shell decal; 2655 box - cream/tuscan - RS; 2657 caboose - light red/tuscan/white - RS. Set box marked #187WX 0-Gauge Freight Outfit, SEARS ROEBUCK No. 59-79F. Circa 1940.
- **248 Elec.,** red/black/Br; 629-629-630 red/red/cream, 8-Wh, N journals. Set box marked Special #1. Circa 1934.
- **249E** Gunmetal - N; 2225T tender - gunmetal; 2660 derrick - cream/light red/green boom; 2620 floodlight - light red/alum light; 2653 hopper - Stephen Girard green;3659 dump - black/red hopper; 2657 caboose - light red/light red/white. Set box marked #6631EX, Quakenbush Hardware, Patterson, N.J. Circa 1939.
- **249E** Black - N; 265T tender - black; boxes marked 1685V-1685V-1687V, vermillion/maroon/ cream - N. Set box marked #6532E. Circa 1937-38.

Note: Same set with 265W tender has set box #6532W.

- **250 Elec. (early)** - dark green/black/Br; 804 tank (early) - gray; 831 lumber - black/8 stakes; 807 peacock/dark green/red. SEARS ROEBUCK, uncat. Circa 1926.
- **250 Elec. (early)** - dark green/black/Br; 629-629-630 dark green/dark green/maroon. SEARS ROEBUCK, uncat. Circa 1927.

Note: Similar to Lionel set #294 but has one less pullman.

- **252 Elec.** - terra cotta/maroon/Br; 902 gondola, 804 tank, 805 box, 807 caboose. SEARS ROEBUCK, uncat. Circa 1931.

Note: Similar to Lionel set #293 which has 803 hopper and 806 cattle, but no 902 lumber or 805 boxcar.

- **252 Elec.,** 831 lumber - green/4 stakes, 804 tank (late) - alum, 807 caboose - light red/light red/cream - N. Set #49K5198, SEARS ROEBUCK, uncat. Circa 1938.
- **253 Elec.,** red; 607-607-607-608 - red/red/cream. Car boxes marked R, set box marked Special #3. Circa 1926-27.
- **253 Elec.,** gray/black/Br.; 607-607-608 maroon/maroon/cream - lettered MACY

SPECIAL under the windows. R.H. MACY CO., New York. Circa 1926. DSS

• **253 Elec.,** dark green, Br trim, cast headlight, disc wheels; 610-612 dark green/dark green/maroon. Set box marked Special #1 for G.B. and 27 on end, uncat. Circa 1927-28. DSS

Note: This set differs from 1925 Gimbels Special #l (page 119) in motor, type of headlight, and type of drive wheels.

• **253 Elec.,** red/black/cream windows/ Br, cast headlight; 607-607-607-608 - red/red/cream, RS - THE LIONEL LINES above windows in gold. 253 box marked 253 RED, car boxes marked 607 RED or 608 RED, set box marked Special #1, sold by Lasalle and Koch Co., uncat. Circa 1929.

• **253E Elec.,** Stephen Girard green/ dark green/ cream, matching 607-607-608. Set box marked 296E - 0 Gauge Set and R.H. MACY & Co. Circa 1936.

• **254 Elec.,** red/black/Br - disc wheels, diecast headlight; 607-607-607-608 red/ red/cream - 8-Wh. Car boxes marked O gauge - R and YELLOW, set box marked Sears Special #3. Circa 1930-31.

• **254 Elec.,** pea green/black/Br - orange stripe and orange hatches, HR; 610-610-612 pea green/pea green/orange. All items stamped on bottom - Made in U.S. of America, made for export. Circa 1931-32.

• **254E Elec.,** pea green/orange ventilators and bottom stripe; 605-605-606 olive green/dark red. 254 Box marked L. GREEN, car boxes marked L. OLIVE. Set box marked Special #10 AMC for 0 gauge track. Circa 1933.

Pg. 120 • **257** Black/orange stripe; 257T tender - black/no stripe; 603-604 red/black/ cream. Set box marked Special #2X. Circa 1931-32.

• **257** Ives - black; 259T tender - black, Ives plate; 1707 Ives litho gondola, 1708 Ives litho cattle, 1709 Ives litho boxcar, 1712 Ives litho caboose. Set box marked #5004, J. L. Hudson Co., uncat. Circa 1932. DSS

Note: Differs from Hornes set #5004 by the addition of 1707 gondola.

• **258 (early)** Black; 257T tender - black, 4-Wh; 803 hopper, 804 tank, 805 box, 807 caboose. Set box marked 49D5175, SEARS ROEBUCK, uncat. Circa 1930.

Note: Same as Lionel set #133 except Lionel set has 806, not 805, and 902 gondola.

• **258 (early)** Black; 258T tender - black, 8-Wh; 902 gondola, 804 tank, 807 caboose. Set box marked 49F5173, SEARS ROEBUCK, uncat. Circa 1931.

Note: Same as Lionel set #133 except Lionel set has 262 loco.

• **258 (early)** Black; 258T tender - black, 8-Wh; 607-607-608. Set box marked 49F5178, SEARS ROEBUCK, uncat. Circa 1931.

Note: Same as Lionel set #236 except Lionel set has 262 loco.

• **258 (early)** Black; 259T tender - black, 4-Wh; 603-603-604 Stephen Girard green/dark green/cream with air tanks. Set box marked 49D5187, SEARS ROEBUCK, uncat. Circa 1933.

Note: Similar to set 49D5164 sold by Sears in 1933 which has 607-607-608 Stephen Girard green/dark green/cream with air tanks.

• **258 (late)** Black; 1689T tender - black; 1679 litho box, 1680 litho tank, 1682 litho caboose. Set box marked 7005 EX, uncat. Circa 1940.

• **258 (late)** Gunmetal; 2689T tender - gunmetal; 1679 litho box - yellow/ maroon; 1680 litho tank - alum SUNX; 1682 litho caboose - brown/brown. Set box marked #7003 Freight Train Outfit, and E4131 SPECIAL. Circa 1941.

• **258 (late)** Black; 1689T tender - black; 654 tank - light gray; 655 box - cream/ tuscan; 657 caboose - light red/tuscan/ white. All cars are RS or decal lettering and black journals. Set box marked #8042, uncat. Circa 1941.

Note: Same set with 2689TX tender marked #8062, uncat. 1941.

• **258 (late)** Gunmetal - RS; 01689W - gunmetal - N; 655 boxcar - tuscan/RS, black journals; 654 tank - light gray/ SUNOCO decal - black trim; 657 caboose - light red/tuscan/white - RS - black trim. Set box marked 8067W - no individual boxes, uncat. Circa 1941.

• **258 (late)** Black; 1689T tender, 1679 litho boxcar, 1682 litho caboose, 2640-2640-2641, uncat. Circa 1942.

• **259E** Black; 259T tender - black, 4-Wh; 629-629-630 red/red/cream - either 4-Wh or 8-Wh, alum observation platform, have journal boxes. Set box marked 49K5155, SEARS ROEBUCK, uncat. Circa 1934.

Note: Same as Sears 49K5155 in 1935 except that set has 8-Wh 259T tender.

• **259** Black - HR; 261T tender - black; 603-603-604 red/black/cream. Set box marked #5226. Sold by Frank & Seder Department Store, Pittsburgh, uncat. Circa 1934.

• **259E** Black; 259T tender - black;

603X-604X orange/terra cotta. Set box marked #5017EX, uncat. Circa 1934.

- **259** Black; 259T tender - black, 4-Wh; 629-629-630 light red/light red/cream, 8-Wh. SEARS ROEBUCK, Philadelphia. Circa 1935-36.

- **259E** Gunmetal - N; 1689T or W tender - gunmetal; 603-603-604 red/black/cream - no air tanks, N journals. Set box marked 6505E or W, uncat. Circa 1935.

Note: Sold through American Auto Accessories stores.

- **259E** Black; 261T tender - black; 1717 litho gondola; 1719 litho box; 1722 litho caboose - N journals on cars, latch couplers. Set box marked #5205E, uncat. Circa 1936.

- **259E** Gunmetal - N; 1689W tender - gunmetal - N; 651 flat, 654 tank, 657 caboose - all cars N trim and journals. Set box marked #6600W and 1937, bought from SEARS ROEBUCK in Philadelphia, uncat. Circa 1937.

- **259E** Gunmetal - N, black oxidized wheels; 1689T tender - gunmetal - N; 804 tank - alum/Sunoco, 809 dump - medium green, 831 lumber - green/4 stakes, 807 caboose - light red/light red/cream - all cars N trim and journals. Set box marked No. 6504E Freight Outfit, uncat. Circa 1937.

- **259E** Black; 1689TW - black, 8-Wh; 654 tank-alum/Sunoco, 651 flat - 4 stakes/green, 657 caboose - light red/light red/cream. Set box marked 79K5970, SEARS ROEBUCK, uncat. Circa 1937-38.

Note: Same as Lionel set #290W cataloged in 1935.

- **259E** Gunmetal - E but not so marked; 1689T tender - gunmetal; 1717 litho gondola; 1719 litho box; 1722 litho caboose - Br journals. Set box marked #6705E, uncat. Circa 1940.

- **259E** Black - N; 1689T tender - black; mixed consist - 3 freight cars and 2 passenger cars. Set box marked #7130, Sears Roebuck No. 59/71, uncat. Circa 1941.

- **259E** Gunmetal - black oxidized wheels; 1689T tender - gunmetal; 1717 litho gondola, 1719 litho box, 1722 litho caboose - N journals. Set box marked #8046 Red Diamond Fast Freight Special. Masbach Hardware Company, North Bergen, N.J. Circa 1938-41.

Pg. 121

- **261E** Black - N; 261T tender - black; 603-603-604 light red/light red/white. Set box marked 5017E. Circa 1935.

- **261E** Black - N; 261T tender - black; 610-610-612 terra-cotta/maroon/cream - N. Set box marked #1520E, Quakenbush Hardware, Patterson, N.J., uncat. Circa 1935.

- **261E** Black - N; 261T tender - black; 603-603 light red/light red/white; 604 red/black/cream. Set box marked #269E, Special set, uncat. Circa 1935.

Note: Same set has been found with red stripe on both 261E and 261T.

- **262E** Black - Br; 262T tender - black - Br; 1680 - Sunoco; 1717 litho gondola; 1719 litho boxcar; 1722 litho caboose. Set box marked 5071E. Gimbels, New York, uncat. Circa 1934.

- **262E** Black - Br; 262T tender - black; 603-603-604 red/black/cream. Set box marked 5018, uncat. Circa 1934.

- **262E** Black - N; 265T tender - black; 1685-1685-1687 vermillion/maroon/cream - black RS lettering. Car boxes marked 1685V or 1687V, and set box marked #6532E. Hearns Department Store, New York, uncat. Circa 1935.

- **262E** Black - N; 261T - black - N; 1717 litho gondola, 1719 litho boxcar; 1719 litho boxcar; 1722 litho caboose - N trim on cars; set box marked 5207E, uncat. Circa 1935-36.

- **264E** Black - N; 259T tender, 8-Wh; 607-607-608. Set box marked 49D5174, SEARS ROEBUCK, uncat. Circa 1936.

- **264E** Light red - steel rim drivers, N; 265W tender - light red, N; 610-610-612 light red/alum/alum - scroll lettering, uncat. Circa 1935-37.

- **264E** Light red - N; 265T tender - light red, N; 1685-1686-1687 vermillion/maroon/cream - black lettering. Set box marked #6511E, uncat. Circa 1936-37.

- **264E** Light red - N; 265W tender - no whistle, light red, type 1 box couplers; 603-603-604 light red/light red/white - aluminum painted observation platform, cars have fish bellies, no air tanks, latch couplers. Set box marked Outfit 6601EX - 0 Gauge Track and 1937, uncat. Circa 1937.

- **264E** Black - N; 264T tender - black, N; 1690-1690-1691 litho light red/light red/cream. Set box marked #6526E, uncat. Circa 1940.

- **289E** Black; 1689 tender - black; 804 tank, 809 dump, 831 lumber, 807 caboose. Set box marked #6504E or W in 1936, and #6544 in 1937, uncat. Circa 1936-37.

Note: While Lionel's total numbering scheme remains to be clarified, it appears that special sets in 1937 were numbered 6200-99, in 1938 were 6300-99, in 1939 were 6400-99, and in 1940 were 6500-99.

Pg. 122 • **902 GONDOLA** - Lionel Craft (boat) sticker on bottom

• **1045X** Wartime operating freight car set - 3651 lumber, 3659 dump, unloading track - all flat black, O. Circa 1942-43.

• **1506** Red; 1509 stoker tender - red; 1514 litho boxcar, 1515 litho tank, 1517 litho caboose. Set box marked 1538, uncat. Circa 1935.

Note: Same as set 1532 but 1514 boxcar added. Also sold by Sears as mail order item 49K5104 in 1935.

• **1506** Red; 1509 stoker tender - red; 1811-1811-1811 litho gray/red and gray/ivory. Set box marked 1540, uncat. Circa 1935.

Note: Similar to set 1534 but 1506 loco and three 1811 pullmans rather than two pullmans and one 1812 observation.

• **1508** Red - mechanical loco; 1509 stoker tender - red; 1518 litho dinner car, 1536 band car, 1536 litho animal car; battery included; cardboard circus tent and circus buildings, composition Mickey Mouse figure. Set box marked 49K5703, SEARS ROEBUCK, uncat. Circa 1935.

Note: Sold only as mail order item by Sears.

• **1508** Red; 1509 stoker tender - red; 1811-1811-1811 litho gray/red and gray/ivory. Set box marked 1539, uncat. Circa 1935.

Note: Same as set 1534 but three 1811 pullmans rather than two pullmans and one 1812 observation.

• **1666E** Black; 1689TW tender - black; 1679 litho box - yellow/maroon; 1680 litho tank - alum/SUNX; 1682 litho caboose - light red/light red/cream. Set box marked #1089W, and Sears Roebuck No. 59/63. Circa 1941.

• **1668** Black; 1689T tender; 3 freight cars. Set box marked R 59/71, SEARS, uncat. Circa 1940.

• **1681** Black; 1681T tender - black/red; 1514 litho box, 1515 litho tank, 1517 litho caboose. Set box marked Special Lionel Outfit 1058. Model Railroad Shop, Dunellen, N.J. Circa 1934.

• **1681E** Black - N; 1661T tender - black/red trim; 1514 litho boxcar, 1515 litho tank, 1517 litho caboose. Set box marked #1058E, uncat. Circa 1934.

• **1688** Black - N; 1689T tender - black, N; 1679 box - litho yellow/medium blue, 1680 tank - alum/MOTOR OIL, 1682 caboose - light red/light red/cream - N journals. Set box marked #6300E, 1938 executive catalog. Circa 1938.

Note: Same outfit with switches is set 6308E.

• **1688** Black - N; 1689T tender - black, N; 1690-1690-1691 light red/light red/cream - N trim. Set box marked 6314E, 1938 executive catalog. Circa 1938.

• **1688** Black; 1689T tender - black; 1679 litho box - yellow/maroon; 1680 litho tank - orange/SHELL; 1682 litho caboose - light red/light red/cream - all cars N or Black journals. Set box marked #7003, uncat. Circa 1939-41.

Note: Variety of accessories offered with these promotional sets (7003 B, C, F, W) or added track with manual switches (7004 B, C, F, W) or added tracks with electric switches (7005 B, C, F, W) in 1941 Dealer's promotion sheet.

• **1689EX** Black or gunmetal - no marker lights; 1689T tender - black or gunmetal - N; 1679X litho box - no journals, 1680X litho tank - no journals, 1682X litho caboose - yellow cupola stripe, no journals. Set box marked 6207E Lionel Jr. Freight Train and Miller Auto Supply #5541. Circa 1936.

Note: Set 6207E with switches added is set #6232E, circa 1937.

• **1689E** Gunmetal - N; 1689T tender - gunmetal, N; 1679 litho box, 1680 litho tank, 1682 litho caboose, 48W whistling station; pair of 1121 switches. Set box marked 6237E Freight Outfit and June 1937 stamp. Circa 1937.

• **1689E or W** Gunmetal - N; 1588T tender - gunmetal; 1512 litho gondola, 1514 litho box, 1515 litho tank, 1517 litho caboose. Box marked #6201E - Lionel Jr. Freight set, uncat. Circa 1937.

• **1689E** Gunmetal; 1689T tender - gunmetal; 1690-1690-1691 light red/light red/cream/dark red frame with fish belly - N trim and journals. Set box marked 6236E; set box, transformer box and instruction sheet all dated 1937, uncat. Circa 1937.

• **1689E** Black; 1588W tender - black, 4-Wh; 1673-1674-1675 Hiawatha orange/Hiawatha gray/Hiawatha orange - Fl, no journals. Set box marked 6244, uncat. Circa 1937.

Note: Same outfit with switches is set 6251W.

• **1689E**

Note: 1689E Gunmetal with 1692 and 1693 litho peacock/peacock/cream passenger cars found with set #6206E, 6206W, or 6233E (switches added). These peacock cars were made for SEARS ROEBUCK in 1936-38.

Pg. 126 • **7 LOCO AND TENDER** - all nickel

• **8E Elec.,** 337, 337,338 with track but no transformer. Set box marked

114 HARMONY DAIRY boxcar - dark olive green

213 production color for next year

381 SS pre-production

79F5196 and Mfg #360E. SEARS ROEBUCK, uncat. Circa 1931.

Note: Lionel set #360 has 332, 337, 338, but Sears set has no 332, and two 337.

• **8E Elec.,** pea green/cream; 337-337-338 pea green/pea green/cream - lettered below windows MACY SPECIAL, celluloid drumhead on observation platform - MACY SPECIAL. Set box marked Special No.2 R.H. Macy Co., New York. Circa 1932. DSS.

• **8E Elec.,** peacock/cream stripe/cream window trim, marked MACY on motor plate. R.H. MACY CO., New York. Circa 1930-31. DSS.

• **8E Elec.,** red/cream windows - diecast headlight, Super Motor; 511 flat - dark green, 515 tank - alum/Sunoco, 517 caboose - pea green/red/Br - all but caboose have N trim and journals. Set box marked 5302EX, uncat. Circa 1934.

• **10 Elec.,** peacock/black frame - combination latch couplers; 112 gondola - gray; 112 gondola - gray; 114 box - orange - CM&St.P, 98237; 113 cattle - green; 117 caboose - maroon/black - NYC&HRRR. Set box marked #4 Special. Circa 1927.

• **10 Elec.,** gray; 332-339-341 gray/gray/maroon. Set box marked Special #5. Circa 1926-28.

• **10 Elec.,** gray/dark green frame - Br; 332-339-341 gray/gray/maroon. Set box marked PO-99, uncat. Circa 1927.

• **35 PULLMAN (early)** - maroon. Circa 1912. Factory repaint. UNIQUE

• **38 Elec.,** royal blue; 35-36 royal blue/gold trim with horizontal embossed rib sides. Shown in 1914 Butler Brothers catalog. Circa 1914.

Note: May be same color as midnight blue Montgomery Ward set, circa 1913.

• **114 BOX,** dark olive green, decal lettering- #898 HARMONY CREAMERY CO. (Pittsburgh). Factory special for dairy promotion. Circa 1920.

• **213 CATTLE** - marked with blue stripe on top and sides for color of next production run. Circa 1937. UNIQUE

• **213 CATTLE,** terra cotta/maroon/maroon door guides - Br trim, N journals. Circa 1930. UNIQUE

• **219 DERRICK,** dark blue/dark green/red boom - N journals. Circa 1926. UNIQUE

• **381E Elec.,** State green/apple green subframe; 418-419-431-490 apple green/apple green/red. Loco box marked Special Green, car boxes mixed - two Lionel and two Ives, three cars lettered Ives, two cars have Ives oiling sticker. Purchased from Lionel factory in 1932, uncat. Circa 1932.

• **381E Elec.,** State green/apple green - O gauge diecast headlights, black oxidized steam type wheels; 214R - white/light blue/N; 220 floodlight - green/black/N; 212 gondola - green/N; 219 derrick - ivory/light red/green boom/light red trim; 217 caboose - light red/light red/aluminum/yellow doors, uncat. Circa 1942.

Pg. 127 • **381 SS Elec.** - originally dark green but plated by a former owner.

• **384E** Black; 384T tender - black; 309-310-312 mojave/mojave/maroon. Set box marked PO-94, Special Set, uncat. Circa 1930.

• **408E Elec.,** peacock/Br windows; 418-419-431-490 peacock/peacock/orange, 6-Wh trucks. Circa 1931-32. UNIQUE

• **408E Elec.,** dark green/Br windows;

402E mustard brown

402E set - mustard brown

1700,1701,1701, 1702 yellow/brown/yellow

418-419-431-490 dark green/dark green/cream - 6-Wh trucks. Circa 1931-32. UNIQUE

Note: 402E special sets are known to exist in cream/red and mustard brown/red.

Pg. 129 • **259E,** Black - N trim and rims on wheels; 1688W tender - black, N, 8-Wh; 1703-1701-1702, light red/light red/ maroon. Set box marked 6218W and box has R.H. Macy shipping label. Circa 1936.

• **265E,** Black; 265T tender - black; 619-617-618 medium blue/no stripe, car boxes stamped SB - ? solid blue or special blue. Circa 1937.

• **616E,** Chrome/red top and nose/red tail, red skirts and vestibules. 617-617-618 to match. Circa 1936.

• **636W,** ''City of Denver'' set

Note: A single 636W streamliner factory repaint - cream sides/brown roof and ends/brown underbody known.

• **752E,** Yellow/brown roof and underbelly, stamped M-10001 on side; 753-753-753-753-754 yellow/brown roof and underbelly - no numbers on cars, UNION PACIFIC above windows and LIONEL LINES below. Circa 1933. UNIQUE.

Note: Reportedly made for display at 1933 Chicago World Fair. Another 752 set exists with motor unit lettered CITY OF SAN FRANCISCO.

Pg. 130 • **1684,** ''Hiawatha'' 027 pre-production loco - Hiawatha orange and gray/ black top; 1673-1674-1675 Hiawatha orange/ Hiawatha gray/Hiawatha orange, Fl. Circa 1936-37.

• **1689 and 1588W,** black or gunmetal; 1673-1674-1675 all red, Fl. Set box marked 6244, (027). Circa 1937.

Note: Set 6244 with switches added is set 6251W.

• **1700,1701,1702,** Hiawatha orange/ Hiawatha gray/Hiawatha orange - Fl. Set box marked No. 5213 Lionel Jr. Streamline Outfit, uncat. Circa 1935.

• **1700E,1701,1702,** Hiawatha orange/ Hiawatha gray/Hiawatha orange. Set box marked #5214 Lionel Jr. Streamliner Outfit, uncat. Circa 1936.

Note: Also found in set boxes #6202E as described above in 1937 master catalog, #6202EX with crossing, 6204 same as 6202E without remote control or transformer, and 6204X same as 6202EX without remote control or transformer, all uncat. Circa 1937.

• **1700,1701,1702,** Hiawatha orange/ Hiawatha gray/Hiawatha orange - not Fl. Set box marked #5218, uncat. Circa 1936.

Note: Same uncataloged set is numbered 6304E in 1938 Executive catalog.

• **1700,1701,1701,1702,** alum/light red/ light red. Set box marked #6205, uncat. Circa 1937.

Pg. 135 • **001 LOCO**

Note: 1938 models have locomotive and tender attached with a drop pin and chain, while 1939-42 models have a spring held pin assembly.

00 display set

1927 miniature

1928 miniature

1929 miniature

Pg. 136 **• 0014 BOX**

Note: Transition car has been found in tuscan with LIONEL LINES decal lettering.

• 0015 TANK

silver/decal - SUNOCO herald, black lettering and #0015

black/decal - SUNOCO herald, black lettering and #2599 - cataloged 1941 but NM

• 0025 TANK

silver/decal - SUNOCO herald, black lettering

Pg. 144 **• 1927 Folder,** 3½" x 5⅞", 12 page folds

• 1928 Miniature catalog, 5¹¹⁄₁₆" x 7¹¹⁄₁₆", 32 pages

• 1929 Miniature catalog, 5¾" x 7⅝", 32 page folds

Pg. 146 **• 1935 Catalog**

Type V - red stripe top and bottom of page 4, caption page 41 "Silver Streak"

Pg. 148 **• 1937 Catalog**

Type V - caption page 22 corrected to "Worm Gear," white background on page 39

Type VI - tan quadrants on page 39, mispelled caption "Worn Gear" bottom of page 22

Note: 1937 and 1938 catalogs also found in black and white.

• 1940 Catalog

Type IV - "Lionel" outlined in white on cover, mistake page 20 - caption "Lumber car will unload"

Type V - White "Lionel" on cover, mistake page 20 - caption "Lumber car will unload"

Accessories 1901-1943

Not long after the first Lionel train appeared, the potential of including various accessory lines in the train offerings was seen. By 1902 Lionel produced an iron bridge, a spring bumper and elevated pillars for their 2⅞" gauge equipment. It is generally true, however, that during the early years of Lionel Standard gauge production they made very few accessory items. Lionel sold wood Schoenhut and metal German stations as part of the line. Beginning in 1908 Lionel included in their catalog the Ives 113 passenger station as the Lionel 121, the Ives large 123 glass dome station as the Lionel 128 and the Ives 116 passenger station as the Lionel 127. In 1914 Lionel last cataloged the glass dome station and only the small Ives design 121 station remained. In 1920 Lionel introduced its own design 121 station. By the mid 1920's, Lionel was making an extensive line of accessories from houses, bungalows, stations and signals to various sized tunnels and street lamps. Many of these accessories by their size and description were made for Standard gauge, but interestingly, numerous items were made strictly for use in either O or Standard gauge, such as different sized telegraph poles and tunnels. Generally the accessories were made to be used with all Lionel production. This production ended in 1942 at the outset of World War II.

Because most accessories were made for many years, numerous color variations occur. As with the trains, the colors change from early items in duller shades such as gray and maroon to later production in cream, terra-cotta and bright green. In the final few years of pre-war production the predominant colors are red, aluminum and white with nickel plates and trim. The accessories in the late colors are considerably more difficult to find. Other sections of this book utilize a uniform format to present the information; the variety of colors and types of accessories preclude this approach. Therefore, the accessories have been broken into groups, each with introductory comments, and developmental and color variation charts as needed. Within each group an ascending numerical listing is employed. The exception to this format is the 2⅞" accessories all of which are listed together. Lionel used many colors on accessories that never appeared on trains. These colors have been added to the color chart.

2⅞" GAUGE

1901-05

The 2⅞" gauge accessories are either track related or supplied power for the train. Thus one sees switches, bumpers, pillars for an elevated track and bridge to break the monotony of a loop of track. All are cast iron except for the wooden track ties. Since most homes were not equipped with electricity at the start of this century, both wet cells and dry cells as well as zinc plunge batteries were available to provide power for the early Lionel trains.

301 FOUR DRY CELLS AND WIRE. 1901-05.

302 COMPLETE PLUNGE BATTERY. 1902.

303 CARBON CYLINDER. 1902.

304 COMPOSITE ZINC. 1902.

305 ELECTRIC SAND, 3 pounds. 1902.

306 GLASS JAR. 1902.

310 TRACK, 12 sections, 12" long, strap steel with wood ties. 1901-05.

320 SWITCH AND SIGNAL, manual, 17½"l, 8"w, 4½"h, strap steel with wood ties. 1902-05.

330 90 DEGREE CROSSING, 6" x 6", strap steel with wood ties. 1902-05.

340 BRIDGE, suspension, 24"l, 6"w, 10"h, cast iron, black, wood ties slotted for rails, to be assembled. 1902-05.

350 **BUMPER,** 4″l, 4″w, 3″h, cast iron, black, mounted on track. 1902-05.

370 **TWO WET CELL BATTERIES.** 1902-03.

380 **ELEVATED PILLARS,** base 6″w, post 8⅜″h, cast iron, black, packed one dozen/box. 1903-05.

310 and 320

340 and 380

350

BRIDGES
1906-42

Though Lionel cataloged a No. 26 passenger foot bridge in 1906-07, the first railroad bridge was introduced in Standard gauge in 1911. O gauge bridges entered the line in 1920. Bridges manufactured by Lionel fall into two basic periods: early (1920-31) and late (1931-42). As with other accessories two basic color schemes exist: earlier subdued colors from 1920 to 1934, and later brighter colors from 1935 through 1942. Steel production predominates with most bridges designed to enable more than one span to be joined creating larger structures. One final group of bridges introduced in 1940 were also offered after World War II. High points are the No. 300 Hell Gate and No. 313 Bascule bridges.

EARLY STANDARD GAUGE BRIDGES
1906-15

26 **PASSENGER FOOTBRIDGE,** 24″l, 17″h, probably of European manufacture, tinplate, two manual semaphores, and two miniature figures. 1906.

103 **BRIDGE,** 28″l, 6½″w, simulated stone, papier-mache ornamentation. Cataloged 1913-15, probably NM.

105 **BRIDGE,** 72″l, 6″w, 6″h, wood, papier-mache ornamentation, five pieces. Cataloged 1911-14, probably NM.

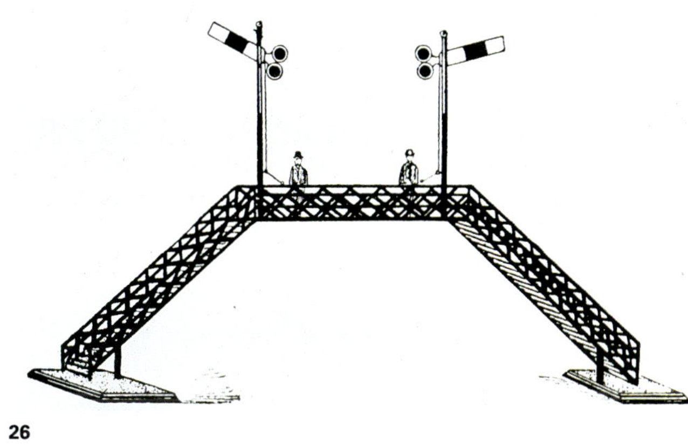

26

105

MIDDLE STANDARD GAUGE BRIDGES
1920-31

100 **TWO APPROACHES,** 28″l, 5½″w, 2″h, stamped steel, simulated concrete. For use in combinations with 104. 1920-31.
cream/black deck
cream/litho gravel
cream/gray

101 **TWO APPROACHES, CENTER SPAN,** 42″l, 6¼″w, 6½″h, see 100 and 104. 1920-31.

102 **TWO APPROACHES, TWO CENTER SPANS,** 56″l, 6¼″w, 6½″h, see 100 and 104. 1920-31.

103 TWO APPROACHES, THREE CENTER SPANS, 70″l, 6¼″w, 6½″h, see 100 and 104. 1920-31.

104 CENTER SPAN, 14″l, 6¼″w, 6½″h, stamped steel with wood finials. For use in combinations with 100 Approaches. 1920-31.
pea green/cream/black
pea green/cream/litho gravel
pea green/cream/gray

Note: Earliest attempt by Lionel to model the "Hell Gate Bridge."

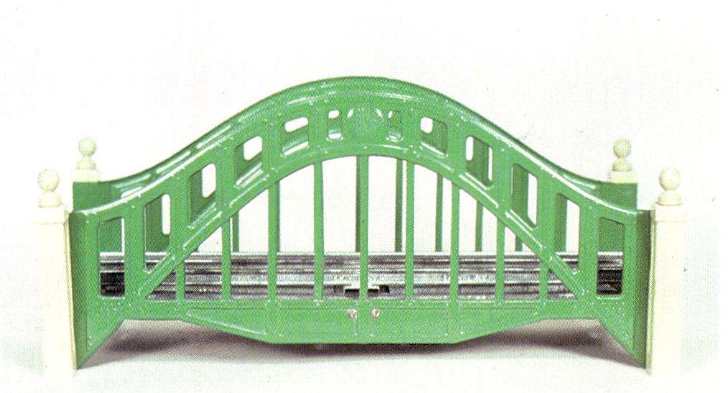

104 pea green/cream/gray

LATE STANDARD GAUGE BRIDGES
1928-42

280 BRIDGE, 14″l, 5½″w, 9″h, steel girder with one section of track. 1931-42.
red/Br
pea green/Br
olive green/N
green/N

Note: 280 bridge has been found with deck cutout to fit O gauge track, box marked **280X**.

281 TWO SPAN,28″l, 5½″w, 9″h, see 280. 1931-33 and 1935-40.

282 THREE SPAN, 42″l, 5½″w, 9″h, see 280. 1931-33 and 1935-40.

300 HELL GATE, 28¾″l, 10⅞″w, 11″h, stamped steel, simulated steel girder, concrete, stone. 1928-42.
pea green/cream/orange/Br trim and plates
pea green/cream/terra-cotta/Br trim and plates
alum/white/red/N stanchions/black railings
alum/white/red/N plates/black stanchions and railings

280 pea green/Br

280X green/N

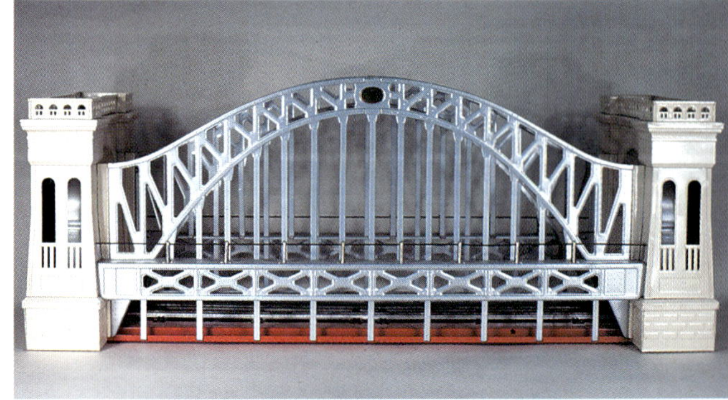

300 alum/white/red

EARLY O GAUGE BRIDGES
1920-31

105 TWO APPROACHES, 21″l, 4¼″w, 2″h, stamped steel, simulated concrete, for use in combinations with 110 Center Span. 1920-31.
cream sides/litho gravel deck
cream/gray
light mustard/gray

106 **TWO APPROACHES, CENTER SPAN,** 31½"l, 5½"w, 4"h, see 105 and 110. 1920-31.

108 **TWO APPROACHES, TWO CENTER SPANS,** 42"l, 5½"w, 4"h, see 105 and 110. 1920-31.

109 **TWO APPROACHES, THREE CENTER SPANS,** 52½"l, 5½"w, 4"h, see 105 and 110. 1920-31.

110 **CENTER SPAN,** 10½"l, 5½"w, 4"h, stamped steel, simulated steel lattice work, with or without wood finials, for use in combinations with 105 Approaches. 1920-31.
pea green/cream/litho gravel deck
pea green/cream/gray
pea green/light mustard/gray

105 cream/gray and **110** pea green/cream/gray

LATE O GAUGE BRIDGES
1931-42

270 **SINGLE SPAN,** 10"l, 6⅜"w, 3"h, steel girder with one section of track. 1931-42.
dark red/Br
red/Br or N
vermilion/N
green/N
light red/N or decal

271 **TWO SPAN,** 20"l, 6⅜"w, 3"h, see 270. 1931-33 and 1935-40.

272 **THREE SPAN,** 30"l, 6¾"w, 3"h, see 270. 1931-33 and 1935-40.

313 **BASCULE,** 21½"l, 10⅛"w, 9¼"h closed, stamped steel, operating, illuminated. 1940-42 and postwar.
alum bridge/green base/cream house/light red roof/orange windows
92 gray/green/cream/light red/orange

314 **GIRDER,** 10"l, 4½"w, 1¾"h, die cast sides, steel deck. 1940-42 and postwar.
alum
92 gray

315 **TRESTLE,** 24½"l, 4½"w, 5¾"h, stamped steel, illuminated. 1940-42 and postwar.
alum
92 gray

316 **TRESTLE,** 24½"l, 4½"w, 5¾"h, stamped steel. Uncat except in 1942 promotional flyer. Circa 1942 and postwar.
alum
92 gray

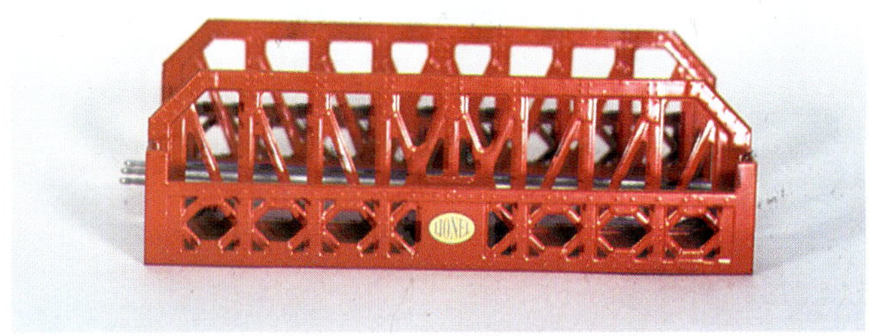

270 light red/decal

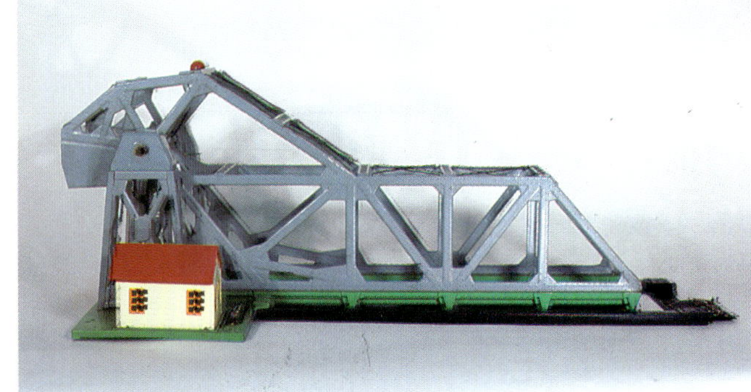

313 92 gray/green

314 92 gray

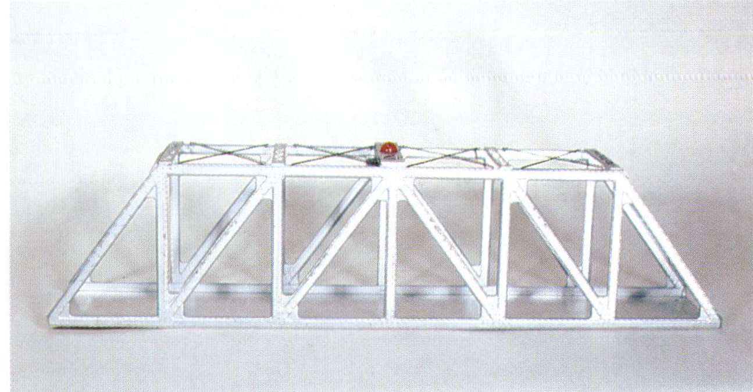

315 alum

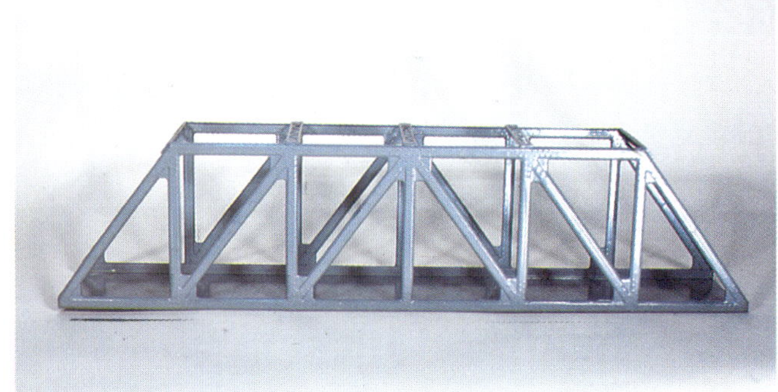

316 92 gray

TUNNELS AND MOUNTAINS
1909- 42

The first tunnels were papier-mache, from 1909 to 1920. The change to metal was made in 1920. Interestingly, Lionel's copywriters really downplayed the paper construction. In the 1925 catalog it says, ". . . with great pleasure we offer the Lionel steel tunnels, which are a wonderful improvement over the old, flimsy, papier-mache ones that users of train outfits were compelled to accept before we introduced ours. . ." In 1932 felt construction gave birth to a new line of very scenic tunnels, while metal tunnels continued to be made. Felt mountains were also made from 1933 to 1936. The longest running number in tunnels, possibly the longest running number in Lionel's entire history, was 119-starting with papier-mache in 1915, changing to metal in 1920, and ending in 1942. Dimensions of tunnels given in Lionel catalogs should be used as a general guide; measurements of actual models can be found to vary. All tunnels were handpainted in various scenic colors. These colors may not correspond to the colors in the color chart.

104 **TUNNEL,**13″l, 9″w, 9″h, Std gauge, brown with cream, gray and green speckled finish. 1909-14.

109 **TUNNEL,** 25″l, 14″w, 12½″h, Std gauge, color, material and finish are unknown. 1913-14.

118 **TUNNEL,** 10″l, O gauge, paper composition with steel brace, hotel on side, color and finish unknown. 1915-20.

118 **TUNNEL,** 8″l, 7″w, 7½″h, O gauge, metal construction, embossed stone portals, handpainted green, red, yellow, gray. 1920-32.

118L **TUNNEL,** same as 118 except illuminated. 1927.

119 **TUNNEL,** 16″l, O or Std gauge, paper composition, with steel brace, hotel on side, color and finish unknown. 1915-20.

119 **TUNNEL,** 12″l, 9″w, 8½″h, O and small Std gauge, metal construction with embossed stone portals, handpainted green, red, yellow, gray. 1920-42.

119L **TUNNEL,** same as 119 except illuminated. 1927-33.

120 **TUNNEL,** 20″l, O or Std gauge, paper composition with steel brace, hotel on side, color and finish unknown. 1915-20.

120 **TUNNEL,**17″l, 12″w, 10″h, O and Std gauge, steel construction with embossed stone portals, mountain road and Swiss chalet, handpainted in green, red, yellow, gray. 1920-27.

120L **TUNNEL,** same as 120 except illuminated. 1927-42.

123 **TUNNEL,** 18½″l, 16¼″w, 10″h, O gauge, 90 degree curve, felt with wood base, house with trees and shrubs, handpainted in various colors. 1933-42.

128 **TUNNEL,** same as metal 118 except illuminated. 1920.

129 **TUNNEL,** same as metal 119 except illuminated. 1920.

130 **TUNNEL,** same as metal 120 except illuminated. 1920.

Note: Numbers 128, 129, 130 have not been found.

130 **TUNNEL,** 26″l, 23″w, 14½″h, O gauge, 90 degree curve, steel construction with embossed stone portals, several chalets, handpainted green, red, yellow, gray. 1924-26.

130L **TUNNEL,** same as 130, except illuminated. 1927-33.

140L **TUNNEL,** 37″l, 24½″w, 20″h, O or Std gauge, 90 degree curve, steel construction with embossed stone portals, several chalets, one light inside each portal, handpainted green, red, yellow, gray. 1927-32.

915 **TUNNEL,** 65″l, 28½″w, 23½″h, O and small Std gauge, 90 degree curve, felt with wood base, handpainted in various colors. 1932-34.

915 **TUNNEL,** 60″l, 28¾″w, 20½″h, O and small Std gauge, 90 degree curve, felt with wood base, handpainted in various colors. 1935.

916 **TUNNEL,** 37″l, 30½″w, 13½″h , O gauge, 90 degree curve, felt with wood base, several chalets, handpainted in various colors. 1932.

916 **TUNNEL,** 29¼″l, 24″w, 12″h, O gauge, 90 degree curve, felt with wood base, three chalets, handpainted in various colors. 1933-42.

917 **MOUNTAIN,** 34″l, 15″w, 9½″h, O and Std gauge, felt with wood base, one chalet, handpainted in various colors. 1932-36.

918 **MOUNTAIN,** 30″l, 10″w, 9½″h, similar to 917. 1932-36.

923 **TUNNEL,** 40″l, 23″w, 16½″h, O or Std gauge, similar to 916, 90 degree curve, felt with wood base, three chalets, handpainted in various colors. 1933-42.

Note: Stamped inside "O G track & STD."

924 TUNNEL, 29¼"l, 20½"w, 13½"h, O-72 gauge, similar to 916, 90 degree curve, felt on wood base, three chalets, handpainted in various colors. 1935-42.

1022 TUNNEL, 18¾"l, 16½"w, 9¼"h, Lionel Jr. and small O gauge, 90 degree curve, felt on wood base, similar to 123 but no houses or trees, handpainted in various colors. 1935-42.

1023 TUNNEL, 13"l, 10"w, 8"h, Lionel Jr. and O gauge, felt, handpainted in various colors. 1934-42.

104 brown/speckled

109

118 (1915-20)

118 and **118L**

119 and **119L**

120

120L

123

130

140L

915 (1932-34)

915 (1935)

916 (1932)

917

918

1023

POWER STATIONS
1926-42

Modeled after the electric power stations and substations found in nearly every town, they were designed to contain a transformer. The 840 power station had a panel board with knife switches to control electrical circuits. Power stations were made from stamped steel and came in three sizes. While the 840 has been located in only one major color scheme both the 435 and 436 have been found in a variety of color combinations.

435 POWER STATION, SMALL, 5¾″l, 4½″w, 5⅜″h, smoke stack - 5¼″, base - 8⅝″ x 6″, removable skylight, type A or B transformers fit inside, Br plates. 1926-38.

436 POWER STATION, MEDIUM, 7½″l, 6″w, 6½″h, smoke stack - 5¼″, base 9¼″ x 7¼″, removable skylight, type T, C, or K transformers fit inside, Br or N plates. 1926-37.

840 POWER STATION, LARGE, 26″l, 21½″w, 18″h, illuminated, with unique light fixture, smokestacks - 8½″, removable skylights, holds two transformers, 6 knife switches. 1928-42.

- *pea green base/mojave floor/cream sides and steps/orange roof and trim/pea green windows/red water tower/red and cream sign/alum stacks/Br plates, handles, knife switches*
- green/Hiawatha gray/cream/orange/Stephen Girard green/red/red and cream/alum/Br plates and N handles and knife switches

Note: Knife switches can be found on sides, front or rear. Bayonet base automobile type bulb 840-97 used for interior light.

FIGURE 13.
435 POWER STATION

Roof	Skylight	Sides	Window Frames	Windows	Door Frames	Door	Plates	Base	Stack
Mojave	Pea Green	Mustard	Terra Cotta	Pea Green	Mojave	Wood Grained	Br	Gray	Red
Terra Cotta	Pea Green	Mustard	Dark Green	Pea Green	Dark Green	Wood Grained	Br	Gray	Red
Terra Cotta	Pea Green	Mustard	Dark Green	Pea Green	Dark Green	Maroon	Br	Gray	Red
Terra Cotta	Red	Cream	Pea Green	Orange	Dark Green	Red	Br	Gray	Red
Terra Cotta	Pea Green	Cream	Pea Green	Orange	Dark Green	Red	Br	Gray	Red
Terra Cotta	Pea Green	Cream	Pea Green	Orange	Pea Green	Maroon	Br	Gray	Red**
Terra Cotta	Red	Cream	Red	White	Red	White	Br	Gray	Alum**
Light Mojave	Red	Cream	Red	White	Red	White	Br or N	Green	Alum**

Note: First color scheme probably NM.
** Pictured

435 three variations

436 light mojave/red/cream

FIGURE 14.
436 POWER STATIONS

Roof	Skylight	Sides	Window Frames	Windows	Door Frames	Doors	Plates	Base	Stack
Mustard	Pea Green	Terra Cotta	Dark Green	Pea Green	Dark Green	Wood Grain	Br*	Gray	Red
Mustard	Pea Green	Terra Cotta	Dark Green	Pea Green	Dark Green	Maroon	Br*	Gray	Red**
Mustard	Pea Green	Terra Cotta	Pea Green	Cream	Dark Green	Wood Grain	Br	Gray	Red
Mustard	Maroon	Terra Cotta	Dark Green	Orange	Dark Green	Red	Br	Gray	Red**
Cream	Pea Green	Terra Cotta	Dark Green	Orange	Dark Green	Red	Br	Gray	Red
Cream	Pea Green	Terra Cotta	Pea Green	Orange	Dark Green	Red	Br	Gray	Red
Cream	Pea Green	Terra Cotta	Pea Green	Cream	Pea Green	Red	Br	Gray	Red
Cream	Pea Green	Terra Cotta	Pea Green	Cream	Pea Green	Red	Br	Mojave	Red
Light Mojave	Red	Cream	Red	White	Red	White	Br	Green	Alum**
Light Mojave	Red	Cream	Red	White	Red	White	N	Green	Alum

* Also found with plates lettered "Edison Service"
** Pictured

840 green base

TOWERS, TELEGRAPH POSTS AND SIGNAL BRIDGES
1920-42

Lionel's trackside structures and signals were interpretations of a wide variety of real railroad construction with an early emphasis on lighting. Later items were integrated into the control of the trains themselves. The telegraph post crossarms carry green glass or porcelain insulators. Extension arms that clip to the track are always black.

60 **TELEGRAPH POST,** stamped steel, 8 ¾"h, crossarm 2½"l, Br cap, Std gauge. 1920-35.
dark green base/yellow post/dark green crossarm
dark gray/dark gray/maroon
gray/gray/maroon
peacock/peacock/maroon
apple green/apple green/maroon
Stephen Girard green/Stephen Girard green/Stephen Girard green
alum/alum/light red

060 **TELEGRAPH POST WITH EXTENSION ARM,** stamped steel, 6 ⅞"h, crossarm 2"l, Br cap, O gauge. 1929-42.
orange base/orange post/maroon crossarm
gray/gray/maroon
green/green/red
alum/alum/light red
92 gray/92 gray/light red/Black cap

71 **TELEGRAPH POST SET,** six 60 posts, 8¾"h, Std gauge. 1921-31.
gray base/gray post/maroon crossarm
peacock/peacock/maroon
apple green/apple green/maroon

071 TELEGRAPH POST SET, six 060 posts, 6⅞"h, O gauge. 1929-42.
orange base/orange post/maroon crossarm
green/green/red
92 gray/92 gray/light red

85 TELEGRAPH POST WITH EXTENSION ARM, stamped steel, 9"h, crossarm 2½"l, Br cap, Std gauge. 1929-42.
orange base/orange post/maroon crossarm
olive green/olive green/maroon
alum/alum/light red
92 gray/92 gray/light red

86 TELEGRAPH POST SET, six 85 posts, 9"h, crossarm 2½"l, Std gauge. 1929-42.
orange base/orange post/maroon crossarm
alum/alum/light red
92 gray/92 gray/light red

92 FLOODLIGHT TOWER, stamped steel, 20¼"h, base 5" x 5", 2 lights. 1931-42.
terra-cotta base/pea green tower/Br lights and trim
light red/alum/N
light red/92 gray/N

93 WATER TOWER, stamped steel, 8"h, base 3⅝" x 3⅝". 1931-42 and postwar.

FIGURE 15.
93 WATER TOWER

Base	Structure	Tank	Center Pipe	Spout	Decal Lettering
Maroon	Terra Cotta	Pea Green	Pea Green	Br	None *
Terra Cotta	Terra Cotta	Pea Green	Pea Green	Br	None
Light Red	*Alum*	*Alum*	*Alum*	*Black*	*LIONEL TRAINS decal* *
Light Rod	92 Gray	Alum	Alum	Black	LIONEL TRAINS decal *
Light Red	92 Gray	92 Gray	Alum	Black	LIONEL TRAINS decal *
Light Red	92 Gray	92 Gray	92 Gray	Black	LIONEL TRAINS decal *

* Pictured

94 HIGH TENSION TOWER, stamped steel, 6 porcelain insulators, came with 25 ft. of copper wire, 22"h, base 5"x5". 1932-42.
terra-cotta base/gray tower/Br trim
light red/alum/N
light red/92 gray/N

096 TELEGRAPH POST, stamped steel, 6½"h, crossarm 2"l, orange base/orange post/red crossarm, Br cap, O. 1934-35.

097 TELEGRAPH POST AND SIGNAL SET, six 096 posts and one 068 warning sign. O. 1934-35.

439 PANEL BOARD, 8¼"h, 7⅛"w, stamped steel, 6 knife switches, can hold two switch controllers, illuminated. 1928-42.
crackle maroon base/Br trim
maroon/Br
alum/Br
red/N
light red/N

Note: Not all panel boards have holes to attach switch controllers.

**440
0440 SIGNAL BRIDGE,** diecast base, stamped steel structure, diecast signal heads, with 440C panel to control train operation, illuminated by 8 bulbs. 1932-35.
terra-cotta base/gray structure/maroon platform/Br trim
light red/alum/light red/N

440N SIGNAL BRIDGE, same as 440/0440 except for number plates. 1936-42.
light red base/alum structure/light red platform/N trim
light red/92 gray/light red/N

1571 TELEGRAPH POSTS, 7"h, stamped steel, Mech. 1933-38.
light red base/pea green post/red double crossarm
black/92 gray/red

Note: Part of Lionel Jr. accessory set 1569.

71 six 60 posts — peacock/maroon

060 green/green/red

071 six 060 posts - green/green/red/

86 six 85 posts - 92 gray/92 gray/light red

92 all three variations

93 five variations

94 light red/alum and terra cotta/gray

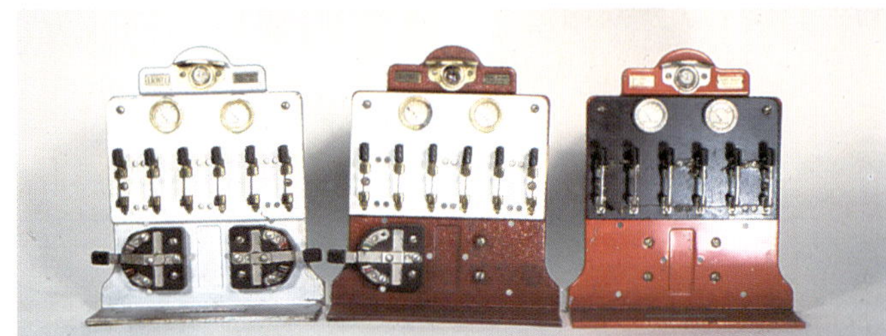

439 alum, crackle maroon, red

440N light red/92 gray and **440C** light red/N

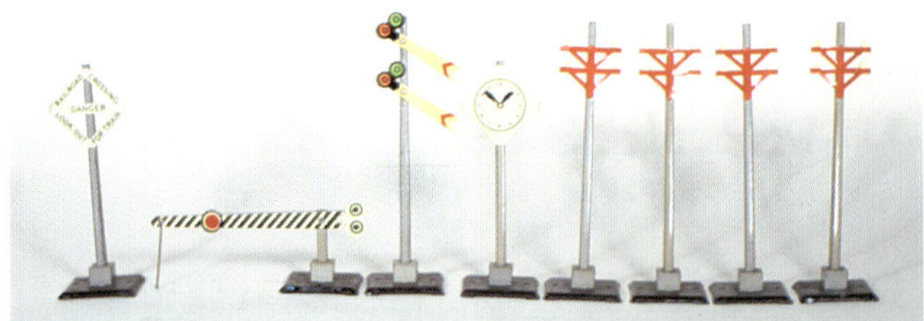

1571 92 gray/red

SEMAPHORES AND SIGNALS

1915-42

Semaphores were among the first accessories to be produced by Lionel, rather than purchased from another manufacturer. They were the predcessors of the wide variety of trackside accessories produced at Irvington. Though early semaphores and signals were illuminated and changed when trains approached, the train control feature was not introduced until 1924. Signals made before 1936 that were designated for O or Standard gauge came with a special section of track and/or the appropriate lockon. Signals made from 1936 on came with a universal lockon and contactor if needed, and are designated by the letter "N".

62 **SEMAPHORE,** 8¾"h, stamped steel, no light, red arm with red, green and yellow discs. 1920-32.
dark green base/yellow post/Br cap
pea green/pea green/Br
apple green/apple green/Br

63 **SEMAPHORE,** 14"h, sheet metal base, sheet metal post, single arm, no light, black base/orange post/dark green ladder/Br trim. 1915-20.

64 **SEMAPHORE,** 14"h, sheet metal base, sheet metal post, double arm, no light, black base/orange post/dark green ladder/Br trim. 1915-20.

65 **SEMAPHORE,** 14"h, sheet metal base, sheet metal post, single arm, with light, black base/cream post/orange ladder/Br trim. 1915-26.

66 **SEMAPHORE,** 14"h, sheet metal base, sheet metal post, double arm, with lights, black base/orange post/dark green ladder/Br trim. 1915-26.

75 **LOW BRIDGE SIGNAL,** (Telltale). 1921. NM

76
076 **BLOCK SIGNAL,** 8¾"h, stamped steel, two lights on arms,special connector base/ post. 1923-29.
mojave
white

Note: May have mojave or black lamp caps with 4 red or 4 green lens in each cap.

78
078 **AUTOMATIC TRAIN CONTROL SIGNAL,** 10¼"h, diecast base, rolled steel post, diecast head, with two bulbs and built in train control. 1924-32.
maroon base/mojave post/dark green ladder/white head
orange/cream/dark green/white

80
080 **SEMAPHORE,** 15"h, diecast base, rolled steel post. 1926-35.
terra-cotta base/mojave post/dark green ladder/Br trim
black/mojave/dark green/Br
light red/alum/orange/N

80N **SEMAPHORE,** same as 80/080 except for number, light red base/alum post/orange ladder/N trim. 1936-42.

82
082 **SEMAPHORE,** 14¾"h, diecast base, rolled steel post. 1927-35.
peacock base/cream post/orange ladder/Br or N trim
green/alum/black/N

82N **SEMAPHORE,** same as 82/082 except for number plates, green base/alum post/ black ladder/N trim. 1936-42.

84
084 **SEMAPHORE,** 15"h, diecast base, rolled steel post, hand operated, dark green base/ cream post/orange ladder/Br trim. 1927-32 (084 in 1928-32).

99
099 **TRAIN CONTROL BLOCK SIGNAL,** 12"h, diecast base and head, red, yellow and green lights. 1932-35.
red base/ivory post/red ladder/Br trim
black/ivory/black/Br
black/light mojave/red/Br

99N **TRAIN CONTROL BLOCK SIGNAL,** same as 99/099 except for number plate, light red base/alum post/light red ladder/N trim. 1936-42.

153 **BLOCK SIGNAL,** 12"h, diecast base and head. 1940-42 and postwar.
green base/alum post/orange ladder/N trim
green/92 gray/orange/N

1572 **SEMAPHORE,** 7"h, stamped steel, not illuminated. 1933-37.
light red base/pea green post
black/92 gray

Note: Part of Lionel Jr. accessory set 1569.

62 pea green/pea green/Br

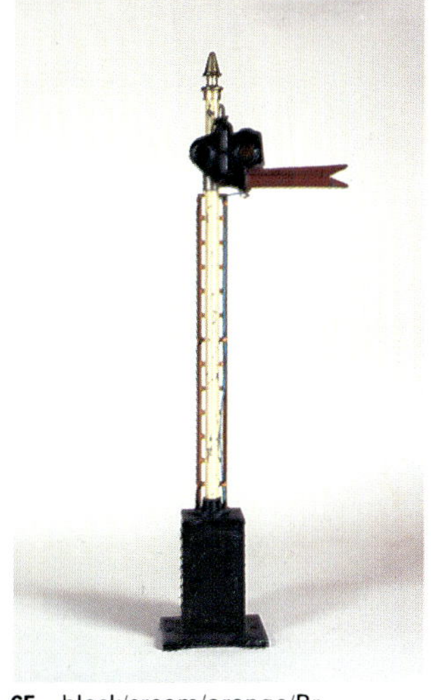

65 black/cream/orange/Br

66 black/orange/dark green/Br

76/076 mojave/black lamp caps

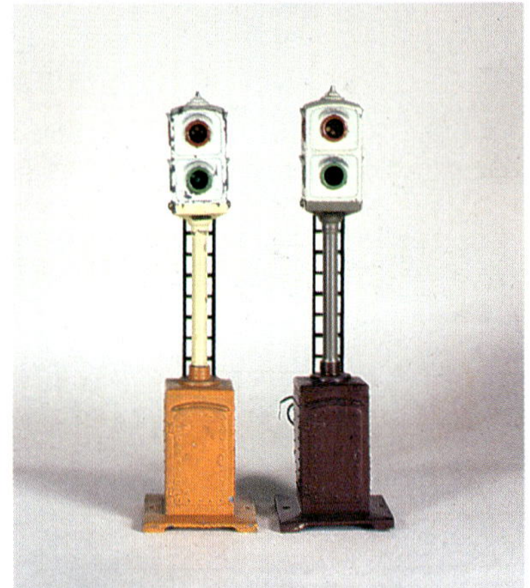

78/078 maroon/mojave and orange/cream

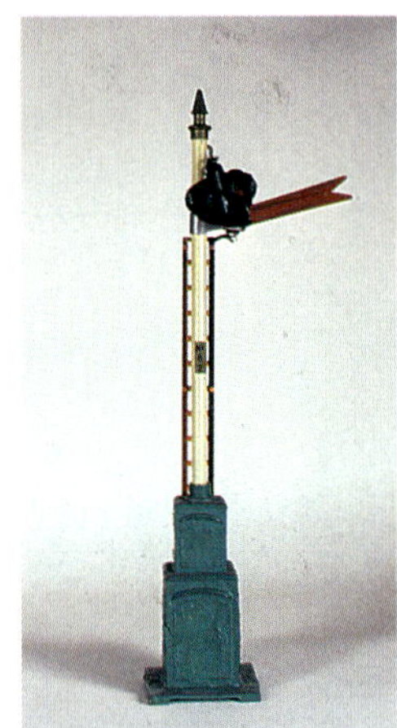

82/082 peacock/cream/Br

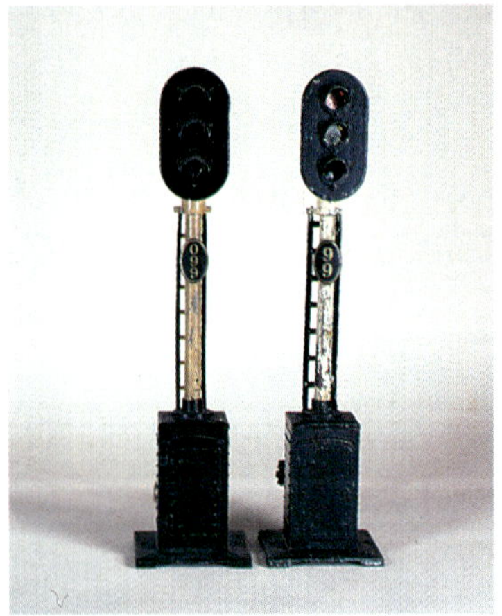

99 ivory post and 099 light mojave post

99N light red/alum/light red/N

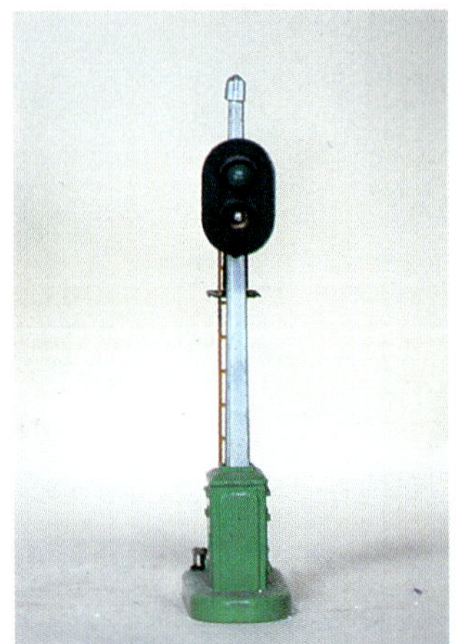

153 green/alum/orange/N

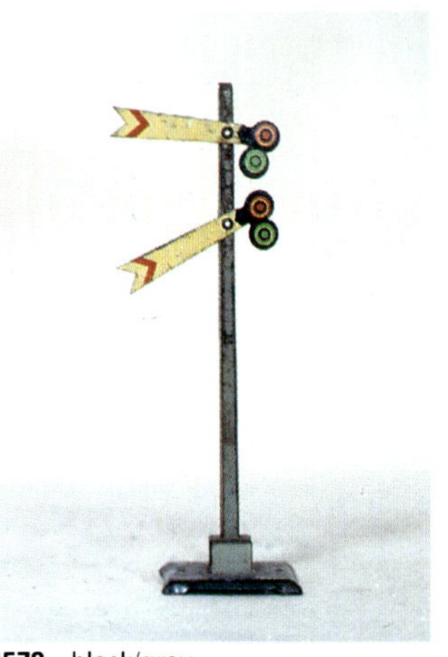

1572 black/gray

CROSSING GATES AND WARNING SIGNS
1920-42

45
045 **AUTOMATIC CROSSING GATEMAN WITH SHANTY,** 7″l, 5¾″w, 4¾″h, stamped steel, man comes out of shanty as train passes, green base/ivory building/vermilion roof/dark blue gateman. 1935-36.

45N **AUTOMATIC CROSSING GATEMAN WITH SHANTY,** same as 45/045 but for either O or Std gauge. 1937-42 and postwar.

Note: Numerous variations of the pole and crossing sign occur. Sign may be found in Br diamond shape or diecast crossbuck. Pole may be solid or open lattice work in gray, alum, or 92 gray.

46 **AUTOMATIC CROSSING GATEMAN,** electric, O gauge. 1936. NM

46 **CROSSING GATE, SINGLE,** 8½″l, 4″w, 3½″h, stamped steel except diecast stile, illuminated, with or without decal identification, special wire base for miniature bulb gave appearance of railroad lantern. 1939-42.
green base/ivory roadway/red stile/black and white main arm/alum pedestrian arm
green/ivory/red/black and white/92 gray

47 **CROSSING GATE, DOUBLE,** 16½″l, 4″w, 3½″h, stamped steel except diecast stile, illuminated, decal identification, special wire base for miniature bulbs gave appearance of railroad lanterns. 1937-42.
green base/ivory roadway/red stiles/black and white main arms/alum pedestrian arms
green/ivory/red/black and white/92 gray

68 **WARNING SIGNAL,** 8½″h, stamped steel, diamond shaped sign, early - lattice post, later - solid post, Br or N caps, white, Std gauge. 1920-39.
dark olive green/Br sign - red lettering
orange/Br - red
maroon/Br - black
pea green/Br
white/Br - red or black
peacock/Br - red

068 **WARNING SIGNAL,** 6½″h, diamond shaped sign, early - lattice post, later - solid post, Br or N cap, O gauge. 1925-42.
orange/Br sign - red lettering
olive green/Br - black
pea green/Br
alum
92 gray

69
069 **WARNING BELL,** 8½"h, stamped steel, lattice post, diamond shaped sign, Br or N caps. 1921-35.
dark green base/yellow post/Br sign - red lettering
white/Br - red
olive green post and base/Br - black
maroon/Br - black
orange/Br - black
red/N - black

Note: Had one bell from 1921-26, two bells 1927-35.

69N **WARNING BELL,** same as 69/069 but for either O or Std gauge. 1936-39.
red/N sign - black lettering
alum/N - black

76 **WATCHMAN'S SHANTY WITH RINGING BELL,** stamped steel, 7"l, 5¾"w, 4¾"h, white/red/Hiawatha orange, bell rings as train approaches. 1939-42.

77
077 **AUTOMATIC CROSSING GATE,** 11" single arm, stamped steel. 1923-35.
black base/black stile/black and white arm/N cap/Br trim
black/black/red and white/N/Br
dark gray/maroon/black and white/N/Br
dark green/maroon/green and white/N/Br
pea green/black/black and white/N/Br

Note: Illuminated from 1930 on.

77N **AUTOMATIC CROSSING GATE,** same as 77/077 except for number, black base/red stile/black and white arm/black cap/N trim. 1936-39.

79 **FLASHING SIGNAL,** 11½"h, diecast base and crossarm, rolled steel post, 2 flashing lights on crossarm, red light in base. 1928-40.
cream post and base/gold crossarm/Br trim
alum/alum/Br or N

83 **TRAFFIC AND CROSSING SIGNAL,** 6¾"h, diecast, illuminated. 1927-42.
mojave base/cream sides/white head
red/cream/flesh
light red/cream/white

87 **RAILROAD CROSSING SIGNAL,** 6¾"h, diecast, illuminated. 1927-42.
mojave base/orange sides/ivory head
mojave/Stephen Girard green/ivory
dark green/Stephen Girard green/flesh
dark green/yellow/ivory
green/yellow/ivory

Note: Celluloid bull's eye may be found in light orange, orange, or red with or without black crescent.

152 **CROSSING GATE,** 10½"l main arm, diecast base. 1940-42 and postwar.
• *light red base and stile/alum main arm/ alum pedestrian arm/N trim*
• light red/92 gray/92 gray/N
• light red/white/white/N

154 **AUTOMATIC HIGHWAY SIGNAL,** two flashing lights on crossarm, 4"l, 2"w, 8⅜"h, diecast base, stamped steel post, crossbuck with 2 red lights. 1940-42 and postwar.
black base/alum post/black crossarm
Hiawatha orange/alum/black
black/92 gray/black

1045 **OPERATING WATCHMAN,** no shanty, 4"l, 4"w, 7"h, stamped steel, swings flag as train approaches, vermilion base/alum or 92 gray post/Br sign/medium or dark blue man. 1938-42 and postwar.

1046 **MECHANICAL GATEMAN WITH GATE,** 1936. NM.

1573 **WARNING SIGNAL,** 6"h, stamped steel, small diamond shape, part of Lionel Jr. 1569 accessory set. 1933-37.
light red base/pea green post/litho sign
black/92 gray/litho

1575 **CROSSING GATE,** 5½" arm, stamped steel, not illuminated. 1933-37.
light red base/pea green post/black, white, and red main arm
92 gray/black, white, and red

Note: 1575 found in 1569 accessory sets only, never for sale separately.

45/045/45N green/ivory/red

46 green/ivory/92 gray pedestrian arm

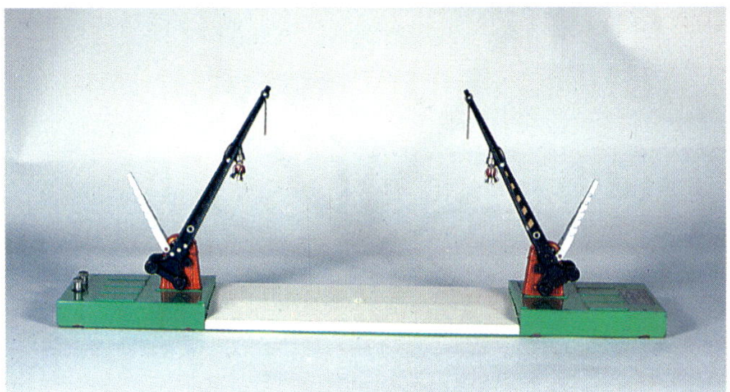

47 green/ivory/alum pedestrian arms

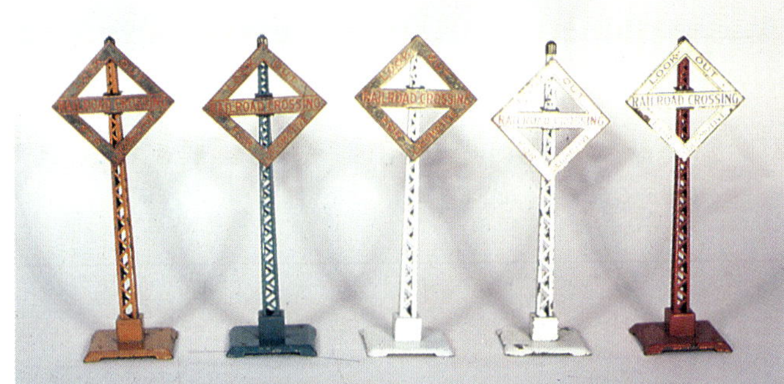

68 orange, peacock, white, maroon

068 olive green, alum, 92 gray

69/069 red, orange, olive green, white, maroon

76 white/red/Hiawatha orange

77N black/white/red

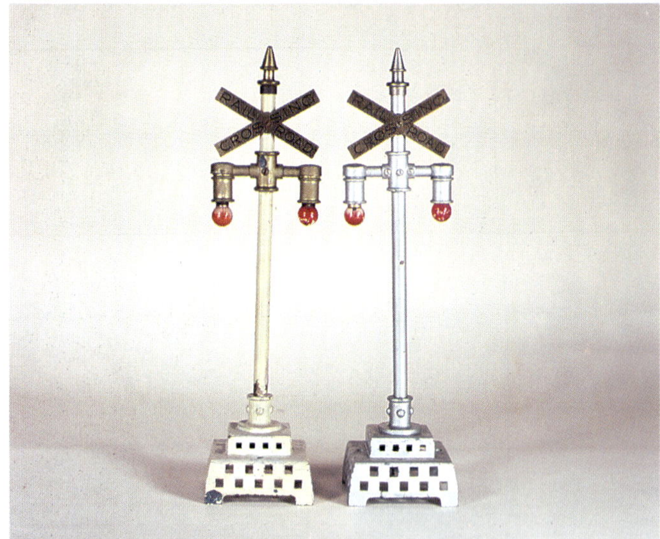

79 cream and alum

152 light red/alum and light red/white

154 alum/Hiawatha orange/black

1045

1573 and 1575 light red/pea green

83 three variations

87 three variations

RAILROAD BUILDINGS
1923-42

092 **SIGNAL TOWER,** 5″l, 4″w, 5½″h, stamped steel except pagoda roof made of brass, no chimney, interior light, number RS on bottom. 1923-28.

- mojave base/white sides/red roof/pea green windows/red doors - NM
- *mojave/terra-cotta/pea green/ivory/maroon*
- light mustard/terra-cotta/pea green/ivory/wood grained or maroon
- ivory/light terra-cotta/pea green/ivory/wood grained

200 **TURNTABLE,** 17″diameter, Std gauge, stamped steel, manual control. 1928-36.
pea green base/red center/Br trim
black/red/Br

437 **ILLUMINATED SWITCH SIGNAL TOWER,** 10¼″l, 8⅜″w, 8⅞″h, stamped steel, 6 knife switches and bracket for switch controllers on back, interior light, bay window. 1926-37.

FIGURE 16.
437 BAY WINDOW SWITCH AND SIGNAL TOWERS

Base	Sides	Stripe	Roof	Windows	Doors	Chimney
Mojave	Orange and Mustard	Cream	Pea Green	Peacock	Maroon	Red*
Mojave	Terra Cotta and Mustard	Cream	Pea Green	Peacock	Maroon	Red
Mojave	Terra Cotta and Cream	Cream	Peacock	Pea Green	Maroon	Brick Litho
Mojave	Terra Cotta and Cream	Cream	Peacock	Orange	Red	Red
Red	Cream	Dark Brown	Orange	Green	Red	Cream*

* Pictured

438 **ILLUMINATED SIGNAL TOWER,** 5″l, 4″w, 12″h, base 6″ x 4¾″, stamped steel except pagoda roof made of brass, interior light, 2 knife switches on back. 1927-40.

Note: Has been found with neither knife switches nor mounting holes.

441 **WEIGHING SCALE,** 29½″l, 9½″w, 4¾″h, Std gauge, stamped steel, diecast beam, brass weights, illuminated, pea green base/cream structure/crackle maroon roof/terra-cotta window frames. 1932-36.

FIGURE 17.
438 SWITCH TOWERS

Base	Structure	Sides	Roof	Windows	Doors	Chimney	Ladder	Plates
Mojave	Pea Green	Orange	Maroon	Ivory	Red	Brick Litho	Br	Br*
Mojave	Pea Green	Orange	Maroon	Ivory	Red	Cream	Br	Br*
Light Mojave	Pea Green	Orange	Red	Ivory	Red	Brick Litho	Br	Br
Black	Alum	White	Light Red	Light Red	Light Red	White	Light Red	N*

* Pictured

442 **DINER,** 10½″l, 5½″w, 3″h, 610 series O gauge car body, wood base with shrubbery, illuminated, ivory body/light red roof/light red trim - RS alum. 1938-42.

444 **ROUNDHOUSE SECTION,** 24″ back, 8¾″ front, 14½″h, stamped steel, illuminated, terra-cotta walls/129 sand beams/pea green roof/dark green skylights/maroon windows and doors/Br trim. 1932-34.

Note: Sheet metal pieces are embossed "Made in Italy." A 444-18 clip was used to hold sections together. Uses special 20″ Std track section.

092 two variations

438 three variations

200 pea green/red

441 pea green/cream/crackle maroon

437 two variations

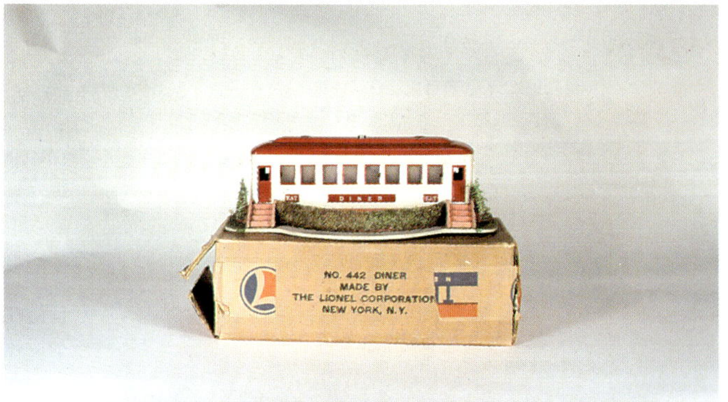

442 cream/red/red

444 terra cotta/sand/pea green

STATION ACCESSORIES
1928-42

157 HAND TRUCK, 1⅝"l, 1⅛"w, 3⅛"h, diecast, red or vermilion chassis/black wheels and skids, see 163. 1930-42.

161 BAGGAGE TRUCK, 5⅛"l, 2⅛"w, 2⅝"h, stamped steel, pea green or green chassis/ black wheels and black or N couplers, see 163. 1930-42.

162 DUMP TRUCK, 4¾"l, 2¾"w, 2½"h, stamped steel, black wheels and black or N couplers, see 163. 1930-42.
peacock dump/orange chassis
peacock/light orange
medium blue/light orange
medium blue/yellow

163 FREIGHT STATION SET, consists of two 157, one 161, and one 162. 1930-42.

Note: Items in set available for separate sale only in 1930-32.

205 LCL CONTAINERS, set of three, 3½"l, 3"w, 4"h, stamped steel, hinged doors, one set of lifting chains, paper labels - "Manufactured under license granted by LCL Container Corp." made to fit 512 and 212 gondolas, dark green/Br trim - gold RS. 1930-38.

Note: No chains after 1932.

208 TOOL SET, consists of six of the following tools in a stamped steel tool box, 4½"l, 2⅝"w, 2⅛"h, shovel, hammer, fork, pincers, pick, sledge, hatchet, hoe or rake, tools are generally nickel plated cast iron, Std. 1928-42.
gray tool box/Br handles/gold RS lettering
gray/Br/black
alum/N/black
92 gray/N/black

Note: Some early tools have wooden handles. Between 1928 and 1932 tool set sold only with work train, thereafter available for separate sale.

209 SET OF 4 BARRELS, natural wood, both barrel and drum shapes, 2¼"h, Std. 1928-42.

0209 SET OF 6 BARRELS, natural wood, both barrel and drum shapes, 1½"h, O gauge. 1930-42 and postwar.

Note: 209 and 0209 between 1930 and 1932 were sold only with work train, thereafter available for separate sale.

308 SET OF YARD SIGNS, 5 diecast metal signs on posts with rectangular base, white/black lettering. 1940-42 and postwar.

812T TOOL SET, consists of Std gauge size tools - spade, pick and shovel sold only with O gauge work train sets. 1930-41.

Note: Not in metal box but in Lionel cardboard box with added end label lettered 812T.

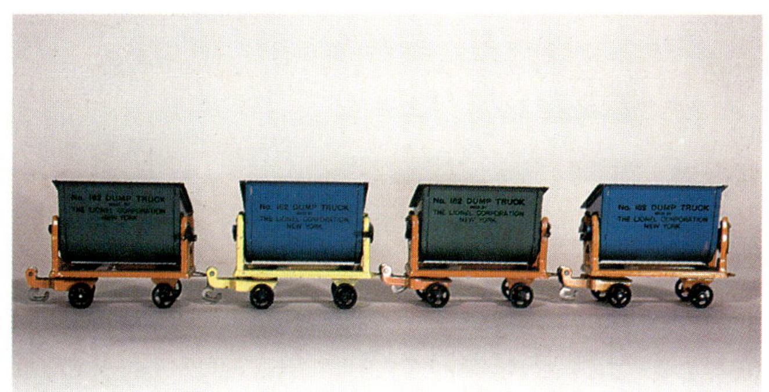
162 four variations

163 two sets

205

208 gray, alum, and 92 gray tool boxes

209

RAILROAD STATIONS

1906-42

The earliest stations sold by Lionel appear to be of German manufacture, but this cannot be verified. Following the introduction of these stations in 1906, Lionel sold the Ives stations through 1916. They were constructed of lithographed steel.

In 1917 Lionel sold stations manufactured by Schoenhut. These stations were quite large and constructed of composition board and wood. Lionel indicated in their 1917 catalog that the No. 121 station ". . . is substantially constructed of sheet steel and is hand enameled. It must not be confused with the cheap lithographic railway stations that have heretofore been sold . . . windows are fitted with glass and sashes slide up and down . . ." These comments are conflicting in that the Schoenhut station did have glass windows but were not of steel construction.

The 1920 catalog still shows the Schoenhut 121 station but deleted the reference to steel construction. A late 1920/21 catalog features the *new* steel stations which carried the numbers 121 as well as 122-124. This style of station was carried for many years. Several smaller stations were introduced in later years. The 129 station terrace was added to complement the early Lionel City station and was used later with the 112 series station.

In 1931 Lionel introduced their second series of stations in two sizes. These stations were replicas of terminal stations with embossed steel walls to represent limestone construction. Lionel also sold small transformer stations which were originally sold as Winner line items. These appeared in the early 1930's.

EARLY STATIONS

1906-42

24 **RAILWAY STATION,** 11″l, 7½″w, 8″h, heavy tin - probably German manufacture, cast lead window frames, maroon base/black and cream simulated brick sides/maroon window and door frames/flat red and black roof/lettered OCEANSIDE. 1906.

25 **OPEN RAILWAY STATION,** 11″l, 11″w, 8″h, heavy tin - probably German manufacture, none identified. 1906.

27 **STATION,** 21″l, 9″w, 10″h, similar to Ives 116, multicolor lithography. 1909-14.

28 **DOUBLE STATION WITH LEADED GLASS DOME,** 18½″l, 22 ½″w, 11″h, similar to Ives 123, multicolor lithography. 1909-14.

121 **SPECIAL STATION,** 14″l, 10″w, 9″h, similar to Ives 113, lettered TICKET OFFICE over window, multicolor lithography. 1909-17.

Note: Usual contemporary Ives 113 same lithography except lettered TELEGRAPH OFFICE over window.

121 **STATION,** 13½″l, 9″w, 13″h, embossed composition board, Schoenhut manufacture, windows fitted with glass, doors swing, various colors. 1917-20.

121X **STATION,** composition board, Schoenhut manufacture, same as 121 but 2 electric lights. 1917-20.

121 **LIONEL CITY STATION,** 13½″l, 9″w, 13″h, embossed stamped steel, no lights. 1920-26.

122 **LIONEL CITY STATION,** same as 121 but one interior light. 1920-31.

123 **LIONEL CITY STATION,** same as 121 but one interior 110-volt light. 1920-23.

124 **LIONEL CITY STATION,** same as 121 but 2 platform corner lights and one interior light. 1920-30 and 1933-36.

125 **LIONELVILLE STATION,** 10¼″l, 7¼″w, 7″h, stamped steel, no embossing, no lights. 1923-25.

126 **LIONELVILLE STATION,** same as 125 but with one interior light. 1923-36.

FIGURE 18.
LIONEL CITY STATIONS

Roof	Sides	Window Frames	Windows	Corner Stones	Doors	Departure Boards	Lights	Base	Chimney	Notes
Pea Green	Flat State Brown	Ivory	Pea Green	Ivory	Pea Green	No	N	Dark Hiawatha Gray	Ivory	124*
Pea Green	Burnt Orange	Mustard	Pea Green	Mustard	Maroon	No	None	Light Gray	Mustard	124
Pea Green	Burnt Orange	Ivory	Pea Green	Dark Ivory	Maroon	Yes	N	Light Gray	Ivory	124
Pea Green	Flat Light Terra Cotta	Light Terra Cotta	Pea Green	Light Terra Cotta	Pea Green	No	N	Flat Gray	Light Terra Cotta	121,122, 123,124
Pea Green	Light Terra Cotta	Mustard	Pea Green	Mustard	Wood Grained	No	N	Light Gray and Yellow Speckled	Mustard	121,122, 123,124*
Pea Green	Terra Cotta	Light Mustard	Pea Green	Light Mustard	Light Red	Yes	Gold Paint	Gray	Light Mustard	122,124
Light Red	Tan	Ivory	White	Ivory	White	Yes	Alum Paint or N	Green	Ivory	124,134
Pea Green	Light Terra Cotta	Mustard	White	Light Terra Cotta	Wood Grained	No	N	Litho Gray & Yellow Speckled	Light Terra Cotta	121,122, 123,124
Pea Green	Burnt Orange	Mustard	Pea Green	Mustard	Maroon	No	N	Litho Gray & Yellow Speckled	Light Terra Cotta	124

* Pictured

FIGURE 19.
LIONELVILLE STATIONS

Roof	Sides	Windows	Ticket Window	Door Frames	Front/Back Doors	Side Doors	Base	Chimney	Notes
Maroon	Crackle Red	Ivory	Br	Ivory	Pea Green	Pea Green	Mojave	Brick Litho	126
Pea Green	Crackle Red	White	Br	Ivory	Pea Green	Pea Green	Mojave	Brick Litho	126
Pea Green	Crackle Red	Ivory	Br	Ivory	Pea Green	Pea Green	Mojave	Brick Litho	126
Pea Green	Brick Litho	White	Br	Dark Green	Stephen Girard Green	Maroon	Flat Light Gray	Brick Litho	126
Pea Green	Brick Litho	White	Br	Dark Green	Mojave	Mojave	Gray	Brick Litho	125,126
Pea Green	Brick Litho	White	Br	Dark Green	Maroon	Mojave	Gray	Brick Litho	125,126*
Pea Green	Crackle Red	White	Br	Ivory	Pea Green	Pea Green	Mojave	Crackle Red	126
Light Red	Mustard	White	Light Red	White	Light Red	Light Red	Green	Mustard	126,136*
Light Red	Cream	White	Light Red	White	Light Red	Light Red	Green	Cream	136*
Light Red	Yellow	White	Light Red	White	Light Red	Light Red	Green	Yellow	136
Light Red	Mustard	White	Light Red	White	Light Red	Light Red	Green	Yellow	136

* Pictured

FIGURE 20.
LIONELTOWN STATIONS

Roof	Sides	Window Frames	Windows	Door Frames	Doors	End Vent	Base	Chimney	Plates	Notes
Maroon	Dark Ivory	Dark Green	Stephen Girard Green	Dark Green	Wood Grained	Stephen Girard Green	Flat Hiawatha Gray	Brick Litho	Br	127
Maroon	Butternut	Dark Green	Stephen Girard Green	Dark Green	Wood Grained	Stephen Girard Green	Flat Gray	Brick Litho	Br	127
Maroon	Mustard	Dark Green	Apple Green	Dark Green	Wood Grained	Light Apple Green	Gray	Brick Litho	Br	127*
Maroon	Mustard	Dark Green	Apple Green	Dark Green	Wood Grained	Peacock	Gray	Brick Litho	Br	127
Dark Red	Ivory	Peacock	Cream	Peacock	Maroon	Orange	Mojave	Brick Litho	Br	127
Red	Ivory	Peacock	Cream	Peacock	Red	Orange	Mojave	Brick Litho	Br	127*
Red	Ivory	Peacock	Cream	Peacock	Maroon	Orange	Mojave	Brick Litho	Br	127
Light Red	White	Peacock	Yellow	Peacock	Light Red	Peacock	Mojave	Brick Litho	Br	127
Light Red	White	Dark Green	Peacock	Dark Green	Maroon	Peacock	Gray	Brick Litho	Br	127
Light Red	White	Green	Yellow	Green	Yellow	Green	Mustard	White	N	127,137
Light Red	Ivory	Peacock	Yellow	Peacock	Light Red	Peacock	Mojave	Yellow	Br	127
Light Red	White	Green	Yellow	Green	Yellow	Green	Light Mojave	White	N	127,137*
Light Red	Ivory	Peacock	Cream	Peacock	Red	Peacock	Light Mojave	Yellow	Br	127

* Pictured

127 LIONELTOWN STATION, 7″l, 3½″w, 4½″h, stamped steel, embossed walls to represent plank siding, one interior light. 1923-36.

128 LIONEL CITY STATION AND TERRACE PLATFORM, terrace in combination with the following stations 121, 122, or 124 stations (1928-30), 112 or 113 stations (1931-34), and 115 stations (1935-42). 1928-42.

129 TERRACE STATION PLATFORM, 31½″l, 18″w, 12″h, stamped steel, torch lights, landscaped flower beds and flagpole, same as 128 but without station. 1928-33 and 1935-42.
light mojave/pea green lattice/gold light posts
cream/cream/alum

24 maroon/black and cream/flat red and black

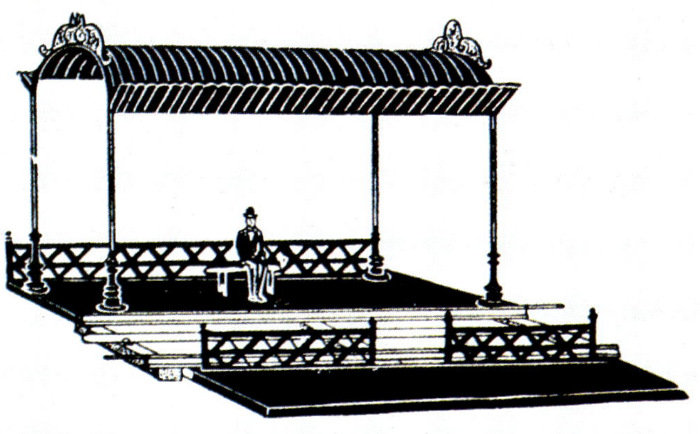
25

121 (1917-20)

28

124 pea green/light terra cotta/mustard

121 Special, multicolor lithography, lettered 'TICKET OFFICE'

125,126,136 three variations

127,137 three variations

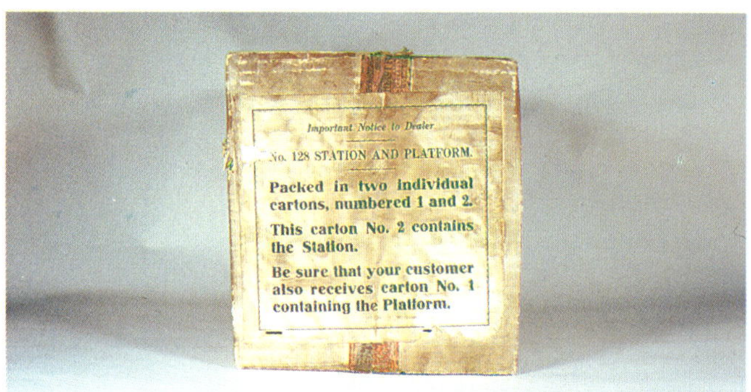

Important Notice to Dealer

No. 128 STATION AND PLATFORM.

Packed in two individual cartons, numbered 1 and 2.

This carton No. 2 contains the Station.

Be sure that your customer also receives carton No. 1 containing the Platform.

128

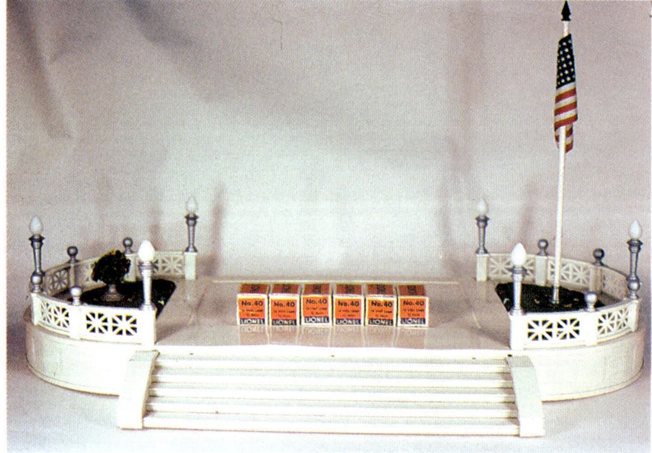

129 sand/cream/alum

LATER STATIONS
1930-42

48W **WHISTLING STATION,** 5½″l, 3¾″w, 3¾″h, same as 1012X and 1560 stations but with whistle, lithographed steel in bright colors. 1937-42.

112 **STATION,** 13¾″l, 9½″w, 9″h, stamped steel, flat base, embossed walls and corners, removable skylight grill, interior light, flat roof, 4 front doors, clock over doors. 1931-35.

- mojave base/apple green roof/pea green skylight/ apple green windows/ maroon doors/ivory sides
- terra-cotta/apple green/pea green/apple green/maroon/129 sand
- light red base, roof, skylight, windows and doors/ivory sides

113 **STATION,** same as 112, but with 2 gold exterior lighting brackets beside doors. 1931-34.

Note: Skylights for 113 have been found in apple green or pea green.

114 **LARGE STATION,** 19¾″l, 9½″w, 9″h, stamped steel, similar to 113 but 6″ longer, 2 interior and 2 exterior lights, 2 removable skylight grills. 1931-34.

- mojave base/apple green roof/pea green or apple green skylights/apple green windows/maroon doors/ivory sides/gold exterior lights
- terra-cotta/apple green/pea green or apple green/apple green/maroon/129 sand/ gold

115 **STATION,** same as 113 but with automatic train control, light red base/beige sides/light red windows, doors, trim and skylight/alum light brackets. 1935-42 and postwar.

116 **LARGE STATION,** same as 114 but with automatic train control, light red base/ beige sides/light red windows, doors, skylights and trim/alum light brackets. 1935-42.

117 **STATION,** same as 115 but without exterior lights. 1936-42.

134 **LIONEL CITY STATION,** same as 124 but with automatic train control. 1937-42.

136 LIONELVILLE STATION, same as 126 but with automatic train control. 1937-42.

137 LIONELTOWN STATION, same as 127 but with automatic train control. 1937-42 and postwar.

155 ILLUMINATED FREIGHT SHED, 18″l, 8″w, 11″h - stamped steel, 2 lights under embossed roof. 1930-42.
- cream foundation and underside roof/ terra-cotta floor/maroon roof/pea green posts - Br trim
- ivory/light red/light gray/alum - N

156 ILLUMINATED STATION PLATFORM, 12″l, 3¼″w, 5⅛″h, bakelite base and roof, diecast posts, 2 lights under roof, bright green base/vermilion roof/alum or 92 gray posts/black fence with or without advertising signs. 1939-42 and postwar.

158 STATION PLATFORM SET, two 156 platforms and 136 station. 1940-42.

1012 TRANSFORMER STATION, 5½″l, 3¾″w, 3¾″h, contains transformer, removable roof, lithographed steel in bright colors. Winner 1930.

1012K STATION, 5½″l, 3¾″w, 3¾″h, same as 1012 but no transformer, shown as part of sets 173 and 173S. 1932-33.

1017 TRANSFORMER STATION, same as 1012 with rheostat for Winner and Lionel-Ives. Winner 1931 and Lionel-Ives 1933.

1027 TRANSFORMER STATION, same as 1017 with spring loaded contactor but for Lionel Jr. 1934.

1028 TRANSFORMER STATION, same as 1027 for Lionel Jr. 1935.

1560 STATION, same as 1012K, for mechanical sets. 1933-37.

48W multicolored lithography

113 terra cotta/apple green/pea green

116 light red/beige/light red/alum

155 cream/terra-cotta/maroon

156

1017 multicolored lithography

LAMPS

1920-42

35 **BOULEVARD LAMP,** 6⅛"h, single diecasting except for plastic lamp shade and ornate cap, clear bulb - O. 1940-42 and postwar.
alum
92 gray

52 **LARGE LAMP POST,** 10½"h, single diecasting, alum, 63-11 opal bulb. 1933-41.

53 **SMALL LAMP POST,** 8½"h, single diecasting, 63-11 opal bulb. 1931-42.
light mojave
light ivory
alum

54 **SMALL DOUBLE GOOSENECK LAMP POST,** 9½"h, cast iron base, rolled sheet metal post, metal filigree and reflectors, frosted bulb. 1929-35.
maroon
pea green
State brown
green

56 **PARK LAMP POST,** 7½"h, diecast base, metal tube post, 2 sheet metal stampings hold the celluloid lamp shade and sheet metal cap, clear bulb. 1924-42 and postwar.
dark gray
gray
mojave
pea green
copper-bronze
alum
green

Note: Copper-bronze apparently found only on 922 illuminated lamp terrace.

57 **BROADWAY LAMP POST,** 7½"h, diecast base, rolled sheet metal post, 2 sheet metal stampings hold celluloid lamp shade, various combinations of BROADWAY, MAIN STREET, 21st STREET, 42nd STREET or FIFTH AVENUE, stamped in silver or black lettering, clear bulb. 1922-42.
gray
orange
yellow

58 **SMALL GOOSENECK LAMP POST,** 7½"h, diecast base, metal tube post, metal filigree and lamp reflector, base cutout, clear round or frosted pear shaped bulb. 1922-42 and postwar.
maroon
brown
peacock
pea green
1685 cream
cream
green
medium green
alum
92 gray

59 **MEDIUM GOOSENECK LAMP POST,** 8⅝"h, cast iron base, rolled sheet metal post, metal filigree and reflector, clear round or frosted pear shaped bulb. 1920-36.
maroon
dark green
mojave
olive green
pea green
State brown
red
light red

61 **LARGE GOOSENECK LAMP POST,** 12¾"h, early - 2⅜" x 2¼" cast iron base, rolled sheet metal post, metal filigree, 1 9/16" diameter reflector; later - 2¼" x 2¼" cast iron base, 1¼" diameter lamp reflector; clear round or frosted pear shaped bulb. 1914-32 and 1934-36.
black
maroon
dark green
mojave
olive green
State brown

63 **LARGE DOUBLE LAMP POST,** 12¾"h, diecast, alum, 63-11 opal bulbs. 1933-42.

64 **HIGHWAY STREET LAMP,** 6¾"h, diecast base, metal tube post, sheet metal arm, diecast bracket, green, 64-15 opal bulb - O. 1940-42 and postwar.

67 **LARGE DOUBLE GOOSENECK LAMP POST,** 12⅝"h, early - 2 9/16" x 2½" cast iron base, rolled sheet metal post, 1 9/16" diameter lamp reflector; later - 2¼" x 2¼" cast iron base, 1¼" diameter lamp reflector; clear round or frosted pear shaped bulbs. 1915-32.
dark green
State green

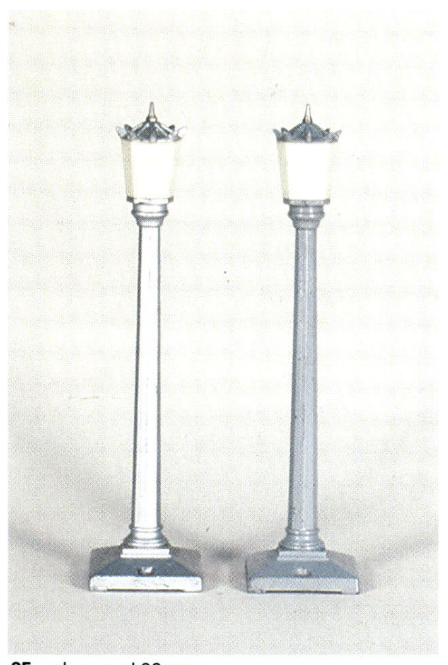

35 alum and 92 gray

54 maroon and pea green

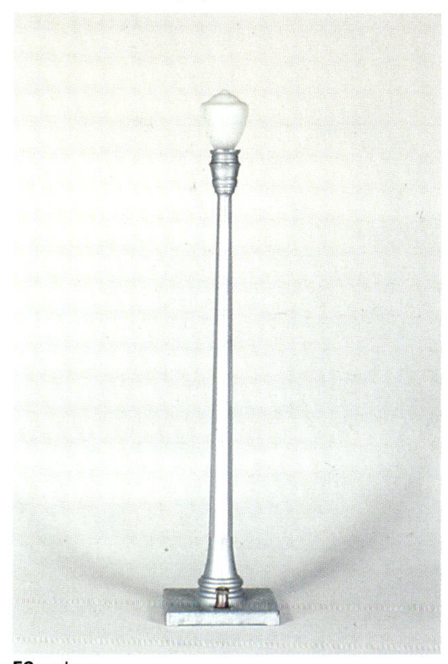

52 alum

56 pea green and green

58 peacock, maroon, and cream

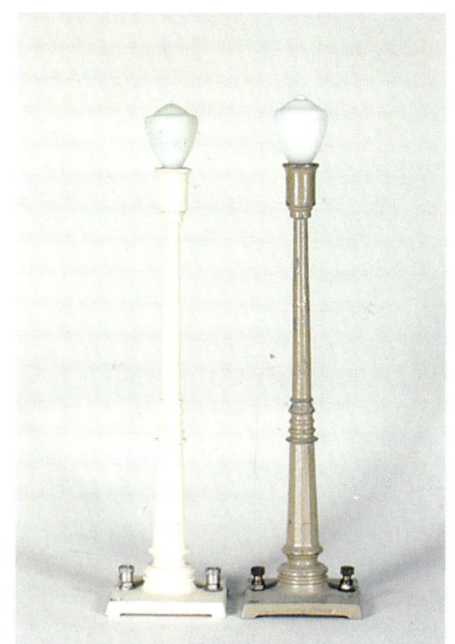

53 light ivory and light mojave

57 yellow and orange

59 dark green and olive green

Comparison of **58, 59, 61**

67 early and late castings - dark green

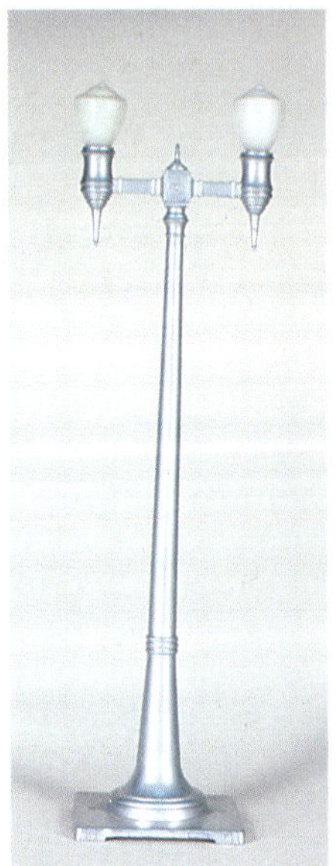

63 alum

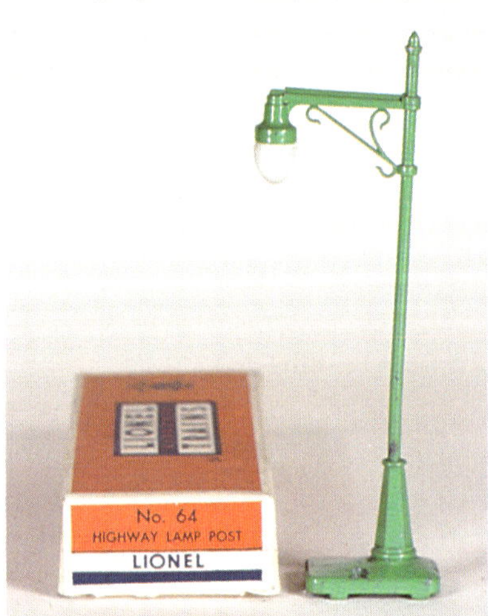

64 green

FLAGS AND CLOCK

1923-42

89 **FLAG STAFF AND FLAG,** 14″h, 2½″ x 2½″ sheet metal base, silk U.S. flag, ivory base and pole, black or gold wood finial. 1923-34.

90 **FLAG STAFF AND FLAG,** 14″h, 4½″ diameter round metal base with miniature grass plot and flower border, silk U.S. flag, ivory pole/green grass plot/black wood finial. 1927-42.

927 **ORNAMENTAL FLAG PLOT,** 14¼″h, oval base 16″l, 9″w, with miniature grass plot, trim hedge and shrubbery, silk U.S. flag, ivory pole/green grass and tan walkways/ black wood finial. 1937-42.

1574 **CLOCK,** stamped steel, part of Lionel Jr. accessory set 1569. 1933-37.
- *light red base/pea green post/cream litho clock face*
- black/92 gray/cream litho

89 and 90

927

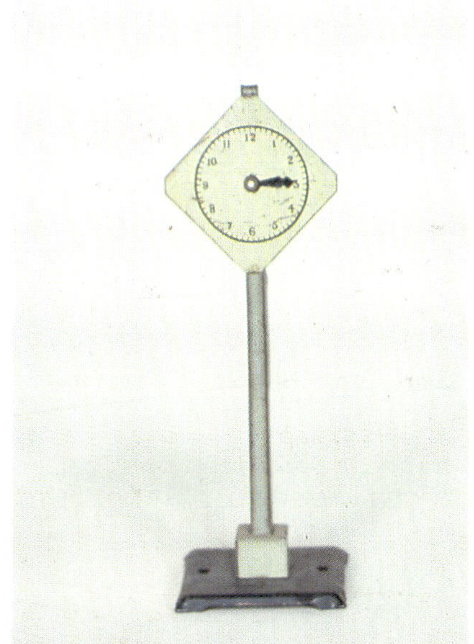
1574 black/92 gray/cream

RESIDENTIAL HOMES AND SCENIC PLOTS
1923-42

Scenic plots appear to have been made from general plans and may have infinite variety. After 1932 bungalows and villas were only available on plots.

184 **BUNGALOW,** 4¾″l, 2¾″w, 4″h, stamped sheet metal, illuminated, one dormer on left side with chimney at back, gabled roof. 1923-32.

Note: Exists with dormer on right side with chimney at back.

185 **BUNGALOW,** same as 184 but no interior light. 1923-24.

186 **BUNGALOW SET (LIONELVILLE),** five 184 illuminated bungalows in assorted colors. 1923-32.

187 **BUNGALOW SET (LIONELVILLE),** five 185 bungalows in assorted colors. 1923-24.

189 **VILLA,** 5½″l, 4⅞″w, 5⅜″h, stamped sheet metal, illuminated, with four third floor dormers, gambrel roof. 1923-32.

Note: Exists without dormers.

191 **VILLA (MANSION),** 7⅛″l, 5⅛″w, 5¼″h, stamped sheet metal, illuminated, hip roof with two dormers. 1923-32.

Note: Also exists without dormers.

Note: 1923-27 catalogs show train room to right of front entry, yet no 191 villa (mansion) has been found this way.

192 **VILLAS AND BUNGALOWS SET (LIONEL MANOR),** two 184 bungalows, one 189 villa, and one 191 villa mansion, in assorted colors. 1923-32.

195 **ILLUMINATED TERRACE,** 22″l, 19″w, composition board with grass, shrubbery and trees, contains - 90 flag, 184 bungalow, two 56 lamp posts, 189 villa, and 191 villa. 1927-30.

910 **GROVE OF TREES,** 16″l, 8″w, wood base covered by imitation grass with grouping of trees. 1932-42.

Note: Cataloged as 16″ x 8¾″ from 1938-42. Most 910 groves have a mound of composition felt rocks.

911 **ILLUMINATED COUNTRY ESTATE,** 16″l, 8″w, wood base covered with shrubbery and trees around 191 villa mansion, numerous variations of shrubbery and trees, 191 usually crackle red, yellow, or light cream sides. 1932-42.

912 **ILLUMINATED SUBURBAN HOME,** 16″l, 8″w, wood base covered with shrubbery and trees around 189 villa, numerous variations of shrubbery and trees, 189 usually ivory sides. 1932-42.

913 ILLUMINATED LANDSCAPED BUNGALOW, 16″l, 8″w, wood base covered with shrubbery and trees around 184 bungalow, numerous variations of shrubbery and trees, 184 usually lithographed. 1932-42.

914 PARK LANDSCAPE, 16″l, 8½″w, wood base with shrubbery, trees and central garden base with flowers. 1932-36.

919 PARK GRASS, 8 ounce cloth bag of green artificial grass. 1932-42 and postwar.

920 ILLUMINATED SCENIC PARK, 57″l, 31½″w, 10″h, wood and felt composition, built in 2 sections, contains 2-189 villas, 2-191 villas and 2-184 bungalows. 1932-33.

921 ILLUMINATED SCENIC PARK, 85″l, 31½″w, 10″h, wood and felt composition, built in 3 sections, 2 end sections same as 920, 921C center section contains 1-189 villa, 1- 191 villa, and 1-184 bungalow and 1-910 grove of trees or 1-914 park landscape or 1-922 illuminated lamp terrace. 1932-33.

921C ILLUMINATED CENTER SECTION OF 921 SCENIC PARK, 28″l, 31½″w, 10″h, as described under 921. 1932-33.

922 ILLUMINATED LAMP TERRACE, 13″l, 3¾″w, 8¼″h, wood base covered with grass and shrubbery and one 56 park lamp post in mojave, pea green, green, or copper-bronze. 1932-36.

185 stucco

186 five variations

FIGURE 21.

184 AND 185 BUNGALOWS

Base	Sides	Main Roof	Entry Roof	Dormer	Main Window	Dormer Window	Chimney	Lattice & Corner	Porch Sides	Bottom Lettering	Chimney Position	Found on 913 Plot	
Gray	Ivory	Dark Green	Dark Green	Ivory	Apple Green	Apple Green	Ivory	—	Ivory	Decal	L. Rear	No	
Gray	Ivory	Pea Green	Pea Green	Ivory	Orange	Orange	Ivory	—	Ivory	Decal	L. Rear	No	
Gray	Ivory	Dark Gray	Dark Gray	Ivory	Apple Green	Apple Green	Ivory	—	Ivory	Decal	L. Rear	No	*
Gray	Flesh**	Orange	Orange	Flesh**	Ivory	Ivory	Ivory	—	Ivory	Decal	L. Rear	No	*
Gray	Cream	Orange	Orange	Light Mojave	Ivory	Ivory	Light Mojave	—	Cream	Decal	L. Rear	No	
Gray	Cream	Red	Red	Cream	Ivory	Ivory	Cream	—	Cream	Decal	L. Rear	No	
Gray	White	Maroon	Apple Green	White	Orange	Orange	White	—	White	Decal	L. Rear	No	*
Hiawatha Gray	Ivory	Dark Green	Dark Green	Ivory	Pea Green	Pea Green	Ivory	—	Ivory	Decal	L. Rear	No	
Hiawatha Gray	White	Apple Green	Apple Green	White	Orange	Orange	White	—	White	Decal	L. Rear	No	*
Speckled Gray & Yellow	Cream	Red	Red	Cream	Pea Green	Orange	Red	—	Cream	Decal	L. Rear	No	
Hiawatha Gray	Yellow	Light Red	Light Red	Light Red	Apple Green	Apple Green	Yellow	—	Yellow	Unknown	L. Rear	Yes	
Hiawatha Gray	Ivory	Apple Green	Apple Green	Apple Green	Orange	Orange	Ivory	—	Ivory	Unknown	L. Rear	Yes	
Mojave	Ivory	Apple Green	Apple Green	Apple Green	Orange	Orange	Ivory	—	Ivory	Unknown	L. Rear	Yes	
Mojave	Cream	Red	Red	Red	Ivory	Ivory	Cream	—	Cream	Unknown	L. Rear	Yes	
Light Mojave	Light Mojave	Terra Cotta	Terra Cotta	Light Mojave	Yellow	Yellow	Light Mojave	—	Light Mojave	Decal	L. Rear	No	
Litho Grass	Litho Ivory Back-ground	Red	Red	Red	Orange	Orange	Red	Green Litho	Litho	Rubber Stamped (RS)	R. Rear	No	
Litho Grass	Litho Ivory Back-ground	Red	Red	Red	Pea Green	Pea Green	Red	Green Litho	Litho	RS	R. Rear	No	
Litho Grass	Litho Ivory Back-ground	Green Litho	Green Litho	White Litho	Orange	Orange	Brick Litho	Green Litho	Litho	RS	L. Rear	No	
Litho Grass	Litho Gray Back-ground	Green Litho	Green Litho	White Litho	Pea Green	Pea Green	Brick Litho	Green Litho	Litho	RS	L. Rear	No	*
Litho Flowers	Litho Ivory Back-ground	Red Litho	Red Litho	White Litho	Orange	Orange	Brick Litho	White Litho	Litho	RS	L. Rear	No	
Litho Flowers	Litho Ivory Back-ground	Red Litho	Red Litho	White Litho	Pea Green	Pea Green	Brick Litho	White Litho	Litho	RS	L. Rear	No	*
Litho Flowers	Litho Ivory Back-ground	Red Litho	Red Litho	White Litho	Pea Green	Pea Green	Brick Litho	White Litho	Ivory	RS	L. Rear	No	
Gray	Stucco**	Maroon	Maroon	Stucco**	Ivory	Ivory	Stucco**	—	Stucco**	Unknown	L. Rear	No	*
Gray	Cream	Red	Red	Cream	Pea Green	Pea Green	Gray	—	Cream	—	R. Rear	Yes	*

* Pictured

** Stucco - textured surface, Ivory color
Flesh - flat finish surface, Mustard color

187 lithographed bungalow set

189 three variations

191 two variations

192 Lionel Manor

910

914

921 left section

921C center section

922 with 56 copper bronze

Standard gauge billboard 1932

FIGURE 22.

189 VILLA

Base	Sides	Main & Porch Roof	Chimney	Chimney Base	Dormer Sides	Doors	Porch Sides	Windows 1st Floor	Windows 2nd Floor	Windows 3rd Floor	Windows Dormers	Lettering	Found on 912 Plot
Pea Green	Ivory	Dark Gray	Brick Litho	Mojave	Ivory	Wood Grained	Ivory	Pea Green	Pea Green	Pea Green	Pea Green	RS	No
Pea Green	Ivory	Dark Gray	Brick Litho	Mojave	Ivory	Light Red	Ivory	Pea Green	Pea Green	Pea Green	Pea Green	RS	No
Pea Green	Ivory	Dark Gray	Light Red	Mojave	Ivory	Wood Grained	Ivory	Pea Green	Pea Green	Pea Green	Pea Green	RS	No
Pea Green	Ivory	Maroon	Brick Litho	Pebble Litho	None	Wood Grained	Ivory	Dark Green	Dark Green	Dark Green	None	Decal	No
Pea Green	Ivory	Dark Gray	Brick Litho	Pebble Litho	None	Wood Grained	Ivory	Dark Green	Dark Green	Dark Green	None	Decal	No
Terra Cotta	Ivory	Peacock	Brick Litho	Mojave	Ivory	Wood Grained	Ivory	Dark Green	Dark Green	Dark Green	Pea Green	RS	No
Terra Cotta	Ivory	Peacock	Light Red	Mojave	Ivory	Light Red	Ivory	Pea Green	Pea Green	Pea Green	Ivory	RS	No
Terra Cotta	Ivory	Peacock	Brick Litho	Mojave	Ivory	Light Red	Ivory	Pea Green	Pea Green	Pea Green	Pea Green	RS	No
Terra Cotta	Ivory	Peacock	Light Red	Mojave	Ivory	Light Red	Ivory	Pea Green	Pea Green	Pea Green	Ivory	—	Yes *
Terra Cotta	Ivory	Peacock	Red	Mojave	Ivory	Maroon	Ivory	Pea Green	Pea Green	Pea Green	Ivory	—	Yes
Terra Cotta	129 Sand	Peacock	Red	Mojave	Ivory	Maroon	Ivory	Pea Green	Pea Green	Pea Green	Ivory	—	Yes
Mojave	Ivory	Dark Gray	Brick Litho	Mojave	Ivory	Wood Grained	Ivory	Dark Green	Dark Green	Dark Green	Pea Green	—	Yes
Light Mojave	129 Sand	Medium Green	Terra Cotta	Terra Cotta	129 Sand	Beige	129 Sand	Light Buff	Beige	Light Buff	Light Buff	—	Yes *
Light Mojave	129 Sand	Green	Terra Cotta	Terra Cotta	129 Sand	Beige	129 Sand	129 Sand	White	White	White	—	Yes
Hiawatha Gray	Light Mustard	Apple Green	Terra Cotta	Terra Cotta	Light Mustard	Ivory	Light Mustard	Ivory	Ivory	Ivory	129 Sand	—	Yes *

* Pictured

FIGURE 23.

191 VILLA (MANSION)

Base	Sides	Roof	Chimney	Windows	Dormer Sides	Porch Roofs	Front Porch Sides	Doors	Railing	Lettering	Found on 911 Plot
Mojave	Dark Red Brick Litho	Pea Green	Brick Litho	Ivory	Pea Green	129 Sand	Ivory	Wood Grained	Dark Green	Decal	No
Mojave	Dark Red Brick Litho	Dark Gray	Brick Litho	Ivory	None	Cream	Ivory	Wood Grained	Dark Green	Decal	No
Mojave	Terra Cotta	Pea Green	Brick Litho	Ivory	Terra Cotta	129 Sand	Ivory	Wood Grained	Br	RS	No
Mojave	Terra Cotta	Pea Green	Brick Litho	Ivory	Pea Green	129 Sand	Ivory	Wood Grained	Pea Green	RS	No
Mojave	Terra Cotta	Pea Green	Brick Litho	Ivory	Terra Cotta	Cream	Ivory	Red	Br	None	Yes
Mojave	Terra Cotta	Pea Green	Brick Litho	Ivory	Terra Cotta	129 Sand	Ivory	Wood Grained	Br	None	Yes
Mojave	Red Crackle	Pea Green	Cream	Ivory	Red Crackle	Cream	Ivory	Ivory	Br	RS	No
Mojave	Red Crackle	Pea Green	Brick Litho	Ivory	Red Crackle	Cream	Ivory	Ivory	Br	None or RS	Yes

FIGURE 23.
191 VILLA (MANSION-cont'd)

Base	Sides	Roof	Chimney	Windows	Dormer Sides	Porch Roofs	Front Porch Sides	Doors	Railing	Lettering	Found on 911 Plot	
Mojave	Red Crackle	Pea Green	Cream	Ivory	Red Crackle	Cream	Ivory	Ivory	Br	None or RS	Yes	
Mojave	Terra Cotta	Pea Green	Brick Litho	Ivory	Pea Green	129 Sand	Ivory	Maroon	Pea Green	RS	No	
Mojave	Terra Cotta	Pea Green	Brick Litho	Ivory	Pea Green	129 Sand	Ivory	Red	Pea Green	None	Yes	
Mojave	Red Crackle	Light Apple Green	Brick Litho	Ivory	None	Cream	Ivory	Wood Grained	Br	None or RS	Yes	
Pea Green	Light Red Brick Litho	Dark Gray	Brick Litho	Ivory	None	Cream	Ivory	Wood Grained	Br	Decal	No	
Pea Green	Dark Red Brick Litho	Light Apple Green	Brick Litho	Ivory	None	Cream	Ivory	Wood Grained	Dark Green	Decal	No	
Pea Green	Dark Red Brick Litho	Pea Green	Brick Litho	Ivory	Pea Green	Cream	Ivory	Wood Grained	Dark Green	Decal	No	*
Pea Green	Dark Red Brick Litho	Light Apple Green	Brick Litho	Ivory	None	Cream	Ivory	Wood Grained	Pea Green	None	Yes	
Pea Green	Light Red Brick Litho	Light Apple Green	Brick Litho	Ivory	None	Cream	Ivory	Brown	Gray	Unknown	No	
Pea Green	Light Red Brick Litho	Gray	Brick Litho	Ivory	None	Cream	Ivory	Wood Grained	Pea Green	Unknown	No	
Light Mojave	Cream	Red	129 Sand	Stephen Girard Green	129 Sand	Light Mojave	Cream	Stephen Girard Green	Br	None	Yes	
Hiawatha Gray	Yellow	Light Red	Yellow	Apple Green	Light Red	Hiawatha Gray	Yellow	Apple Green	N	None	Yes	
Hiawatha Gray	Yellow	Light Red	Yellow	Apple Green	Yellow	Hiawatha Gray	Yellow	Apple Green	N	None	Yes	*
Hiawatha Gray	Red Crackle	Pea Green	Brick Litho	Ivory	Red Crackle	Cream	Ivory	Wood Grained	Br	Unknown	No	
Hiawatha Gray	Cream	Light Red	Cream	Apple Green	Light Red	Hiawatha Gray	Cream	Apple Green	Gray	None	Yes	
Hiawatha Gray	Cream	Light Red	Cream	Apple Green	Cream	Hiawatha Gray	Cream	Apple Green	Gray	None	Yes	
Hiawatha Gray	Cream	Light Red	Cream	Pea Green	Light Red	Hiawatha Gray	Cream	Pea Green	Gray	None	Yes	
Hiawatha Gray	Cream	Light Red	Cream	Pea Green	Light Red	Hiawatha Gray	Cream	Pea Green	Br	Unknown	No	

* Pictured

SCENIC RAILWAYS AND LAYOUTS
1923-41

131 **CORNER ELEVATION,** steel. 1924-28.

131W **LAYOUT,** consists of 225 loco, 2235 tender, 3659 dump, 3652 gondola, 3651 lumber, 2657 caboose, 97 coal elevator, track O gauge. 1940.

132 **CORNER GRASS PLOT,** steel. 1924-28.

133 **HEART SHAPED GRASS PLOT,** steel. 1924-28.

134 **OVAL GRASS PLOT,** steel. 1924 and 1927-28.

135 **CIRCULAR GRASS PLOT,** steel. 1924-28.

136 **LARGE ELEVATION,** steel. 1924-28.

172 **LAYOUT,** contains 150 Elec. loco, three 600 pullmans, track O gauge, 88 rheostat, 68 warning sign, 62 semaphore, 118 tunnel. 1923.

173 **LAYOUT,** contains 150 Elec. loco, two 603 pullmans, one 604 observation, track O gauge, 88 rheostat, six 60 telegraph posts, 106 bridge, 118 tunnel. 1923.

173 **LAYOUT,** 42″l, 48″w platform table with 18″ folding legs, 248 Elec. loco, two 629 pullmans, 630 observation, 435 power station, Y transformer, pair 021 switches, track O gauge, two 184 bungalows, 1012X station, hand made tunnel, four 060 telegraph posts. 1932.

173 **LAYOUT,** same as above but with 259E steam loco, 259T tender, 603 pullman, 604 observation, 1560 station, 88 controller. 1933.

173 **LAYOUT,** same as above but with type L transformer. 1934.

174 **LAYOUT,** contains 154 Elec. loco, 602 baggage, two 601 pullmans, track O gauge, 88 rheostat, pair 022 switches, 106 bridge, 121 station, six 60 telegraph posts, 62 semaphore, 68 crossing sign, 119 tunnel. 1923.

174 **LAYOUT,** same as above but with 153 Elec. loco, two 603 pullmans, 604 observation. 1924-25.

Note: Catalog cut shows #253 Loco.

174 **LAYOUT,** same as above but with 252 Elec. loco, two 607 pullmans, 608 observation, two 62 semaphores, 068 warning signal. 1926-27.

174 **LAYOUT,** same as above but with pair 021 switches, 122 station. 1928.

174 **LAYOUT,** same as above but with 253 Elec. loco, one 62 semaphore, 89 flag staff. 1929-31.

175 **LAYOUT,** contains 254E Elec. loco, two 610 pullmans, 612 observation, 080 semaphore, 069 warning signal, 90 flag staff, 106 bridge, pair 012 switches, 437 signal tower, 119L tunnel, two 56 lamps, eight 60 telegraph posts, 81 rheostat, track O gauge. 1928-29.

176 **LAYOUT,** contains 156 Elec. loco, two 610 pullmans, 612 observation, track O gauge, 88 rheostat, 109 bridge, eight 60 telegraph posts, 62 semaphore, 121 station, 119 tunnel, pair 022 switches. 1923.

176 **LAYOUT,** same as above but with 253 Elec. loco, two 610 pullmans, 612 observation. 1924-25.

Note: Cut shows #254 Loco.

176 **LAYOUT,** contains 260E steam loco, two 710 pullmans, 712 observation, 080 semaphore, 069 warning signal, 90 flag staff, 106 bridge, pair 012 switches, 437 signal tower, 119L tunnel, two 56 lamps, eight 060 telegraph posts, 81 rheostat, track O gauge. 1930-31.

177 **SCENIC RAILWAY,** 72″l, 48″w, platform table with removable legs, contains accessories and trains - two span bridge, 069 signal, 62 semaphore, 119 tunnel, six illuminated metal houses, 124 station, five 60 telegraph poles, 150 Elec. loco, two 603 pullmans, 604 observation, two 022 switches, track; platform landscaped, packed in wood box, O gauge. 1922.

177 **SCENIC RAILWAY,** 78″l, 57″w, platform table with removable legs, contains accessories and trains - 191 villa, 189 villa, five 184 bungalows, two 104 span bridge, 110 bridge, 124 station, two 59 lamp posts, five 58 lamp posts, 57 lamp post, 62 semaphore, 69 warning signal, three 60 telegraph posts, 89 flagstaff, 150 Elec. loco, 603 pullman, 604 observation, 33 Elec. loco, 35 pullman, 36 observation, track, O and Std gauge. 1923.

178 **SCENIC RAILWAY,** 60″l, 36″w platform table, contains accessories and trains -069 electric signal, five 60 telegraph posts, two span bridge, 62 semaphore, 124 station, 118 tunnel, four illuminated metal houses, 150 Elec. loco, two 603 pullmans, 604 observation, landscaped platform, packed in wood box, O gauge. 1922- 23.

180 **SCENIC RAILWAY,** 36″l, 36″w, platform only, contains accessories and trains - 62 semaphore, 89 flagstaff, two 60 telegraph poles, two 58 lamp posts, three 184 bungalows, 127 station, 150 Elec. loco, two 600 pullmans, track O gauge. 1923.

183 **SCENIC RAILWAY,** 144″l, 60″w, 2 sections, platform table with removable legs, contains accessories and train - two span bridge, foot bridge, 69 warning signal, 62 semaphore, 120 tunnel, 9 illuminated houses, 124 station, two 67 lamp posts, eleven 60 telegraph posts, 38 Elec. loco, two 35 pullmans, 36 observation, track, packed in wood box, Std gauge. 1922.

189W **LAYOUT,** consists of 225 loco, 2225 tender, three 3659 dumps, 2657 caboose, 97 coal elevator, track O gauge. 1938-39.

198 **SCENIC RAILWAY,** 60″l, 42″w, 2 sections, composition board layout with mountains and sky backdrop (72″l, 28″w); contains accessories - 076 block signal, 077 crossing gate, 069 warning signal, 56 lamp post, 58 lamp post, 80 flagstaff, 184 bungalow, 189 villa, 191 villa, 092 signal tower; contains steel display pieces - 130 tunnel, 131 corner elevation, 132 corner grass plot, two 133 heart shaped grass plots, 134 oval grass plot, three 505 trees, two 504 bushes, O gauge. 1924-28.

199 **SCENIC RAILWAY,** 90″l, 60″w, three section composition board layout with mountains and sky backdrop (72″l, 28″w); contains accessories - 124 station, 189 villa, 191 villa, three 184 bungalows, 092 signal tower, five 60 telegraph posts, two 61 lamp posts, three 58 lamp posts, 57 lamp post, 89 flag, 66 semaphore, 78 automatic control, 77 crossing gate, 69 warning signal, 120 tunnel; contains steel display pieces - 136 large elevation, 131 corner elevation, 132 corner grass plot, two 133 heart shaped grass plots, two 134 oval grass plots, 135 circular grass plot, sixteen 505 trees, eight 504 bushes, Std gauge. 1924-28.

Note: Make up of scenic railways may differ year to year.

269W **LAYOUT,** consists of 225 loco, 2235 tender, 3651 lumber, two 2652 gondolas, 2657 caboose, 165 magnetic crane, track O gauge. 1940.

273W **LAYOUT,** consists of 226 loco, 2226 tender, three 3811 lumber, 2817 caboose, 164 lumber loader, track O gauge. 1940.

405 **LAYOUT,** contains 402 Elec. loco, 5 steam loco, 418 pullman, 419 combine, 490 observation, 11 flat, 12 gondola, 13 cattle, 14 box, 15 tank, 16 ballast, 17 caboose, track Std gauge, three pairs 22 switches, two 23 bumpers, 121 station, 191 villa, 189 villa, four 184 bungalows, K transformer, 69 warning signal, two 77 crossing gates, eight 60 telegraph posts, 89 flag staff, 65 semaphore, 66 semaphore, 120 tunnel, 101 bridge, two 59 lamps, four 57 lamps. 1924-26.

405 **LAYOUT,** contains 9E Elec. loco, 424, 425 pullmans, 426 observation, 81 rheostat, 921 park, 917 mountain, 155 freight station, 915 tunnel, 80 semaphore, pair 223 switches, 114 station, 550 figures, 90 flag staff, 438 signal tower, 436 power house, 440 signal bridge, T transformer, track Std gauge. 1932.

405 **LAYOUT,** same as above but with a K transformer. 1933.

407 **LAYOUT,** contains 408E Elec. loco, 380E Elec. loco, two 81 rheostats, 418 pullman, 419 combine, 490 observation, 431 diner, 211 lumber, 212 gondola, 213 cattle, 214 box, 215 tank, 216 coal, 217 caboose, 218 dump, 219 crane, 84 semaphore, K transformer, three pair 222 switches, two 23 bumpers, track Std gauge, 124 station, 189 villa, 191 villa, three 184 bungalows, 438 signal tower, 101 bridge, 140L tunnel, twelve 60 telegraph posts, 78 train control, 80 semaphore, two 77 crossing gates, 89 flag staff, two 76 block signals, 69 warning signal, 436 power station, 437 switch tower, two 67 lamp posts, four 56 lamps, two 57 lamps, two 59 lamps. 1927-29.

407 **LAYOUT,** contains 408E Elec. loco, 390E steam loco, two 81 rheostats, 412, 413, 414 pullmans, 416 observation, 212 gondola, 217 caboose, 218 dump, 219 crane, K transformer, four pairs 222 switches, two 23 bumpers, set 208 tools, set 209 barrels, track Std gauge, 128 station, 300 bridge, 140L tunnel, twelve 85 telegraph posts, 78 train control, 80 semaphore, two 77 crossing gates, 69 warning signal, 840 power house, two 67 lamps, four 56 lamps, 87 signal, 79 flashing signal, 195 terrace. 1930-31.

424 **LAYOUT,** contains 42 Elec. loco, 18 pullman, 19 combine, 190 observation, 12 gondola, 13 cattle, 14 box, 15 tank, 16 ballast, 17 caboose, two 67 lamps, two 65 semaphores, one 66 semaphore, pair 21 switches, 217 interior car lighting set, track Std gauge, type K transformer, 121 station, 120 tunnel. 1923.

500 **PINE BUSHES.** 1927-28.

501 **SMALL PINE TREES.** 1927-28.

502 **MEDIUM PINE TREES.** 1927-28.

503 **LARGE PINE TREES.** 1927-28.

504 **ROSE BUSHES.** 1924-28.

505 **OAK TREES.** 1924-28.

506 **PLATFORM,** composition board, painted, 2 sections. 1924- 28.

507 **PLATFORM,** composition board, painted, 3 sections. 1924- 28.

508 **SKY BACKGROUND,** composition board, painted, 2 sections. 1924-28.

509 **MOUNTAINS,** composition board, painted. 1924-28.

510 **CANNA BUSHES.** 1927-28.

831W **LAYOUT,** consists of 225 loco, 2235 tender, 3659 dump, 3652 gondola, 3651 lumber, 2757 caboose, 97 coal elevator, track O gauge. 1941.

869W **LAYOUT,** consists of 225 steam loco, 2235 tender, 3651 lumber, two 2652 gondolas, 2757 caboose, 165 magnetic crane, track O gauge. 1941.

878W **LAYOUT,** consists of 226 steam loco, 2226 tender, 2812 gondola, 3811 lumber, 3814 merchandise, 2957 caboose, 164 lumber loader, track O gauge. 1941.

1007 **LAYOUT** (Winner), consists of 43¼"l, 29½"w platform similar to layout 1053E, 1035 steam loco, 1016 tender, 1020 baggage, 1011 pullman, 1019 observation, 1017 transformer-station, track O27 gauge, special tunnel mountain, 913 estate. 1932.

1053E **LAYOUT,** consists of 43¼"l, 29½"w special platform, 1651E steam loco, two 1690 pullmans, 1691 observation, track O27 gauge, 1017 transformer-station, special tunnel mountain, 913 estate. 1933.

1057E **LAYOUT,** similar to layout 1053E, but with 1681E steam loco. 1934.

1066E **LAYOUT,** same as 1053E but with 1700E power car, 1701 coach, 1702 observation. 1935-36.

1095W **LAYOUT,** consists of 1666E loco, 2689W tender, 3659 coal, 2680 tank, 2620 floodlight, 2657 caboose, 96 coal elevator, pair 1121 switches, 1040 transformer, track O27 gauge. 1938-40.

1099 **LAYOUT,** consists of 1666 loco, 2689 tender, three 3651 lumber, 2657 caboose, 164 lumber loader, track O27 gauge, pair 1121 switches, 1041 transformer. 1940.

1195W **LAYOUT,** same as 1095 but with 2666 tender, 2672 caboose, 97 coal elevator, 1041 transformer. 1941.

1199W **LAYOUT,** same as 1099 but with 2666 tender, 2672 caboose. 1941.

1526 **LAYOUT,** consists of litho base, animals, house, bridge, tunnel cut outs, 1506L mechanical steam loco, 1502 tender, 1512 gondola, 1514 box, 1517 caboose, track O27 gauge. 1933.

1527 **LAYOUT,** same as above but with 1813 baggage, 1811 pullman, 1812 observation. 1933.

1528 **LAYOUT,** consists of 1506L mechanical loco, 1502 tender, 1813 baggage, 1811 pullman, 1812 observation, six 1571 telegraph posts, 1574 clock, 1573 warning signal, 1560 station, 1572 semaphore, pair 1550 switches, track O27 gauge. 1933-34.

1536 **LAYOUT,** Mickey Mouse circus outfit. 1935.

1537 **LAYOUT,** same as 1526 but with 1508 loco, 1509 tender. 1935.

1552 **LAYOUT,** consists of 1511 mechanical loco, 1516 tender, two 1811 pullmans, 1812 observation, 1046 gateman (NM), six 1571 telegraph posts, 1572 semaphore, 1574 clock, track mechanical O27 gauge. 1936.

199

96 MANUAL COAL ELEVATOR, 11½"l, 6"w, 12"h, steel construction with bakelite base, manual conveyor, electric dump, black base/alum struts/yellow house sides/light red roof/light red windows and ladders. 1938-40.

97 REMOTE CONTROL COAL ELEVATOR, same as 96 but electric conveyor. 1938-42 and postwar.
- *black base/alum struts/yellow house sides/light red roof/light red windows and ladders*
- black/92 gray/yellow/light red/light red
- black/92 gray/brown/orange/black

98 ELEVATED COAL STORAGE BUNKER, same as 97 but no conveyor mechanism, electric controlled coal chute, black base/alum struts/yellow house sides/light red roof/light red window and ladders. 1939-40.

160 COAL OR LOG UNLOADING BIN, 8⅜"l, 3¼"w, bakelite, black. 1938-42 and postwar.

164 REMOTE CONTROL LOG LOADER, 11¼"l, 10¾"w, 9"h, sheet metal, bakelite base and roof, diecast posts, electric powered, load of logs. 1940-42 and postwar.
- green base/cream loading platform posts/alum conveyor struts/light red or vermilion roof
- green/cream/92 gray/light red

165 MAGNETIC CRANE, 6"l, 6½"w, 10"h, cab and boom of 2660 mounted on stamped steel base and girder superstructure, electrically operated winch, motor, and magnet, green base/alum or 92 gray girders/cream cab sides/light red roof and ladder/bakelite boom. 1940-42.

Note: Can be found with green, medium green, dark green or olive green boom.

186 LOG LOADING OUTFIT, contains 164 log loader, 3651 operating lumber car, RCS track, 160 unloading bin, load of logs. 1940-41.

188 COAL ELEVATOR, CAR AND TRACK SET, contains 97 electric coal elevator, 3659 operating dump car, RCS track, 160 unloading bin, and two 206 bags of artificial coal. 1938-41.

206 BAG OF ARTIFICIAL COAL, ½ pound. 1938-42 and postwar.

207 BAG OF ARTIFICIAL COAL, ¼ pound. 1938-42.

96

97 black/92 gray/yellow/light red

98 black/alum/yellow/light red

164 green/cream/92 gray/light red

165 green/92 gray/cream/light red

FIGURES
1910-18, 1932-36

32 **SET OF 12 SEATED FIGURES,** composition material, for use in trolleys, molded to sit on pins in seats, various colors, Std. 1910-18.

550 **SET OF 6 STANDING FIGURES,** hollow cast, 3″h, set includes 551 engineer, 552 conductor, 553 porter, 554 male passenger, 555 female passenger, 556 red cap; hand-painted in various colors as listed below, set available 1932-36, figures available for separate sale only in 1932.

Note: Base of figures marked J. Hill & Co., England.

551 **ENGINEER**
medium blue jacket and pants/alum oil can
dark blue/alum

552 **CONDUCTOR,** black jacket and pants.

553 **PORTER AND STEPBOX,** dark blue jacket and pants/yellow stepbox.

554 **MALE PASSENGER**
dark brown overcoat and hat
mojave overcoat and hat

555 **FEMALE PASSENGER**
gray overcoat and hat
pea green coat with light brown trim
dark red coat with dark brown trim
State brown coat with dark brown trim

556 **RED CAP,** dark blue jacket and pants/red hat.

32

550 three variations

ACCESSORY SETS
1921-37

70 **ACCESSORY OUTFIT,** two 62 semaphores, one 59 lamp post, one 68 warning signal, two extra globes, Std. 1921-32.

193 **AUTOMATIC ACCESSORY OUTFIT,** one 0-76 block signal, one 0-78 block signal, one 0-80 semaphore, one 0-77 crossing gate, O. 1927-29.

194 **AUTOMATIC ACCESSORY OUTFIT,** same as 193 but Std. 1927-29.

196 **ACCESSORY SET,** one 127 station, six 60 telegraph poles, one 62 semaphore, one 68 warning signal, two 55 bulbs (12 volt), two 39 bulbs (12 volt), one 27 bulb (12 volt), O or Std. 1927.

1569 **LIONEL JR. ACCESSORY SET,** one 1574 clock, one 1573 warning signal, one 1572 semaphore, one 1575 crossing gate, four 1571 telegraph poles, Mech. 1933-37.
light red base/pea green post
black/92 gray

70

194

196

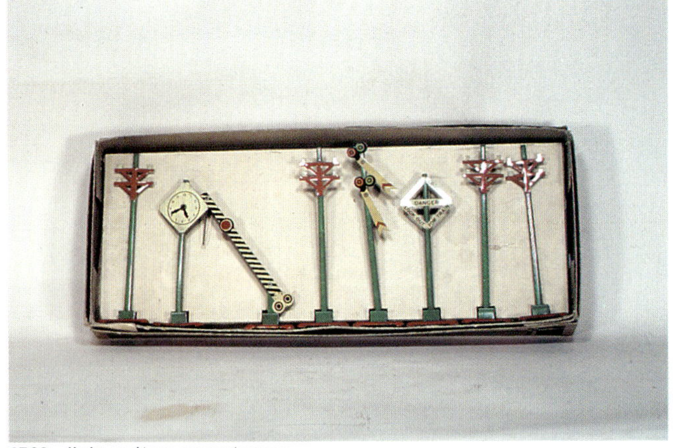

1569 light red/pea green/cream

BILD-A-MOTOR AND ATTACHMENTS

1928-31

1 O gauge motor. 1928-29.

1 O gauge motor with gear set (3 speeds) and reverse unit. 1930-31.

2 Std gauge motor. 1928-29.

2 Std gauge motor with gear set (3 speeds) and reverse unit. 1930-31.

43 Std gauge gear set, converts a Std gauge Bild-a-Loco into #2 Bild-a-Motor. 1929.

0-43 O gauge gear set, converts an O gauge Bild-a-Loco into #1 Bild-a-Motor. 1929.

LUBRICANT

1934-42

925 Tube of lubricant, 2 ounces. 1934-42 and postwar.

926 Tube of lubricant, small. 1942.

LIGHT BULBS AND CAR LIGHTING KITS
1911-31

27 **CAR LIGHTING KIT,** three 3½ volt DC bulbs, sockets and socket holders, contacts, and 5 feet of wire. 1911-21.

Note: Sockets and holders may be wood or porcelain.

27 **CAR LIGHTING KIT,** three 8 volt AC bulbs, sockets and socket holders, contacts, and 5 feet of wire. 1922-23.

111 **LAMP RENEWAL SET,** 8½″l, 7½″w, 2¼″h, 36 bulbs in individual wooden cases indexed in box. 1920-31.

217 **CAR LIGHTING KIT,** three 8 volt AC bulbs, sockets and socket holders, contacts, and 5 feet of wire. 1914-21.

217 **CAR LIGHTING KIT,** three 14 volt AC bulbs, sockets and socket holders, contacts, and 5 feet of wire. 1922-23.

270 **CAR LIGHTING KIT,** two 3½ volt DC bulbs, sockets and socket holders, contacts, and 3 feet of wire. 1915-21.

270 **CAR LIGHTING KIT,** two 8 volt AC bulbs, sockets and socket holders, contacts, and 3 feet of wire. 1922-23.

271 **CAR LIGHTING KIT,** two 8 volt AC bulbs, sockets and socket holders, contacts, and 3 feet of wire. 1915-21.

271 **CAR LIGHTING KIT,** two 14 volt AC bulbs, sockets and socket holders, contacts, and 3 feet of wire. 1922-23.

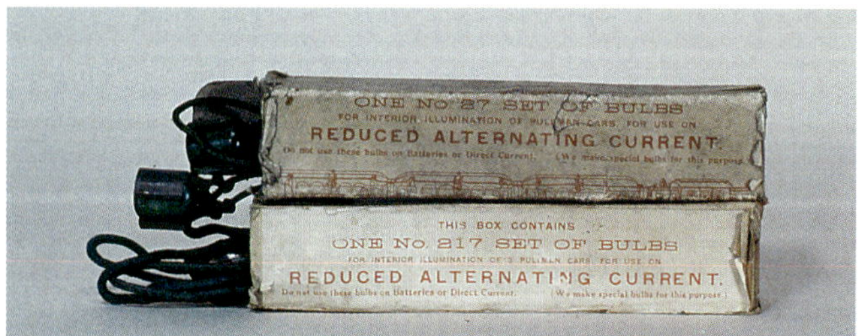

27 and 217

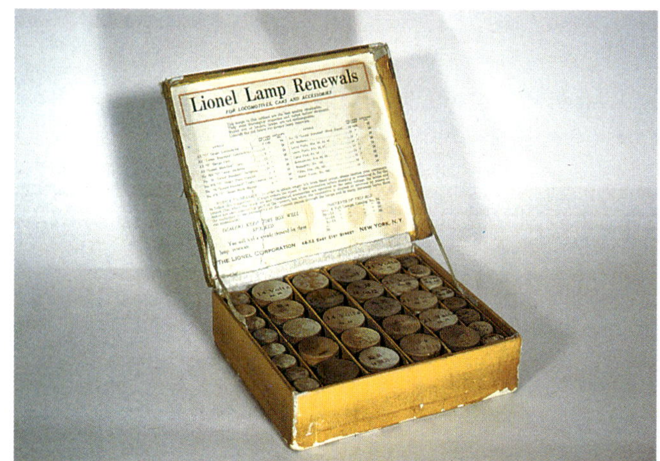

111 lamp renewal set

TRACK MOUNTED REVERSING TRIPS
1906-18

60 **SPRING PLUNGER,** stamped steel, one pair. 1906.

60 **LEAF SPRING,** stamped steel, one pair. 1909-13.

62 **REVOLVING CAM,** stamped steel, one pair. 1914-18.

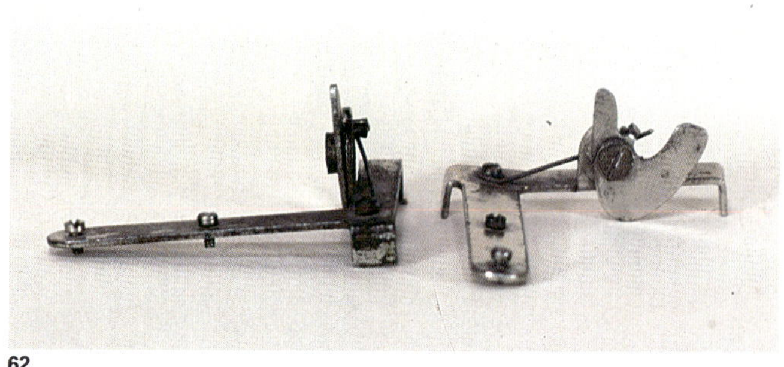

62

BUMPERS, TRACK CONNECTORS, LOCKONS, AND TRACK CLIPS
1906-42

23 **BUMPER,** stamped steel, black, 2 spring plungers with 2 strap steel bands, Std. 1906.

23 **BUMPER,** stamped steel, black, 2 spring bars with solid sides, Std. 1909-13.

23 **BUMPER,** stamped steel, 2 spring bars with cut-out sides, Std. 1914-33.
yellow-orange
black
red
green

0-23 **BUMPER,** stamped steel, one spring bar, cut-out sides, black or red, O. 1915-33.

25 **BUMPER,** diecast with light on top, Std. 1928-42.
cream/red stripes/Br trim
black/Br or N

0-25 **BUMPER,** diecast with light on top, O. 1928-42 and postwar.
cream/Br or N trim
black/Br or N
black/red stripes/Br or N

1025 **BUMPER,** diecast with light, same as 0-25 but mounted on 0-27 straight track, black/N trim, 0-27. 1940-42 and postwar.

41 **ACCESSORY CONNECTOR,** O. 1936-42 and postwar.

153C ACCESSORY CONNECTOR WITH TRACK CLAMP, O. 1941-42 and postwar.

159 BLOCK CONTROL CONNECTOR, controls 2 trains on same track, O. 1940-42 and postwar.

OTC LOCKON, O. 1923-36.

STC LOCKON, Std. 1923-36.

UTC LOCKON, universal - O or Std. 1936-42.

23 black

23 yellow-orange

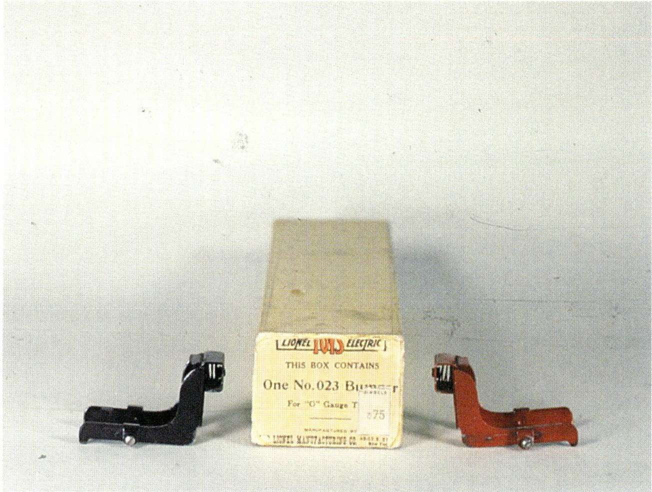

0-23 black and red

25 cream/red

0-25 black

TRACK, CROSSINGS, AND SWITCHES
1906-42

Lionel produced many varieties of track in many gauges. No attempt is made here to chronicle the evolution of track, but merely chart the various types shown in the catalogs. There are some significant milestones which deserve mention.

The first Standard gauge track formed a 36″ diameter circle and had three ties on both curved and straight with split pins in the center rail. These early ties were just a thin channel section. Later track ties were a heavier gauge metal with rounded bases. Track then formed a 42⅞″ circle when measured from end-of-tie to end-of-tie. Lionel was not consistent with the measurements in their catalogs. Split-pin track was last detailed in the 1913 catalog, but the catalog cuts were not changed until the 1920 folder. Curved track mounted on four ties appeared in 1915 and five-tie curved in 1931. Straight track always had three ties until 1931 when it evolved to four ties per section. The roundhouse 444 required a special 20″ section of track. Track ties remained unpainted tinplate until the mid-1930's. Lionel documented black oxidized ties in 1937, but they may have done this as early as 1934 with the advent of 072.

O gauge was first cataloged in 1915 and eight sections constitute a 28½″ diameter circle. This may be center-rail to center-rail and therefore consistent with later 31″ diameter designations. Track ties were unpainted tinplate the same as Standard gauge until the mid-1930's when Lionel started to oxidize all ties black. In 1933 Lionel introduced 027 (27″ diameter) track, an adaptation of Ives O gauge first used in Lionel Winner lines in 1932. It has remained basically unchanged. 1934 was the first year for 072 (72″ diameter) tubular track and was followed in 1935 by 072 solid T-rail. In 1937 the 700E came with a display board with one special length of T-rail track. 072 tubular curved track was also produced in several post-war years. 027 mechanical track was a first for Lionel in 1933. The major variation was "stoker" curved track for the Mickey Mouse sets.

OO gauge track was first cataloged in 1938 as a three-rail 27″ diameter circle. Two-rail track was introduced in 1939 with a wider circle 48″ in diameter.

As with track, Lionel made many switch combinations. The earliest standard gauge switches had cast iron switch stands, a carryover from 2⅞″ gauge. Catalogs indicate these were used through 1915. The manual switch with electric light appeared in 1915 and changed little until 1931. Switches were not sold in pairs until 1922. Electrically operated switches were first cataloged in 1926. Enclosed bottoms were introduced in 1931 and switch bases were painted pea green. Black bases came in the mid-1930's. The non-derailing feature introduced in 1931 was not cataloged as a new item (223) until 1932.

O gauge non-derailing switches were first cataloged in 1933, 072 gauge switches had the non-derailing feature when introduced in 1935. In 1938, O gauge switches were first made with molded Bakelite bases. 1938 also heralds the beginning of OO gauge, and three-rail switches were introduced. Two rail OO switches were never made.

STANDARD GAUGE TRACK, CROSSINGS, AND SWITCHES

1906-42

Track dimensions were taken from catalogs.

1/2C **TRACK,** ½ section curved - 7″, 2 ties. 1906.

1/2C **TRACK,** ½ section curved - 8½″, 3 ties. 1934-42.

C **TRACK,** curved - 14″, 3 ties - 36″ diameter circle (8 sections). 1906.

C **TRACK,** curved - 16½″, 3 ties - 42″ diameter circle (8 sections). 1908-14.

C **TRACK,** curved - 16½″, 4 ties - 42″ diameter circle (8 sections). 1915-19.

C **TRACK,** curved - 16″, 4 ties - 42″ diameter circle (8 sections). 1920-30.

C **TRACK,** curved - 16″, 5 ties - 42″ diameter circle (8 sections). 1931-42.

CC **TRACK,** curved - 16½″, same as third C with electrical connections. 1915-19.

CC **TRACK,** curved - 16″, same as fourth C with electrical connections. 1920-22.

1/2S **TRACK,** ½ section straight - 6″, 2 ties. 1906.

1/2S **TRACK,** ½ section straight - 7½″, 2 ties. 1908-19.

1/2S **TRACK,** ½ section straight - 7″, 2 ties. 1932-42.

S **TRACK,** straight - 12″, 3 ties. 1906.

S **TRACK,** straight - 14″, 3 ties. 1908-30.

S **TRACK,** straight - 14″, 4 ties. 1931-42.

SC **TRACK,** straight 14″, with electrical connections, 3 ties. 1915-22.

SCS **TRACK,** curved - 2 insulated rails, for automatic accessories, 5 ties. 1933-42.

SS **TRACK,** straight - 2 insulated rails, for automatic accessories, 3 ties. 1922-30.

SS **TRACK,** straight - 2 insulated rails, for automatic accessories, 4 ties. 1931-42.

20 **CROSSING,** 90°, depressed center. 1909-26.
Note: Apparently misprinted as 23 in the 1912 catalog.

20 **CROSSING,** 90°, fibre center and solid metal base. 1927-32.

20 **CROSSING,** 90°, Bakelite center and solid metal base. 1933-42.

20X **CROSSING,** 45°, fibre center. 1928-32.

21 **CROSSING,** 90°. 1906.

21 **SWITCH,** manual, with light. 1915-22.

21 **SWITCH,** manual, with light, and fibre rails. 1923-25.

22 **SWITCH,** manual, cast iron switch stand. 1906-15.
Note: May have switch target in red and green or red and white.

22 **SWITCH,** manual, with stamped steel switch stand. 1916-22.

22 **SWITCH,** manual, fibre rails. 1923-25.

210 **SWITCHES,** manual with light, and fibre rails. 1926-42.

210L **SWITCH,** manual, left hand. 1926-42.

210R **SWITCH,** manual, right hand. 1926-42.

220 **SWITCHES,** manual, no light. 1926.

222 **SWITCHES,** electric with light. 1926-32.

222L **SWITCH,** electric with light, left hand. 1926-32.

222R **SWITCH,** electric with light, right hand. 1926-32.

223 **SWITCHES,** electric, non-derailing with light. 1932-42.

223L **SWITCH,** electric, non-derailing with light, left hand. 1932-42.

223R **SWITCH,** electric, non-derailing with light, right hand. 1932-42.

225 Pair of 222 switches and one 439 control panel. 1929-32.

SS track

22 early - cast iron switch stand

O GAUGE TRACK, CROSSINGS, AND SWITCHES

1915-42

Track dimensions are taken from catalogs.

1/2 O-C **TRACK,** ½ section curved - 6½", 2 ties. 1934-42 and postwar.

O-C **TRACK,** curved - 11½", 3 ties, 28½" diameter circle (8 sections). 1915-19.

O-C **TRACK,** curved - 11", 3 ties - 30" diameter circle (8 sections). 1920-42 and postwar.

O-CC **TRACK,** curved - 11½", same as first O-C with electrical connections. 1915-19.

O-CC **TRACK,** curved - 11", same as second O-C with electrical connections. 1920-22.

O-CS **TRACK,** curved - 11", 2 insulated rails for automatic accessories, 3 ties. 1933-42 and postwar.

1/2 O-S **TRACK,** ½ section straight - 5", 2 ties. 1932-42 and postwar.

O-S **TRACK,** straight - 10¼", 3 ties. 1915-42 and postwar.

O-SC **TRACK,** straight - 10¼", same as O-S with electrical connections, 3 ties. 1915-22.

O-SS **TRACK,** straight - 10¼", 2 insulated rails, for automatic accessories, 3 ties. 1922-42 and postwar.

O-11 **SWITCHES,** electric, with light, non-derailing. 1933-37.

O-11L **SWITCH,** electric, with light, non-derailing, left hand. 1933-37.

O-11R **SWITCH,** electric, with light, non-derailing, right hand. 1933-37.

O-12 **SWITCHES,** electric, with light. 1927-33.

O-12L **SWITCH,** electric, with light, left hand. 1927-33.

O-12R **SWITCH,** electric, with light, right hand. 1927-33.

O-13 **PAIR** of O-12 switches and one 439 panel board. 1929-31.

O-20 **CROSSING,** 90°, solid metal center. 1915-25.

O-20 **CROSSING,** 90°, fibre center. 1926.

O-20 **CROSSING,** 90°, solid metal base and fibre center. 1927-32.

O-20 **CROSSING,** 90°, solid metal base and Bakelite center. 1933-42 and postwar.

O-20X **CROSSING,** 45°, metal center. 1917-25.

O-20X **CROSSING,** 45°, fibre center. 1926-32.

O-20X **CROSSING,** 45°, Bakelite center. 1933-42 and postwar.

O-21 **SWITCHES,** manual with light. 1915-22.

O-21 **SWITCHES,** manual with light and fibre rail. 1923-26.

O-21 **SWITCHES,** manual with light, fibre rail and solid metal base. 1927-37.

O-21L **SWITCH,** manual with light, fibre rail and solid metal base, left hand. 1927-37.

O-21R **SWITCH,** manual with light, fibre rail and solid metal base, right hand. 1927-37.

O-22 **SWITCHES,** manual. 1915-22.

O-22 **SWITCHES,** manual with fibre rail. 1923-26.

O-22 **SWITCHES,** electric with light and molded base, switch motor can be mounted on either side. 1938-42 and postwar.

O-22L **SWITCH,** electric, same as above O-22, left hand. 1938-42 and postwar.

O-22R **SWITCH,** electric, same as above O-22, right hand. 1938-42 and postwar.

O-42 **SWITCHES,** manual with molded base, switch mechanism may be mounted on either side. 1938-42 and postwar.

O-42L **SWITCH,** manual, same as above O-42, left hand. 1938-42 and postwar.

O-42R **SWITCH,** manual, same as above O-42, right hand. 1938-42 and postwar.

RCS **TRACK,** straight, 10″, remote control uncoupling. 1938-42 and postwar.

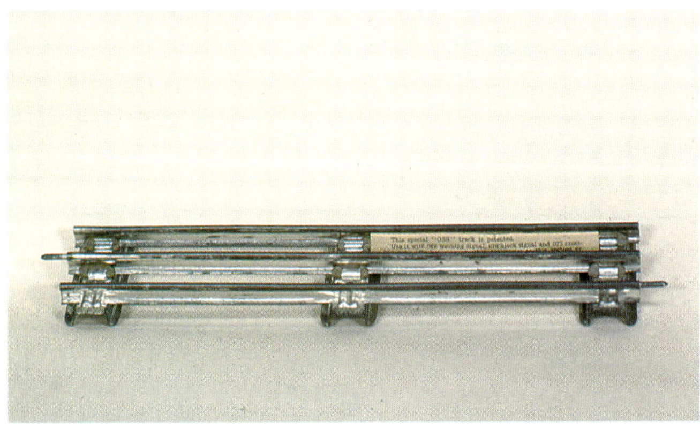

0-SS track

0-20 90° crossing

0-22 manual switches (early)

0-72 TRACK, CROSSINGS AND SWITCHES
1934-42

711 **SWITCHES,** electric, switch motor can be mounted on either side. 1935-42.

711L **SWITCH,** electric, left hand. 1935-42.

711R **SWITCH,** electric, right hand. 1935-42.

720 **CROSSING,** 90°. 1935-42.

721 **SWITCHES,** manual, switch mechanism can be mounted on either side. 1935-42.

721L **SWITCH,** manual, left hand. 1935-42.

721R **SWITCH,** manual, right hand. 1935-42.

760 **TRACK PACK,** 16 sections of 761 curved track. 1938-42 and postwar.

761 **TRACK,** curved - 14″, 6 ties, 72″ diameter circle (16 sections). 1934-42 and postwar.

762 **TRACK,** straight - 15″, 6 ties. 1934-42.

762-S **TRACK,** straight - 15″, 2 insulated rails for automatic accessories. 1934-42.

0-72 SOLID T-RAIL TRACK, CROSSINGS AND SWITCHES
1935-42

730 **CROSSING,** 90°. 1935-42.

731 **SWITCHES,** electric, switch motor can be mounted on either side. 1935-42.

731L **SWITCH,** electric, left hand. 1935-42.

731R **SWITCH,** electric, right hand. 1935-42.

771 **TRACK,** curved - 14″, 10 ties. 1935-42.

772 **TRACK,** straight - 15″, 10 ties. 1935-42.

772S **TRACK,** straight, 2 insulated rails for automatic accessories. 1940-42.

773 **FISH PLATE SET,** 100 screws, 100 nuts, 50 plates, wrench. 1936-42.

0-27 TRACK, CROSSINGS AND SWITCHES
1933-42

1013 **TRACK,** curved - 9½″, 27″ diameter circle (8 sections). 1933-42 and postwar.

1018 **TRACK,** straight - 9″. 1933-42 and postwar.

1019 **TRACK,** straight - 9″ remote control uncoupling. 1938-42 and postwar.

1021 **CROSSING,** 90°. 1933-42 and postwar.

1024 **SWITCHES,** manual. 1935-42 and postwar.

1024L **SWITCH,** manual, left hand. 1935-42 and postwar.

1024R **SWITCH,** manual, right hand. 1935-42 and postwar.

1121 **SWITCHES,** electric. 1937-42 and postwar.

TRACK, CROSSINGS, AND SWITCHES FOR MECHANICAL TRAINS
1933-38

MS **TRACK,** straight. 1933-38.

MWC **TRACK,** curved - 9½″, 27″ diameter circle (8 sections). 1933-38.

SMC **TRACK,** curved - 9½″, for Mickey Mouse sets with stoker tender. 1935-36.

1550 **SWITCHES,** manual. 1933-37.

1555 **CROSSING,** 90°. 1933-37.

OO GAUGE TRACK, CROSSINGS AND SWITCHES
1938-42

OO-31 **TRACK,** 2 rail curved - 13″, 48″ diameter circle (12 sections). 1939-42.

OO-32 **TRACK,** 2 rail straight - 12″. 1939-42.

OO-34 **TRACK,** 2 rail curved, with electrical connection. 1939-42.

OO-51 **TRACK,** 3 rail curved - 7″, 27″ diameter circle (12 sections). 1939-42.

OO-52 **TRACK,** 3 rail straight - 7″. 1939-42.

OO-54 **TRACK,** 3 rail curved with electrical connection. 1939-42.

OO-61 **TRACK,** 3 rail curved - 7″, 27″ diameter circle (12 sections). 1938.

OO-62 **TRACK,** 3 rail straight - 6¾″. 1938.

OO-63 **TRACK,** ½ section, 3 rail curved - 3½″. 1938-42.

OO-64 **TRACK,** 3 rail curved, with electrical connection. 1938.

OO-65 **TRACK,** ½ section, 3 rail, straight - 3⅜″. 1938-42.

OO-66 **TRACK,** ⅚ section, 3 rail, straight - 5⅝″. 1938-42.

OO-70 **CROSSING,** 90°, 3 rail. 1938-42.

OO-72 **SWITCHES,** electric, 3 rail. 1938-42.

OO-72L **SWITCH,** electric, 3 rail, left hand. 1938-42.

OO-72R **SWITCH,** electric, 3 rail, right hand. 1938-42.

Note: 61, 62 and 64 may represent number errors in 1938 catalog as all subsequent years they are numbered 51, 52, and 54. No 2 rail switches were made.

RUBBER ROADBED
1931-39

O-30 **CURVED,** O. 1931-39.

O-31 **STRAIGHT,** O. 1931-39.

O-32 **CROSSING,** 90°, O. 1931-39.

O-33 **CROSSING,** 45°, O. 1931-39.

O-34 **SWITCHES,** right and left hand, O. 1931-39.

30 **CURVED,** Std. 1931-37.

31 **STRAIGHT,** Std. 1931-37.

32 **CROSSING,** 90°, Std. 1931-37.

33 **CROSSING,** 45°, Std. 1931-37.

34 **SWITCHES,** right and left hand, Std. 1931-37.

WHISTLE AND REVERSING CONTROLLERS
1935-42

65 Three button, metal box, red buttons/black border and lettering on N plate. 1935.

66 Three button, same as 65 but plate marked 66, O. 1936-39.

67 Three button, same as 66 but plate marked 67, Std. 1936-39.

Note: 65, 66, and 67 are different electrically.

166 Three button, similar to 66 but plate marked 166. 1938-39.

167 Two button, Bakelite box, maroon buttons/black box. 1940-42 and postwar.

167X Two button, similar to 167 but for OO. 1940-42.

168 Two button, brown Bakelite box, red buttons, similar to 167 but for 2 train Magic Electrol set. 1940-42.

REVERSING AND UNCOUPLING CONTROLLERS
1933-42

88 Reversing, one red button. 1933-42 and postwar.

169 Reversing and uncoupling, two buttons, Teledyne. 1940.

169X Reversing and uncoupling, similar to 169. 1941-42.

VOLTAGE REDUCERS AND INVERTERS
1906-42

20 DC Shunt resistor, ON/OFF switch. 1906.

107 DC reducer, 110 or 220 volts. 1911-13.

107 DC reducer, 110 volts. 1914-38.

170 DC reducer, 220 volts. 1914-38.

171 DC to AC Inverter, 110 volts. 1936-42.

172 DC to AC Inverter, 220 volts. 1938-42.

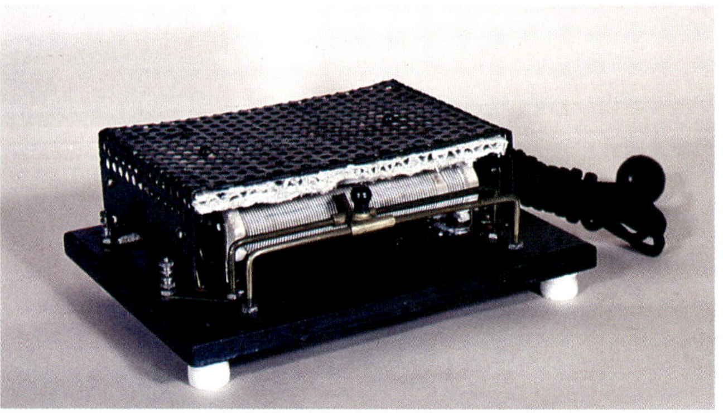

107

CIRCUIT BREAKERS
1930-42

91 2 terminals, State brown, Br light cover. 1930-33.

91 3 terminals, State brown, N light cover. 1934-42.

91 State brown

CONTROLLING RHEOSTATS
1912-42

81 Sliding, black base/dark green cover over coil, ON/OFF switch. 1927-33.

88 Sliding, black base/white coil. 1915-27.

95 Sliding, red push button. 1934-42.

108 Rotary for batteries. 1912-14.

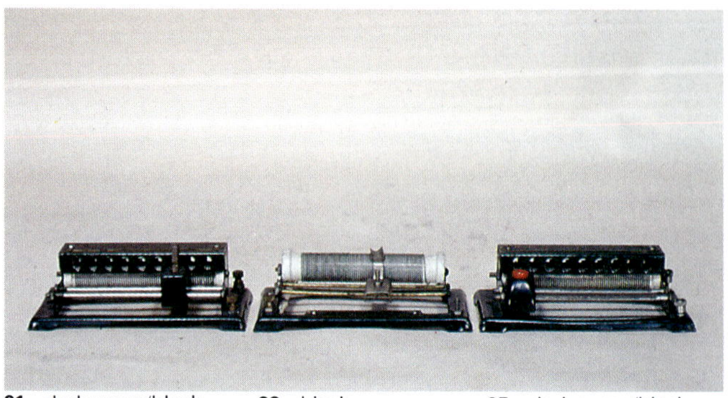

81 dark green/black **88** black **95** dark green/black

TRANSFORMERS

During the early years Lionel used direct current motors in their locomotives. Power was supplied by wet cells and dry cells since few homes had electricity. In 1906 Lionel introduced an alternating current transformer and a direct current reducer (No. 20) which used an incandescent lamp to cut down the house voltage. During the early teens Lionel had AC and DC reducers for both 110 and 220 volts although the numbers were not always listed in the catalogs.

In 1914 Lionel introduced two new transformers for 110 volts, 60 cycles; Type "L" and "K" with cast iron cases. In 1915 Lionel designated their transformers "Multivolt". These designs continued through 1921. Lionel introduced in 1922 the more familiar version of the "Multivolt" transformer in stamped steel cases. Various models of this design were made through 1938.

In 1939 the "TRAINmaster" transformers were introduced. This design incorporated Bakelite cases, circuit breakers and continually variable voltage output. These units were produced through 1942 and postwar. Refer to the chart for years of production of various models.

Type F

Type L (Red Comet)

Type T

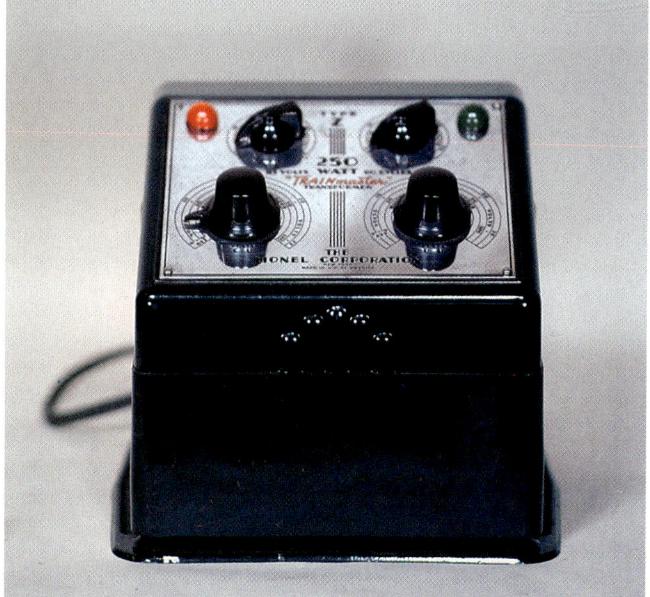

Type Z

FIGURE 24.
TRANSFORMERS

Rating	1906	1907	1908	1909	1910	1911	1912	1913	1914	1915	1916	1917	1918	1919	1920	1921	1922	1923	1924	1925
25w																				
35w																				
40w											A					A	A	A	A	A
50w										S	S	S								
75w										Q			B	B	B	B	C	C	C	C
75w										T	T	T								
75w																				
100w																		T	T	T
110w																	T			
150w									K	K	K	K	T	T	T	T	K	K	K	K
200w													K	K	K	K				
250w																				
110v AC REDUCER	no #			106	no #	106	106	106	106											
220v AC REDUCER	no #			160	no #	160	160	160	160											
110v DC REDUCER	20			107	107	107	107	107	107	107	107	107	107	107	107	107	107	107	107	107
220v DC REDUCER									170	170	170	170	170	170	170	170	170	170	170	170
60w																				
BATTERY RHEOSTAT				no #			108													

OTHER LIONEL PRODUCTION

Lionel produced a large variety of non-train items, some of which are avidly sought by collectors. Only those items of general interest are included here.

43 **PLEASURE BOAT,** 17″, stamped steel, vermilion hull bottom/white hull sides/cream top, Br or N trim - 2 figures sit forward, cradle stand for display. 1933-36 and 1938-41.

Note: No figures in boats in 1933-34.

44 **RACING BOAT,** 17″, stamped steel, green hull bottom/white hull sides/dark brown top/N trim - 44 on sides, 2 figures sit at back, cradle stand for display. 1935-36.

49 **AIRPORT,** 58″ diameter circular cut out cardboard base, full color lithography. 1937-39.

50 **AIRPLANE,** red, stamped steel, pylon and controls. 1936.

Note: Base sold separately.

51 **AIRPORT,** square cut out cardboard airport base, full color lithography. 1936 and 1938.

55 **AIRPLANE,** red and alum, stamped steel, pylon and controls. 1937-39.

Note: Base sold separately.

80 **RACING AUTOMOBILE SET,** one car - brass body painted orange or red, two figures, starting post, 36″ diameter circle (8 sections). 1912-16.

81 **RACING AUTOMOBILE SET,** same as 80 with 30″ diameter circle (8 sections). 1912-16.

84 **TWO RACING AUTOMOBILES SET,** one 80 set and one 81 set. 1912-16.

85 **TWO RACING AUTOMOBILES SET,** same as 84 set but with 8 sections of straight track. 1912-16.

TRANSFORMERS (continued)

Rating	1926	1927	1928	1929	1930	1931	1932	1933	1934	1935	1936	1937	1938	1939	1940	1941	1942
25w										1028	1029	1029	1029	1029			
35w												1039	1039	1039	1039		
40w	A	A	A	A	A	A/F	F	F	F	F	F/1030	F/1030				1037	1037
50w								U	L	L	L	L	L				N
75w	C	C	C	C	C	C		C	C	C	C	C		Q	Q	Q	Q
75w							B	B	B	B	B	B	B	W	W	W	W
75w								W					H	H			
100w	T	T	T	T	T	T	T	T	T	T	T	T	T	R	R	R	R
110w																	
150w	K	K	K	K	K	K	K	K	K	K	K	K	K	V	V	V	
200w																	
250w														Z	Z	Z	Z
110v AC REDUCER																	
220v AC REDUCER																	
110v DC REDUCER	107	107	107	107	107	107	107	107	107	107	107	107	107				
220v DC REDUCER	170	170	170	170	170	170	170	170	170	170	170	170	170				
60w							A	A	A	A	A	A	1040	1040	1041	1041	1041
STATION							1017*	1017	1027								
STATION							1012*										
220 VOLT/150w						K	K	K									
220 VOLT/100w							T	T									
220 VOLT/60w							A	A									
220 VOLT/75w							B	B									

*Winner Cat.

A **RACING AUTOMOBILE TRACK,** straight track section, 14", stamped tinplate. 1912-16.

I **RACING AUTOMOBILE TRACK,** curved track section, 30" diameter circle (8 sections), stamped steel. 1912-16.

L **RACING AUTOMOBILE TRACK,** curved track section, 36" diameter circle (8 sections), stamped steel. 1915-16.

O **RACING AUTOMOBILE TRACK,** curved track section, 36" diameter circle (8 sections), stamped steel. 1912-14.

125 **TRACK TEMPLATE,** for all gauges except Std. 1938.

455 **ELECTRIC RANGE,** operating, 25"l, 11"w, 33"h, light green and white porcelain/N trim/Br plate. 1930 and 1932-33.

1500 **LOCOSCOPE,** picture viewer with 75 pictures. 1939.

Note: Two film strips - one of trains, other of World's Fair scenes.

43 pleasure boat

44 racing boat

49 airport

55 red/alum plane

80 racing automobile - orange

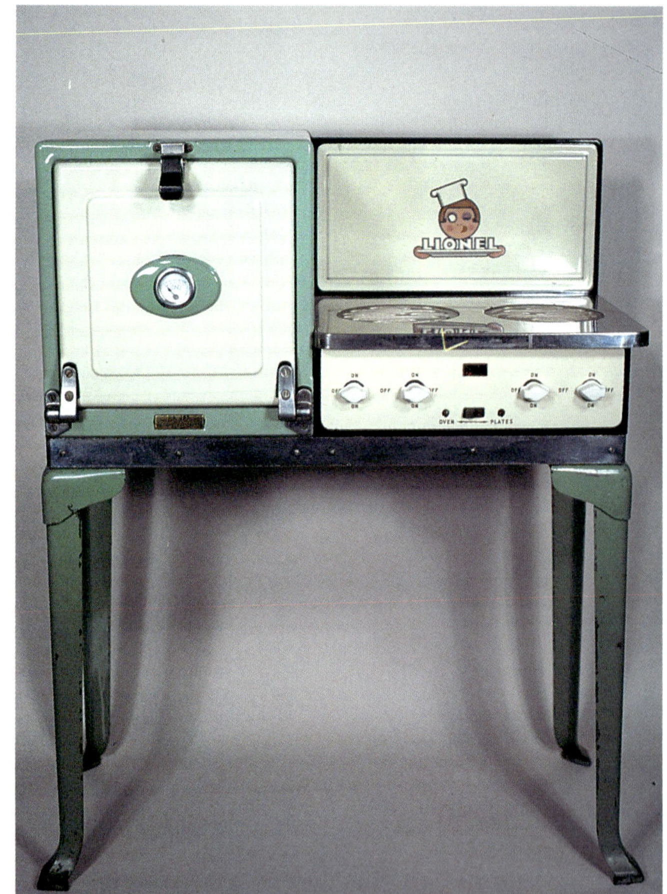

455 stove

1500 Locoscope

Lionel paper

Lionel Engineers Club Certificate

Lionel Engineers Club Pin

Paperweight of 402 Elec.

Lionel Paper Clip Tray

Peerless **Type R** motor

11 flatcar box "ELECTRIC RAILWAYS"

"MANUFACTURING" O gauge set box

113 cattle car box "LIONEL SYSTEM"

Comprehensive Numerical Listing and Index

1901-1969

The comprehensive numerical list serves two purposes—an index to this book through the listed page numbers, and a compilation of all numbers known to have been used by Lionel from 1901 through 1969. Though this book covers only prewar Lionel, it was obvious to the committee that Lionel continued the same numbering system after World War II. Thus to arbitrarily end the list at 1943 was to leave even more holes in the sequence. Therefore postwar trains and other Lionel items not detailed in this book are listed but without page numbers. In the first thousand numbers Lionel often repeated the same number for several different train items. All items with the same number have been listed in chronological order of appearance. Occasionally the numbers are preceded by a prefix number and a dash. Prior to World War II Lionel often designated an item by a number in Standard gauge, i.e. 22, and then used the same number for an equivalent O gauge item but prefixed by an O, i.e. O-22. Unfortunately after the war Lionel used this same convention to distinguish O and HO items, the latter now preceded by an O and a dash. To alleviate some of the confusion, the committee has taken the liberty of adding an H in front of the HO numbers. Thus they read as HO-057, etc. though Lionel used only O-057 in the catalogs. Further, we added a dash in O gauge listings so they read O-30, rather than 030. Using this same notation OO gauge items are prefixed by OO and a dash, thus OO-2. Standard gauge items have no prefix number or dash. On all items where indicated, the gauge designation is given in the description using the following abbreviations: 2⅞" (2⅞ inch gauge), Std (Standard gauge), O (O gauge), 027 (027 track, O gauge), 072 (072 track, O gauge), Super O (Super O track, O gauge), OO (OO gauge), HO (HO gauge) and mech (mechanical train sets). The only exceptions to Lionel's designations have been the committee's decisions to list small Ives sets of 1931-32, Lionel-Ives trains of 1933, and Lionel Junior items as 027 even though they predate Lionel's first use of that term. These trains are however the same size and style as the later 027 trains. After the description and gauge, the first year cataloged is noted in parentheses, or if uncataloged, the designation uncat appears. All dates refer to Lionel consumer catalogs, except when noted as Advance catalogs, Master catalogs, Winner catalogs, Executive catalogs or Ives catalogs for 1931-1932. It was apparent that Winner and Ives 1931-32 fit into the Lionel master list, and the latter did not follow the old Ives numbering system. They are included for completeness. Set numbers in the list are designated with inclusive dates (year first cataloged — year last cataloged). Following the dates of these sets the type of train set is indicated by Pass (passenger), Fgt (freight), or Mixed (passenger and freight). The abbreviation NM means never made on items before 1943, but after this date items marked NM though cataloged may or may not have been made. The 0000 number was used by Lionel to indicate a pre-production model. The abbreviation oper. is used to distinguish operating accessories or cars. Catalog numbers are found which include an alphabetical suffix which provides additional information as to make up of the set or item; see listings below. It is believed that the same catalog number with a suffix was produced in the same year as one without a suffix. Example: 147 and 147W were both produced in 1939.

A	Accessory display
B	Bell, bridge
C	Contactor, electrical component, center section of park, remote control couplers on special set
E	Electric reverse
E/W	Electric reverse and whistle
F	Flagman (1045)

G Green bulb
K Kit, transformer
KW Kit with whistle, transformer
L Lighted, locomotive and tender, left hand, transformer
LT Locomotive and tender
LTS Locomotive, tender and smoke
M Motor
N Accessory operated with special track section
P Platform
R Refrigerator car, red bulb, right hand, racing accessory
S Special insulated track section, pre-production super model
Special Uncataloged
SS Pre-production super model
T Tender, tool set, transformer
TW Tender only with whistle
TX Uncataloged tender
U U build it kit
W Whistle
WX Special set with whistle
X Special variation, crossover track

Finally it should be noted that while this list is as complete as possible at present, uncovering of additional Lionel paper and set boxes in the future will no doubt fill in more of the gaps in the sequence.

Catalog Number	Description-Gauge (first year catalogued)	Page No.
1	Trolley, motor car–Std (1906)	93
1	Trolley, trailer–Std (1907)	93
1	Dealer Display, assortment–Std (1916)	
1	Gimbels Special set–0 (uncat 1925)	119
1	Snellenberg Special set–0 (uncat 1927)	119
1	Gimbels Special set–0 (uncat 1927-28)	166
1	Rosenbaum Special set–0 (uncat 1927)	119
1	Bild-A-Motor–0 (1928)	211
1	Bild-A-Motor with gears–0 (1930)	211
1	A.M.C. Special set–0 (uncat 1932)	120
1	Special set–0 (uncat circa 1929)	166
1	Special set–0 (uncat circa 1934)	165
1A	Dealer Display, track, transformer & accessories–0 (1940)	
1H	Special set–0 (uncat 1931)	119
00-1	Loco, steam–00 (1938)	135, 170
00-1 T or W	Tender–00 (1938)	117, 135
2	Countershafting (1905)	
2	Trolley, motor car– Std (1906)	93, 163
2	Trolley, trailer–Std (1906)	93, 155
2	Dealer Display, assortment–Std (1916)	
2	Kaufmann and Baer Special set–0 (uncat 1925)	119
2	Macy Special set– Std (uncat 1928)	126
2	Bild-A-Motor–0 (1928)	211
2	Bild-A-Motor with gears–Std (1930)	211
2	Special set–Std (uncat 1928)	126
2	Macy Special set–Std (uncat 1930)	126, 127
2	Special set–Std (uncat 1931)	126
2	Special set–0 (uncat 1931)	120
2	Macy Special set–Std (uncat 1932)	126, 169
2	Kaufmann Special set–Std (uncat 1931)	126
2	Dealer Display, signals & lamps–0 (1940)	
2X	Special set–0 (uncat circa 1931)	166
00-2	Loco, steam–00 (1939)	135
00-2 T or W	Tender–00 (1939)	117, 135
3	Trolley, motor car–Std (1906)	93, 94
3	Trolley, trailer–Std (1906)	93, 94
3	Power truck with reverse–Std (1910)	
3	Trolley trailer truck–Std (1915)	
3	Dealer Display, assortment–0/Std (1916)	
3	Special set–0 (uncat circa 1926-27)	165
3	Sears Special set–0 (uncat circa 1930-31)	166
3	Special set–Std (uncat 1931)	126
3	Dealer Display, T-rail track–0 (1937)	
3	Dealer Display, 3 step stand–0 (1940)	
00-3	Loco, steam–00 (1939)	135
00-3 T or W	Tender–00 (1939)	117, 135
4	Trolley, motor car–Std (1906)	94, 156
4	Trolley, trailer–Std (1908)	94
4	Dealer Display, assortment–0/Std (1916)	
4	Special set–Std (uncat 1927)	169
4	Loco, elec.–0 (1928)	8, 155, 157
4	Dealer Display, sets & accessories–027 (1938)	
4U	Loco, elec.–0 (1928)	8, 164
00-4	Loco, steam–00 (1939)	135
00-4 T or W	Tender–00 (1939)	117, 135
5	Loco, steam–Std (1906)	58
5	Tender–Std (1906)	115
5	Dealer Display, assortment–0 (1916)	
5	Special set–Std (uncat 1926-28)	169
5	Dealer Display (1932)	
5 Special	Loco, steam–Std (1906)	58
6	Loco, steam–Std (1906)	58, 160
6	Tender–Std (1906)	115
6	Dealer Display, assortment–0 (1916)	
6	Dealer Display, accessories (1939)	
6 Special	Loco, steam–Std (1908)	58
7	Loco, steam (4-6-0)–Std (1907) NM	58
7	Loco, steam (4-4-0)–Std (1910)	58, 168
7	Tender–Std (1910)	115
7	Counter Display (1937)	
7	Dealer Display, operating accessories (1939)	
8	Trolley, motor car–Std (1909)	94
8	Loco, elec.–Std (1925)	67
8	Special set with 8 loco–Std (uncat 1925-26)	126
8	Special set with 8 loco–Std (uncat 1931-32)	126
8	Dealer Display, trains with magic remote control–027 (1938)	
8	Dealer Display, self demonstrator for accessories (1940)	
8E	Loco, elec.–Std (1926)	67, 161
8E	Macy loco, elec.–Std (uncat 1930)	70, 161
8E	Special set with 8E loco–Std (uncat 1928)	126
8E	Macy Special set with 8E loco–Std (uncat 1928-30)	126
8E	Special set with 8E loco–Std (uncat circa 1930-31)	168, 169
8E	Special set with 8E loco–Std (uncat circa 1932)	169
8E	Macy Special set with 8E loco–Std (uncat 1932)	126
8E	Special set with 8E loco–Std (uncat circa 1934)	169
9	Trolley, motor car–Std (1909)	94
9	Loco, elec.–Std (1929)	67
9	Special set with 9 loco–Std (uncat 1928)	126
9	Dealer Display, oper. cars–0 (1939)	
9E	Loco, elec. (0-4-0)–Std (1928)	67
9E	Loco, elec. (2-4-2)–Std (1931)	67
9E	Special set with 9E loco–Std (uncat 1928-30)	126
9E	Special set with 9E loco–Std (uncat 1936)	126
9U	Loco, elec.–Std (1928)	67
9U	Special set with 9U loco–Std (uncat 1929)	126

2261	Set–0 (1956) Fgt.
2263	Set–0 (1956) Fgt.
2263EW	Loco, steam with tender–0 (1938) 12
2263W	Tender–0 (1938) 111
2265	Loco, steam with tender–0 (1938)
2265T/W	Tender–0 (1938) 111
2265	Set–0 (1956) Fgt.
2267	Set–0 (1956) Fgt.
2269	Set–0 (1956) Fgt.
2270	Set–0 (1956) Pass.
2271	Set–0 (1956) Fgt.
2273	Set–0 (1956) Fgt.
2274	Set–0 (1956) Pass. "Congressional"
2274W	Set–0 (1955) Pass.
2275	Set–0 (1957) Fgt.
2276	Set–0 (1957) Pass. "Budd cars"
2277	Set–0 (1957) Fgt.
2279	Set–0 (1957) Fgt.
2281	Set–0 (1957) Fgt.
2283	Set–0 (1957) Fgt.
2285	Set–0 (1957) Fgt.
2287	Set–0 (1957) Fgt.
2289	Set–Super O (1957) Fgt.
2291	Set–Super O (1957) Fgt.
2292	Set–Super O (1957) Pass.
2293	Set–Super O (1957) Fgt.
2295	Set–Super O (1957) Fgt.
2296 or W	Set–Super O (1957) Pass. "Canadian"
2297 or WS	Set–Super O (1957) Fgt.
2321	Loco, FM diesel, Lackawanna–0 (1954)
2322	Loco, FM diesel, Virginian–0 (1965)
2328	Loco, diesel GP-7, Chicago & N.W.–027 (1955 advance) NM
2328	Loco, diesel GP-7, Burlington–027 (1955)
2329	Loco, elec, rectifier, Virginian–0 (1958)
2330	Loco, elec, GG-1–0 (1950)
2331	Loco, FM diesel, Virginian–0 (1955)
2332	Loco, elec, GG-1–0 (1947)
2333	Loco, diesel F-3, AA, Santa Fe or N.Y.C.–0 (1948)
2337	Loco, diesel GP-7, Wabash–027 (1958)
2338	Loco, diesel GP-7, Milwaukee Road–027 (1955)
2339	Loco, diesel GP-7, Wabash (1957)
2340-1	Loco, elec, GG-1, maroon–0 (1955)
2340-25	Loco, elec, GG-1, green–0 (1955)
2341	Loco, FM diesel, Jersey Central–0 (1956)
2343	Loco, diesel F-3, AA, Santa Fe–0 (1950)
2343C	Loco, diesel F-3, B, Santa Fe–0 (1950)
2344	Loco, diesel F-3, AA, N.Y.C.–0 (1950)
2344C	Loco, diesel F-3, B, N.Y.C.–0 (1950)
2345	Loco, diesel F-3, AA, Western Pacific–0 (1952)
2346	Loco, diesel GP-9, Boston and Maine–027 (1965)
2347	Loco, diesel GP-7, C.& O.–027 (uncat 1962)
2348	Loco, diesel GP-9, M.St.L.–027 (1958)
2349	Loco, diesel GP-9, Northern Pacific–0 (1959)
2350	Loco, elec., New Haven–0 (1956)
2351	Loco, elec., Milwaukee Road–0 (1957)
2352	Loco, elec., P.R.R.–0 (1958)
2353	Loco, diesel F-3, AA, Santa Fe–0 (1953)
2353C	Loco, diesel F-3, B, Santa Fe–0 (1954)
2354	Loco, diesel F-3, AA, N.Y.C.–0 (1953)
2354C	Loco, diesel F-3, B, N.Y.C.–0 (1954)
2355	Loco, diesel F-3, AA, Western Pacific–0 (1953)
2356	Loco, diesel F-3, AA, Southern–0 (1954)
2356C	Loco, diesel F-3, B, Southern–0 (1954)
2357	Caboose–0 (1948)
2358	Loco, elec., Great Northern–0 (1959)
2359	Loco, diesel GP-9, B.& M.–027 (1961)
2360-1	Loco, elec., GG-1, maroon, one stripe–0 (1957)
2360-10	Loco, elec., GG-1, maroon, 5 stripes–0 (1956)
2360-25	Loco, elec., GG-1, green–0 (1956)
2363	Loco, diesel F-3, AB, Illinois Central–0 (1955)
2365	Loco, diesel GP-7, C.& O.–027 (1962)
2367	Loco, diesel F-3, AB, Wabash–0 (1955)
2368	Loco, diesel F-3, AB, B.& O.–0 (1956)
2373	Loco, diesel F-3, AB, Canadian Pacific–Super O (1957)
2378	Loco, diesel F-3, AB, Milwaukee Road–0 (1956)
2379	Loco, diesel F-3, AB, Rio Grande–Super O (1957)
2383	Loco, diesel F-3, AA, Santa Fe–Super O (1958)
2400	Pullman–027 (1948) "Maplewood"
2401	Observation–027 (1948) "Hillside"
2402	Pullman–027 (1948) "Chatham"
2403	Tender w/bell–027 (1946)
2404	Vista dome–027 (1964)
2405	Pullman–027 (1964)
2406	Observation–027 (1964)
2408	Vista dome–027 (1966)
2409	Pullman–027 (1966)
2410	Observation–027 (1966)
2411	Flat w/load–027 (1946)
2412	Vista dome–027 (1959)
2414	Pullman–027 (1959)
2416	Observation–027 (1959)
2419	Wrecker caboose–027 (1946)
2420	Wrecker caboose w/light–0 (1946)
2420-20	Bulb, 14 volt–clear (1946)
2421	Pullman–027 (1950) "Maplewood"
2422	Pullman–027 (1950) "Chatham"
2423	Observation–027 (1950) "Hillside"
2426	Tender–0 (1946)
2429	Pullman–027 (1952) "Livingston"
2430	Pullman–027 (1946)
2431	Observation–027 (1946)
2432	Vista dome–027 (1954) "Clifton"
2434	Pullman–027 (1954) "Newark"
2435	Pullman–027 (1954) "Elizabeth"
2436	Observation–027 (1954) "Summit", "Mooseheart"
2440	Pullman–027 (1946)
2441	Observation–027 (1946)
2442	Pullman–0 (1946)
2442	Pullman–027 (1956) "Clifton"
2443	Observation–0 (1946)
2444	Pullman–0 (1956) "Newark"
2445	Pullman–0 (1956) "Elizabeth"
2446	Observation–0 (1956) "Summit"
2452	Gondola–027 (1945)
2452X	Gondola–027 (1946)
2454	Box–027 (1946)
2456	Hopper–0 (1948)
2457	Caboose–0 (1945)
2458	Box, automobile–0 (1945)
2460	Operating crane–0 (1946)
2461	Transformer car–027 (1947)
2465	Tank, double dome–027 (1946)
2466T/W/WX	Tender–027 (1946)
2472	Caboose–027 (1946)
2481	Pullman–027 (1950) "Plainfield"
2482	Pullman–027 (1950) "Westfield"
2483	Observation–027 (1950) "Livingston"
2501	Set–Super O (1958) Fgt.
2502	Set–Super O (1958) Pass.
2503	Set–Super O (1958) Fgt.
2505	Set–Super O (1958) Fgt.
2507	Set–Super O (1958) Fgt.
2509	Set–Super O (1958) Fgt.
2511	Set–Super O (1958) Fgt.
2513	Set–Super O (1958) Fgt.
2515	Set–Super O (1958) Fgt.
2517	Set–Super O (1958) Fgt.
2518	Set–Super O (1958) Fgt.
2519	Set–Super O (1958) Fgt.
2521	Set–Super O (1958) Fgt.

11384 Special set–027 (uncat 1963)
11385 Set–027 (1963) Fgt.
11395 Set–027 (1963) Fgt.
11405 Set–027 (1963) Pass.
11420 Set–027 (1964) Fgt.
11430 Set–027 (1964) Fgt.
11440 Set–027 (1964) Fgt.
11450 Set–027 (1964) Fgt.
11460 Set–027 (1964) Fgt.
11470 Set–027 (1964) Fgt.
11480 Set–027 (1964) Fgt.
11490 Set–027 (1964) Pass.
11500 Set–027 (1964-66) Fgt.
11510 Set–027 (1964) Fgt.
11520 Set–027 (1965-66) Fgt.
11530 Set–027 (1965-66) Fgt.
11540 Set–027 (1966) Fgt.
11550 Set–027 (1965-66) Fgt.
11560 Set–027 (1965-66) Fgt.
11590 Set–027 (1966) Pass.
11600 Set–027 (1968) Fgt.
11710 Set–027 (1969) Fgt.
11720 Set–027 (1969) Fgt.
11730 Set–027 (1969) Fgt.
11740 Set–027 (1969) Fgt.
11750 Set–027 (1969) Fgt.
11760 Set–027 (1969) Fgt.
12502 Gift pak–027 (1962) Pass.
12512 Gift pak–027 (1962) Fgt.
12700 Set–0 (1964) Fgt.
12706 Set–0 (uncat 1964) Fgt.
12710 Set–0 (1964-66) Fgt.
12720 Set–0 (1964) Fgt.
12730 Set–0 (1964-66) Fgt.
12740 Set–0 (1964) Fgt.
12750 Set–0 (1964) Fgt.
12760 Set–0 (1964) Fgt.
12770 Set–0 (1964) Fgt.
12780 Set–0 (1964-66) Pass.
12800 Set–0 (1965-66) Fgt.
12820 Set–0 (1965) Fgt.
12840 Set–0 (1966) Fgt.
12850 Set–0 (1966) Fgt.
13008 Set–Super O (1962) Fgt.
13018 Set–Super O (1962) Fgt.
13028 Set–Super O (1962) Fgt.
13036 Set–Super O (1962) Pass.
13048 Set–Super O (1962) Fgt.
13058 Set–Super O (1962) Fgt.
13068 Set–Super O (1962) Fgt.
13078 Set–Super O (1962) Pass.
13088 Set–Super O (uncat 1962) Pass.
13098 Set–Super O (1963) Fgt.
13108 Set–Super O (1963) Fgt.
13118 Set–Super O (1963) Fgt.
13128 Set–Super O (1963) Fgt.
13138 Set–Super O (1963) Fgt.
13148 Set–Super O (1963) Pass.
13150 Set–Super O (1964-66) Fgt.
14003 Set–HO (1962) Fgt.
14013 Set–HO (1962) Fgt.
14023 Set–HO (1962) Fgt.
14033 Set–HO (1962) Fgt.
14043 Set–HO (1962) Fgt.
14054 Set–HO (1962) Pass.
14064 Set–HO (1962) Fgt.
14074 Set–HO (1962) Fgt.
14084 Set–HO (1962) Fgt.
14098 Set–HO (1962) Fgt.
14108 Set–HO (1962) Pass.
14133 Set–HO (1963) Fgt.
14143 Set–HO (1963) Fgt.
14153 Set–HO (1963) Fgt.
14163 Set–HO (1963) Pass.
14173 Set–HO (1963) Pass.
14183 Set–HO (1963) Fgt.
14193 Set–HO (1963) Fgt.
14203 Set–HO (1963) Fgt.
14233 Set–HO (1963) Fgt.
14240 Set–HO (1964-66) Fgt.
14250 Set–HO (1964) Fgt.
14260 Set–HO (1964-66) Fgt.
14270 Set–HO (1964) Fgt.
14280 Set–HO (1964-66) Fgt.
14290 Set–HO (1964) Pass.
14300 Set–HO (1964-66) Fgt.
14310 Set–HO (1964-66) Fgt.
14320 Set–HO (1965-66) Pass.
15903 Racing set–HO (1962)
16020 Speedway 250 Racing set–0 (1963)
16030 Speedway 600 Racing set–0 (1963)
16040 Speedway 750 Racing set–0 (1963)
16050 Speedway 1000 Racing set–0 (1963)
16090 Raceway Twin Chicane–0 (1965)
16100 Raceway Loop-the-loop–0 (1965)
16110 Raceway Skill tilt-skyway leap–0 (1965)
16130 Raceway Big Eight–0 (1966)
17010 Raceway 33 Racing set–HO (1963)
17020 Raceway 66 Racing set–HO (1963)
17030 Raceway 99 Racing set–HO (1963)
17130 Raceway Malibu Twister–HO (1964)
17140 Raceway Loop-the-loop–HO (1964)
17160 Raceway Pretzel Bender–HO (1964)
17170 Raceway Monte Carlo–HO (1964)
17180 Raceway Flag tag–HO (1964)
17200 Raceway Matterhorn–HO (1966)
19244 Set–027 (uncat 1963) Fgt.
19428 Sears Special set–0 (uncat 1963) Fgt.
19703 Set–0 (uncat circa 1968) Fgt.
21000 Chemcraft beginner's set (1962)
21010 Chemcraft junior lab (1962)
21030 Chemcraft student lab (1962)
21040 Chemcraft collegiate lab (1962)
21050 Chemcraft senior lab (1962)
21060 Chemcraft master lab (1962)
21070 Chemcraft master deluxe lab (1962)
21080 Accessory gift pak (1962)
21090 Accessory gift pak (1962)
21100 Accessory gift pak (1962)
21310 Chemcraft beginner's set (1965)
21320 Chemcraft junior lab (1965)
21340 Chemcraft student lab (1965)
21360 Chemcraft senior lab (1965)
21380 Chemcraft master lab (1965)
21410 Chemcraft beginner's set (1966)
21420 Chemcraft junior lab (1966)
21440 Chemcraft student lab (1966)
21460 Chemcraft senior lab (1966)
21480 Chemcraft master lab (1966)
22000 Microcraft junior set (1962)
22020 Microcraft senior set (1962)
22030 Microcraft research set (1962)
22040 Microcraft lab master (1962)
22050 Microcraft senior lab master (1962)
22060 Microcraft senior lab master deluxe (1962)
22070 Microcraft accessory set (1962)
22080 Four-in-one slide kit (1962)
22090 Microcraft student microscope (1962)
22100 Microcraft master microscope (1962)
22310 Microcraft beginner's set (1965)
22320 Microcraft junior set (1965)
22340 Microcraft student set (1965)
22350 Microcraft senior lab master (1965)
22360 Microcraft lab master (1965)

"A great man is one who has not lost the child's heart."

Mancius
Chinese philosopher
372-289 B.C.

Wrap-around front and back covers of 1913-1914 Lionel catalog.